LEARNING ITALIAN

STEP BY STEP AND REGION BY REGION

Kristina Olson, PhD

THE
GREAT
COURSES®

FSC
www.fsc.org

MIX
Paper from
responsible sources
FSC® C011935

RAINFOREST ALLIANCE
CERTIFIED

THE GREAT COURSES®

4840 Westfields Boulevard | Suite 500 | Chantilly, Virginia | 20151-2299
PHONE: 1.800.832.2412 | FAX: 703.378.3819 | www.thegreatcourses.com

Leadership

PAUL SUIJK	President & CEO
BRUCE G. WILLIS	Chief Financial Officer
JOSEPH PECKL	SVP, Marketing
JASON SMIGEL	VP, Product Development
CALE PRITCHETT	VP, Marketing
MARK LEONARD	VP, Technology Services
DEBRA STORMS	VP, General Counsel
KEVIN MANZEL	Sr. Director, Content Development
ANDREAS BURGSTALLER	Sr. Director, Brand Marketing & Innovation
KEVIN BARNHILL	Director of Creative
GAIL GLEESON	Director, Business Operations & Planning

Production Team

KATRINA YUMPING	Producer
WALTER JACOB	Content Developer
LISA PERSINGER ROBERTSON MASHA STOYANOVA	Associate Producers
JAMES NIDEL	Graphic Artist
OWEN YOUNG	Managing Editor
MAHER AHMED KATY MERRY HANNAH CORY SIVAKOFF ANDREW VOLPE OWEN YOUNG	Editors
CHARLES GRAHAM	Assistant Editor
EDDIE HARTNESS	Audio Engineer
ROBERTO DE MORAES	Director
GEORGE BOLDEN MICHAEL CALLAHAN ERICA CORSO RICK FLOWE PAUL SHEEHAN	Camera Operators
VALERIE WELCH	Production Assistant

Publications Team

FARHAD HOSSAIN	Publications Manager
BLAKELY SWAIN	Senior Copywriter
RHOCHELLE MUNSAYAC	Graphic Designer
JESSICA MULLINS	Proofreader
ERIKA ROBERTS	Publications Assistant
WILLIAM DOMANSKI	Transcript Editor

Copyright © The Teaching Company, 2020

Printed in the United States of America

Kristina Olson, PhD
Associate Professor of Italian
George Mason University

Kristina Olson is an Associate Professor of Italian and the Italian Program Coordinator at George Mason University, where she has taught Italian language, literature, and cinema since 2005. She earned her PhD in Italian from Columbia University.

Professor Olson is the author of *Courtesy Lost: Dante, Boccaccio, and the Literature of History* and several articles on Dante, Boccaccio, and Petrarch. She is the coeditor of *Open City: Seven Writers in Postwar Rome*; *Boccaccio 1313–2013*; and the second edition of *Approaches to Teaching Dante's "Divine Comedy"* with the Modern Language Association.

Professor Olson is the president of the American Boccaccio Association and previously served as vice president and treasurer. She was also the vice president of the Dante Society of America for two years and a councilor for three years. She serves on the editorial boards of *Bibliotheca Dantesca*, an international journal dedicated to Dante studies, and *Dante Studies*, the annual publication of the Dante Society of America, and she is an executive committee member for the Modern Language Association's Languages, Literatures, and Cultures forum on Medieval and Renaissance Italian.

Alyssa Falcone, PhD
Ives Visiting Professor of the Humanities
Youngstown State University

Alyssa Falcone, coauthor of this workbook, is the David and Helga Ives Visiting Professor of the Humanities at Youngstown State University, where she teaches Italian language and literature and Italian American culture. She has previously held appointments at the University of Alabama and George Mason University. She earned her master's degree at Boston College and her PhD at Johns Hopkins University. While her main area of expertise is early modern Italian literature, she also conducts research on the concept of labor in Italian American art and literature. ▪

TABLE OF CONTENTS

INTRODUCTION

LEZIONE GUIDES

SUPPLEMENTARY MATERIALS

ACKNOWLEDGEMENTS

This workbook was written by Alyssa Falcone and Kristina Olson. Dr. Olson also thanks Dr. Nicola Di Nino for his assistance.

LEARNING ITALIAN
Step by Step and Region by Region

This course takes you on a journey through the 20 regions of Italy as you learn the nuts and bolts of the language: its grammar and vocabulary. The course introduces you to the Italian language and cultures of the Italian-speaking world, with the goal of helping you achieve intermediate-level communicative competence in the language. The course is designed for learners with no prior experience of the language, but those who have had some prior exposure to the language will also draw benefit from it.

The guiding principle of this course is that a language learned in context is retained more effectively and for a longer period of time. Following this principle, grammar and vocabulary are introduced via gradually longer texts in Italian at the start of each lesson that describe each region's geography, history, and artistic and regional traditions. By analyzing this content, you'll move steadily from recognizing discrete grammatical elements and vocabulary while only understanding the gist of the text to comprehending an increasing amount of it. These introductory texts incorporate and rehearse grammatical elements that are treated individually and in depth within the lessons.

The presentation of grammatical concepts in this course reflects the sequence that is generally covered in the first year of college-level Italian, including the present, past perfect, imperfect, present progressive, and future tenses of the indicative mood, as well as the imperative mood of verbs. Lessons involve detailed explanations and examples of these different concepts. Animated skits and dialogues in the video lessons introduce more conversational aspects of the language and put new grammatical structures into practice.

This workbook accompanies the video lessons and offers ample opportunities for grammatical and lexical practice. It also includes the introductory texts in Italian with accompanying English translations. It's recommended that you read the associated workbook lesson before watching a particular video lesson, as this will help you feel more grounded in the material. This workbook also includes a glossary and lists of resources for further study. Additionally, it features a list of recommended films and books by region to help you immerse yourself in the language and regional cultures. As you work through this course, it is helpful to watch Italian films and TV shows, read the headlines of an Italian newspaper each day, and even find conversation groups in your local area or online. This course is intended to be a substantial part of a multidimensional strategy to learn the Italian language in context. ∎

LEZIONE 1

BENVENUTI TO ITALIAN AND ITALY'S 20 REGIONS!

Buon giorno! Mi chiamo Kristina Olson.
Sono una professoressa d'italiano a George
Mason University. Benvenuti al corso!

Hello! My name is Kristina Olson. I am
a professor of Italian at George Mason
University. Welcome to the course!

VOCABOLARIO NUOVO E UTILE / NEW AND USEFUL VOCABULARY

Buon giorno!	Hello! Good day!	**Buona sera!**	Good evening!
Ciao!	Hi! Goodbye! [informal]	**Arrivederci!**	Goodbye! [formal]
Come sta?	How are you? [formal]	**Come stai?**	How are you? [informal]
Sto...	I'm (doing)...	**bene, male**	well, poorly
Mi chiamo...	My name is...	**Piacere!**	Nice to meet you!
la montagna	mountain	**l'isola**	island
il fiume	river	**il lago**	lake
la penisola	peninsula	**il mare**	sea
la capitale	capital (of a country)	**il capoluogo**	capital (of a region)
nord	north	**sud**	south
est	east	**ovest**	west
la mattina	morning	**il mezzogiorno**	midday*
il pomeriggio	afternoon	**la notte**	night

* Italians also use this word (as a proper noun) to refer to the South of Italy.

RIPASSO GENERALE / GENERAL REVIEW

A. Notes about Italian History, Culture, and Language

Italian is one of the most beautiful languages in the world, and it has an incredibly rich history behind it. If you've studied a Romance language (Spanish, French, Portuguese, etc.) before, you may find that there are many similarities in structure, syntax, and vocabulary—but be aware that there are also many, many differences! Italy was not formally unified as a nation until 1861. Before that, it was split into many different regions, kingdoms, duchies, and territories, all of which shifted around over time. There are echoes of these divisions even today; the farther apart you move from city to city, the more linguistic differences you will notice. A

Milanese will have a hard time understanding a Neapolitan, but while each region has its local dialects, almost all Italians learn what's called Standard Italian at school. This national (and now global) standard was derived from the Florentine dialect, mostly thanks to Dante!

B. Key(s) to Italian Pronunciation

For the most part, Italian pronunciation is not terribly difficult, but there are some tricks and rules you will want to memorize. Here are the sounds of the Italian alphabet, spelled out as they are pronounced in Italian:

A	ah (as in *papa)*	**N**	ennay
B	bee	**O**	oh (as in *snow*)
C	chee	**P**	pee
D	dee	**Q**	koo
E	ay (as in *hay*) or eh (as in *end*)	**R**	erray (typically rolled)
F	effay	**S**	essay
G	jee	**T**	tee
H	acca (AH-kah)	**U**	oo (as in *boot*)
I	ee (as in *jeep*)	**V**	voo
L	ellay	**Z**	zeta
M	emmay		

The letters *J, K, W, X,* and *Y* do not appear in Italian words—only in those borrowed from other languages.

One thing to keep in mind is that pronunciation is not arbitrary in Italian like it commonly is in English. All letters will almost always have the same sound on their own. Vowels can change their sounds a little bit when combined with each other. For example, to pronounce an Italian word with the combination *ai*, simply think of the original pronunciation for both letters and then blend them together: "ah" + "ee" = "ahee," like the sound of the long "i" in the English word *hi*. So if you see the Italian word *mai* (in English: *never*), you know to pronounce it like the English word *my*, not *may*.

In learning Italian, you'll have to pay particular attention to the sounds that the letters *C* and *G* make with vowels: They take a "hard" sound with the letters *A*, *O*, and *U*, and they take a "soft" sound ("ch-" or "j-") with the letters *E* and *I*. To maintain a hard *C* or *G* sound with the letters *E* and *I*, you'll have to add the letter *H*. To maintain a soft *C* or *G* sound with the letters *A*, *O*, and *U*, you'll have to add the letter *I*.

Hard C sound:	CA, CHE, CHI, CO, CU	
	(pronounce: KAH, KAY, KEY, KO, KOO)	
Soft C sound:	CIA, CE, CI, CIO, CIU	
	(pronounce: CHA, CHAY, CHEE, CHO, CHU)	
Hard G sound:	GA, GHE, GHI, GO, GU	
	(pronounce: GAH, GAY, GHEE, GO, GU)	
Soft G sound:	GIA, GE, GI, GIO, GIU	
	(pronounce: JA, JAY, JEE, JOE, JU)	

After memorizing these, you'll start to notice that we commonly mispronounce many Italian words, such as *bruschetta* ("broo-SKET-tah")!

The pronunciations of a few consonant combinations are also particular to Italian. The most difficult are *GN* and *GL*. The *GN* combination is similar to the Ñ in Spanish. Pronounce it as you would the sound in the middle of the word *onion*, with a "nyuh" sound. *Gnocchi* should sound like "NYOH-kee." *GL* will be pronounced like the middle of the word *million*, with a "lyuh" sound. Pretend that the G isn't there and that there is a slight "y" sound accompanying the *L*. The word *famiglia* will thus sound like "fa-MI-lyah."

C. The Use of Subject Pronouns

Since Italian verbs are very clearly different among the six conjugations, it is not always necessary to include the subject pronouns along with them. Subject pronouns are typically only added for emphasis or clarification. Here are the subject pronouns in Italian:

	singular	plural
first person	**io** (I)	**noi** (we)
second person	**tu** (you [informal])	**voi** (you [plural, informal])
third person	**lui/lei/Lei** (she/he/you [formal])	**loro/Loro** (they/you [plural, formal])

When you meet a new verb, put the forms into a table like this (or a different format that works better for you). Try labeling the verbs from 1 to 6, with *io* as 1, *tu* as 2, *lui/lei/Lei* as 3, *noi* as 4, *voi* as 5, and *loro/Loro* as 6. Then, roll a die and see if you can come up with the correct verb conjugation for whichever number you roll, and repeat the exercise until you've mastered the verb.

D. *Essere* vs. *stare*: A Quick Guide

Essere and *stare* both mean "to be" in Italian. They have different usages, but they are not quite as complicated as the differences between *ser* and *estar* in Spanish. *Essere* is more common and used to convey permanent states of being, while *stare* is more temporary. For example, you would use *essere* to describe characteristics of someone's personality ("I am tall, funny, and smart"), whereas you would use *stare* to ask how someone is feeling ("How are you [doing] today?").

Here are the conjugations of the two verbs (note that the subject pronouns are included since they are new to you, but in the future, they will appear less and less in this workbook):

· · · · · ·
Essere

	singular	plural
first person	**io** sono	**noi** siamo
second person	**tu** sei	**voi** siete
third person	**lui/lei/Lei** è*	**loro/Loro** sono

*Don't forget the accent on the third person singular form! Otherwise you are saying the word for *and* (in Italian: *e*).

· · · · ·
Stare

	singular	plural
first person	**io** sto	**noi** stiamo
second person	**tu** stai	**voi** state
third person	**lui/lei/Lei** sta	**loro/Loro** stanno

Note the difference in usage of the two verbs in the second person singular (*tu*) form:

Come sei?   **What are you like?**

Come stai?   **How are you doing?**

Now that you know the conjugations, try to use them immediately!

E. Informal vs. Formal Speech

In general, you will use informal speech with friends, family members, and children. When conversing with people who are unfamiliar to you, who are higher in authority than you, or who work in service industries, you will use formal speech. Here's a good tip: If you are unsure, simply default to the formal. If your interlocutor finds it too stuffy, he or she will tell you, *"Dammi del tu!"* ("Give me the *tu*/informal form!"). In Italy, it's better to be polite first and then switch to the informal, rather than the other way around.

The formal form of speech mostly lies in the verbs that you use, but it is not limited just to that. You will use the *Lei* form of verbs, which means that the verbs will be in the third person singular, or plural (*Loro*) if speaking to a group.* It might sound strange, but try to think of it as addressing "His/Her Royal Highness," and it will come more easily to you. Even though lei means *she* as a pronoun, Lei is used with both men and women.

*In the South of Italy, it is more common to use the *voi* (second person plural) form of verbs to indicate formal speech. Sometimes it is also common to hear the *voi* used for the formal plural, even outside of the Southern regions.

ATTIVITÀ / ACTIVITIES

Cristina ed[1] Elisa sono due studentesse americane e sono a Roma per la prima volta. Incontrano un'altra studentessa italiana, Giovanna, a un bar[2] e si presentano.

▶ Cristina and Elisa are two American students and they are in Rome for the first time. They meet up with another Italian student, Giovanna, at a café and introduce themselves.

1. Scrivi le parole giuste negli spazi vuoti. (Write the correct words in the blanks.)

siete	mi chiamo	arrivederci	sono di
	come stai	piacere	grazie

Cristina: Ciao, Elisa! 1. _____?

---

1 The word *e* (*and*), when preceding another *e*, will commonly change to *ed* for ease of pronunciation. It is similar to how in English we say "an elephant" instead of "a elephant."

2 In Italy, *il bar* is the word for a café or coffee shop. A place that serves alcoholic drinks would be called *il pub*.

Elisa:	Buon giorno, Cristina! Sto bene, e tu?
Cristina:	Sto benissimo, 2. _____! Ecco[3] un'altra studentessa.
Elisa:	Ciao! Come ti chiami?
Giovanna:	Ciao! 3. _____ Giovanna, e tu? Come ti chiami?
Elisa:	Mi chiamo Elisa.
Cristina:	Mi chiamo Cristina.
Giovanna:	4. _____! Io sono di Firenze. E voi? Di dove 5. _____?
Elisa:	Io sono di Filadelfia, e Cristina è di New York.
Giovanna:	Bene! Ci vediamo a scuola, allora[4]!
Cristina:	6. _____!
Elisa:	Buona giornata[5]!

2. Per ogni frase, scrivi *I* per informale e *F* per formale. (For each sentence, write *I* for informal and *F* for formal. Note: Some may be both formal and informal!)

1. Buon giorno! _____

2. Come sta? _____

3. Arrivederci! _____

4. Come stai? _____

5. ArrivederLa! _____

6. Piacere! _____

3. Rispondi alla domanda "Come stai?" con la risposta che corrisponde alla foto. (Respond to the question "*Come stai?*" appropriately, given the picture.)

1. _____   2. _____   3. _____   4. _____

4. Scrivi il pronome che corrisponde alla forma di *essere e stare*. (Fill in the appropriate subject pronoun for the conjugations of *essere* and *stare*.)

1. _____ siete

2. _____ stiamo

3. _____ sei

4. _____ state

....

3 Here is

4 Then

5 Have a good day!

5. _____ sono

6. _____ stanno

7. _____ sto

8. _____ siamo

9. _____ stai

10. _____ sta

11. _____ è

5. *Esercizio di scrittura: Una cartolina*

Write a short postcard to your new Italian pen pal. Introduce yourself (My name is…. I am from….). Ask the person how he or she is doing and where he or she is from in Italy. Then, choose an appropriate closure.

_____

_____

_____

_____

ANSWER KEY

1.

1. Come stai
2. grazie
3. Mi chiamo
4. Piacere
5. siete
6. Arrivederci

2.

1. *I* or *F*
2. *F*
3. *I*
4. *I*
5. *F*
6. *I* or *F*

3.

1. Sto così così.
2. Sto benissimo!
3. Sto bene.
4. Sto male.

4.

1. voi
2. noi
3. tu
4. voi
5. io *or* loro
6. loro
7. io
8. noi
9. tu
10. lui/lei/Lei
11. lui/lei/Lei

5. Results may vary. Sample:

Ciao amico/a! Come ti chiami? Mi chiamo Elisa. Come stai? Io sto bene. Di dove sei in Italia? Io sono di Filadelfia. Arrivederci!

NAMES OF ITALIAN REGIONS (*REGIONI*) AND THEIR CAPITALS (*CAPOLUOGHI*)

Regione	Capoluogo	English Name (if different)
Abruzzo	L'Aquila	
Valle d'Aosta	Aosta	
Basilicata	Potenza	
Calabria	Catanzaro	
Campania	Napoli	Naples
Emilia-Romagna	Bologna	
Friuli–Venezia Giulia	Trieste	
Lazio	Roma	Rome
Liguria	Genova	
Lombardia	Milano	Milan
Le Marche	Ancona	
Molise	Campobasso	
Piemonte	Torino	Turin
Puglia	Bari	
Sardegna	Cagliari	
Sicilia	Palermo	
Trentino–Alto Adige	Trento	Trent
Toscana	Firenze	Florence
Umbria	Perugia	
Veneto	Venezia	Venice

NOUNS AND ARTICLES / SICILY

Oggi parliamo della Sicilia. La Sicilia è l'isola più grande dell'Italia e del mare Mediterraneo. È un'isola triangolare. Si chiama anche Trinacria. Ecco la bandiera della Sicilia. La Sicilia ha una storia ricca e lunga, dai tempi dei greci e dei romani fino ad oggi. Ci sono tanti templi antichi a Siracusa. C'è un vulcano attivo: il monte Etna! C'è anche lo Stretto di Messina con i mostri Scilla e Cariddi del poema di Omero!

▶ Today we will speak about Sicily. Sicily is the biggest island in Italy and the Mediterranean Sea. It is a triangular island. It is also called Trinacria. Here is the Sicilian flag. Sicily has a rich and long history from the times of the Greeks and the Romans up until today. There are many ancient temples in Siracusa. There is an active volcano: Mount Etna! There is also the Strait of Messina, with the monsters Scylla and Charybdis from Homer's poem!

VOCABOLARIO NUOVO E UTILE / NEW AND USEFUL VOCABULARY

Bentornato/a!	Welcome back!	**Cominciamo!**	Let's begin!
Parliamo di...	Let's talk about...	**Si chiama...**	He/she/ it is called...
Ci vediamo!	Bye! (*literally*: We'll see each other!)	**Alla prossima!**	Until next time!
il vulcano	volcano	**la bandiera**	flag
la storia	history, story	**il tempo**	time
il tempio	temple	**lo stretto**	strait
il mostro	monster	**il punto**	point, tip
grande	big, great	**ricco/a**	rich
lungo/a	long	**greco/a**	Greek
romano/a	Roman	**antico/a**	ancient, old
attivo/a	active		
C'è...	There is... [singular]	**Ci sono...**	There are... [plural]
Ecco...	Here is... (Behold! Aha!)	**dove**	where
Dov'è...?	Where is...?	**Dove sono...?**	Where are...?

RIPASSO GENERALE / GENERAL REVIEW

A. Notes about Sicily

Sicily is the largest island in the Mediterranean and also the largest Italian island. It has a long, fascinating history that reaches back centuries. Having the geographical location that it does—right in the middle of the Mediterranean—Sicily has been host to numerous foreign invaders over the span of history, which contributes to many of its cultural particularities. Traveling around the island, you can see traces of Greek, Norman, Byzantine, North African, and Spanish influences, among many others. The language is very difficult to understand if you've only studied Standard Italian. Sicily may be very well known for crime and poverty, but its beauty and riches are much more worthy of celebration!

B. Genders of Nouns in Italian

By now you have probably noticed that every noun in Italian is accompanied by a small word like *il, lo, la*, etc. These are definite articles (discussed more fully in section e. below), which correspond to the gender of the noun. Unlike Latin and German, which have masculine, feminine, and neuter nouns, Italian only has masculine and feminine, which are generally easily identifiable by their endings (-*o* for masculine and -*a* for feminine). However, many words end in -*e* and could be either masculine or feminine—they must be memorized, for the most part. There are some tricks to learn for some of these nouns ending in -*e*:

- Nouns ending in -*ione* (similar to the -*tion*/-*sion* ending in English) are almost always feminine.

  > *la stazion*e / the station
  > *l'organizzazione* / the organization
  > *la regione* / the region

- Nouns that end in -*tore* typically denote a masculine person, especially a profession.

  > *l'attore* / the actor
  > *il pittore* / the painter
  > *lo scrittore* / the writer

- Nouns that end in -*trice* are feminine and can sometimes match up to the -*tore* nouns above. You may also see these for regular objects, such as *la calcolatrice* / the calculator.[1]

  > *l'attrice* / the actress
  > *la pittrice* / the painter
  > *la scrittrice* / the writer

There are many more rules for the gender of nouns, and some are more intricate than others, but don't get overwhelmed! For now, remember the -*o*/-*a* rule, and if you are unsure of a new word that ends in -*e*, try to look for an article or adjective that accompanies it, which will give you more hints.

---

1 Nowadays, the -*trice* ending may be eschewed in favor of a gender-neutral ending that applies to both sexes; while the noun will be the same, the article will change to reflect the gender. This is more prevalent in nouns ending in -*nte*, such as *il/la cantante* (male/female singer, respectively). Women are also beginning to drop the -*essa* ending for professions, such as in *poetessa* (poet) and *avvocatessa* (lawyer), as it is seen as slightly diminutive. Instead, you may see *la poeta* or *l'avvocata*. This is not universal, however.

C. Regular and Irregular Gendered Endings

As previously mentioned, the regular endings for nouns are -*o*, -*a*, and -*e* for singular nouns. In general, these are very regular, but in Italian, there are always exceptions to the rule! You will eventually notice, for example, that many body parts are very irregular in Italian in terms of gender, especially between singular and plural. Did you know that *hand* is feminine (*la mano*), even though it ends in -*o*? Just looking at *mano*, you'd be tempted to say it was masculine, but the article says otherwise. Here are some irregularities in nouns that you'll want to memorize:

- Nouns that end in -*tà* are feminine and generally correspond to English nouns ending in -*ty*.

    > *l'università* / the university
    > *la città* / the city
    > *la diversità* / the diversity

- Nouns that end in -*si* (similar to the -*sis* ending in English) are feminine, even though they end in -*i*, which usually signifies a masculine plural word.

    > *la crisi* / the crisis
    > *l'analisi* / the analysis
    > *la tesi* / the thesis
    > *la diagnosi* / the diagnosis

- Nouns that are of foreign origin (you'll recognize them right away!) are always masculine. These can be from any language other than Italian.

    > *lo sport* / sport
    > *l'autobus* / bus
    > *i jeans* / jeans

Sometimes a noun will look regular, but it might be an abbreviation, such as *auto* (feminine, short for *automobile*, or car), *foto* (feminine, short for *fotografia*, or photograph), and *bici* (feminine, short for *bicicletta*, or bicycle). Other feminine words that fall into this category are *la radio* (short for *radiotrasmettrice*, or radio), *la metro* (short for *metropolitana*, or subway), and *la moto* (short for *motocicletta*, or motorcycle). One word that looks feminine but is actually masculine is *il cinema* (short for *cinematografo*, or movie theater). In fact, many nouns that end in -*ma* (such as *problema*, *tema*, and *dramma*) are also masculine!

Again, don't despair about the many irregularities of genders in the Italian language. English does not have gendered nouns, which makes it difficult to learn another language that does have them, but it will get easier as you go along.

D. Indefinite Articles

An article is a small word that accompanies every noun in Italian. There are two types of articles: indefinite and definite. Indefinite articles are only used in the singular, since they mean "a" or "one," whereas definite articles can be either singular or plural. Just as nouns have genders, articles also have genders. When it is unclear which gender a noun belongs to, an article will clear up that ambiguity.

Here are the four different indefinite articles:

Gender	Article	When Used	Example
feminine	un'	before a vowel	un'amica
feminine	una	before a consonant	una stazione
masculine	un	before most masculine nouns	un mare
masculine	uno	before masculine nouns beginning with *s* + consonant, *x, y, z, ps, pn, gn*	uno studente

Not too difficult! The only one to really concentrate on is the last category (*uno*), since it is very particular in the rules of its usage. Anytime you see a word beginning in *s* + a consonant, a little red flag should pop up in your brain. A word simply beginning in *s* + a vowel (*sacco, sole, sasso*) will simply use *un*, but with a consonant (*studente, sciocco, sposo*), you'll need to switch to *uno*. The same applies to nouns beginning with *ps, pn,* and *gn*; these may seem odd, but they do exist in Italian—for example, *psicologo* (psychologist), *pneumotorace* (pneumothorax), and *gnocco* (dumpling-type pasta). Keep on the lookout for masculine words that begin with *x, y,* and *z,* too; they also use *uno* instead of *un* (e.g., *uno xilofono, uno yoghurt, uno zoo*)

E. Definite Articles

Definite articles function in the same way as indefinite articles, but instead of denoting "a" or "one," they are used to mean "the." There are more definite articles than indefinite ones because definite articles can be used in the plural, too. This lesson only covers the singular ones. Pay attention to how they correspond to the rules for indefinite articles:

Gender	Article	When Used	Example
feminine	l'	before a vowel	l'amica
feminine	la	before a consonant	la stazione
masculine	l'	before a vowel	l'amico
masculine	il	before most masculine nouns beginning with a consonant	il mare
masculine	lo	before masculine nouns beginning with *s* + consonant, *x, y, z, ps, pn, gn*	lo studente

Did you notice that these articles have almost all of the same rules as the indefinite ones? There is only one additional definite article in the singular: *l'*. It is short for *lo*, not *il*, and it precedes masculine nouns beginning with a vowel.

F. *Ecco, C'è,* and *Ci sono*

These three words are very helpful in Italian, as they are used for expressing the presence of things. They are quite similar to each other but also particular in their usage.

Ecco can be used on its own (*Ecco!*) to mean *Here (it is)!* or *Behold!* or *Aha!* If you are looking for your keys and you finally find them, you might exclaim *Eccole!* (*Here they are!*).

C'è and *Ci sono* are used to enumerate objects or people in a space, or merely to express their existence. *C'è* is used for singular objects (*there is a...*), whereas *ci sono* (*there are...*) is used for plural ones. Note that these contain the third person conjugations of *essere*, but they are different from *è* and *sono*, which mean *he/she/it is* and *they are*.

What objects do you see around you or in your purse or backpack? How many are there? You can use these words to list the objects you see.

- *Ecco una matita.* (Here is a pencil.)
- *C'è un computer.* (There is a/one computer.)
- *Ci sono due studenti.* (There are two students.)

The last one will be easier to use once you learn numbers and plurals. For now, try to use *ecco* and *c'è* to point out nouns that you already know.

> Antonio e Lucia sono marito e moglie e vivono a Palermo, in Sicilia. Questo fine settimana fanno una gita insieme a vedere il loro figlio, Tommaso, e sua moglie, Giuseppina, a Catania.

> ┄┄┄┄▶ Antonio and Lucia are husband and wife and they live in Palermo, Sicily. This weekend they are taking a trip together to see their son, Tommaso, and his wife, Giuseppina, in Catania.

1. Scrivi le parole giuste negli spazi vuoti. (Write the correct words in the blanks.)

si chiama   vulcano   tempio   grande

bentornati   attivo   greco

Tommaso:	Ciao, Mamma! Ciao Papà! Come va? 1. _____ a Catania!
Antonio e Lucia:	Ciao, carissimo! Va tutto bene. Ciao, Giuseppina!
Giuseppina:	Ciao!
Tommaso:	Cosa volete vedere oggi?
Lucia:	Io voglio tanto visitare un 2. _____ antico come questo (*points to map*). È 3. _____ o romano?
Giuseppina:	È romano. È 4. _____ e bellissimo!
Antonio:	E poi prendiamo[1] un bel gelato.
Tommaso:	Ma certo[2]! Ci sono altre cose da vedere, però!
Antonio:	Possiamo salire[3] quella montagna?
Giuseppina:	Non è una montagna, è un 5. _____! 6. _____ Monte Etna.
Lucia:	Mamma mia! C'è qualche pericolo[4]?
Tommaso:	No, non è 7. _____ a questo momento.
Antonio:	Benissimo! Allora, andiamo!

1 Let's order (*literally*: Let's take)

2 Certainly

3 Climb

4 Is there any danger?

2. Per ogni parola, scrivi *F* per femminile e *M* per maschile. (For each word, write *F* for feminine and *M* for masculine. Note: If you are unsure, look at the article!)

1. la rana (*frog*) _____

2. il fiore (*flower*) _____

3. la stazione (*station*) _____

4. la mano (*hand*) _____

5. lo spaghetto (*strand of pasta*) _____

6. l'università (*college*) _____

7. la giraffa (*giraffe*) _____

8. lo zaino (*backpack*) _____

9. il pane (*bread*) _____

10. il leone (*lion*) _____

3. Per ogni parola nell'esercizio precedente, scrivi l'articolo indeterminativo appropriato. (For every word in the previous exercise, write the correct indefinite article.)

1. _____rana

2. _____fiore

3. _____stazione

4. _____mano

5. _____spaghetto

6. _____università

7. _____giraffa

8. _____zaino

9. _____pane

10. _____leone

4. In ogni spazio, scrivi *c'è* o *ci sono* per ogni oggetto. (In each space, write *c'è* or *ci sono* for each object. Pay attention to singular vs. plural!)

1. _____una chiesa

2. _____tre (*three*) stazioni di treno

3. _____due (*two*) biblioteche

4. _____uno zoo

5. _____cinque (*five*) banche

6. _____un ufficio postale

7. _____una questura (*police station*)

5. *Esercizio di scrittura: La Sicilia*

Using the chart below, write a few sentences about things you can find in various cities in Sicily using *c'è*, *dov'è*, *è*, and *si chiama*. Search Google for more interesting things to see and do in these cities!

_____

_____

_____

_____

_____

_____

City	Landmark(s)
Palermo	Museo Archeologico Regionale Antonio Salinas; Palazzo dei Normanni; Teatro Massimo Vittorio Emmanuele
Catania	Monte Etna; Fontana dell'Elefante; Cattedrale di Sant'Agata
Siracusa	Castello Maniace; Teatro Greco; Tempio di Apollo
Taormina	Isola Bella; Corso Umberto (shopping); Palazzo Corvaja
Agrigento	Casa Natale di Luigi Pirandello; Chiesa Santa Maria dei Greci; Tempio di Zeus Olimpio
Ragusa	Duomo di San Giorgio; Grotta delle Trabacche; Giardino Ibleo
Cefalù	Lavatoio Medievale (Medieval Washhouse); Museo Mandralisca; Abbazia (Abbey) di Thélema
Messina	Fontana di Nettuno; Orologio Astronomico (Astronomical Clock); Chiesa della Santissima Annunziata dei Catalani
Enna	Rocca di Cerere (Ceres) Geopark; Museo Archeologico di Aidone; Necropoli di Realmese
Acireale	Museo Opera dei Pupi (Puppets); Fortezza del Tocco; Pinacoteca (Art Gallery) Zelantea

ANSWER KEY

1.

1. Bentornati
2. tempio
3. greco
4. antico
5. vulcano
6. Si chiama
7. attivo

2.

1. F
2. M
3. F
4. F
5. M
6. F
7. F
8. M
9. M
10. M

3.

1. una
2. un
3. una
4. una
5. uno
6. un'
7. una
8. uno
9. un
10. un

4.

1. c'è
2. ci sono
3. ci sono
4. c'è
5. ci sono
6. c'è
7. c'è

5. Answers will vary. Example:

Dov'è un museo archeologico? C'è un museo archeologico a Palermo. Si chiama il Museo Archeologico Regionale Antonio Salinas. È grande!

Ecco la Sicilia. La Sicilia è un'isola. C'è un vulcano attivo: il monte Etna. C'è uno stretto vicino a Messina. C'è una città importante ad ovest che si chiama Palermo. Palermo è il capoluogo della Sicilia. C'è un teatro greco importante a Taormina. C'è un duomo bellissimo a Catania.

Here is Sicily. Sicily is an island. There is an active volcano: Mount Etna. There is a strait close to Messina. There is an important city to the west which is called Palermo. Palermo is the capital of Sicily. There is an important Greek theater in Taormina. There is a beautiful cathedral in Catania.

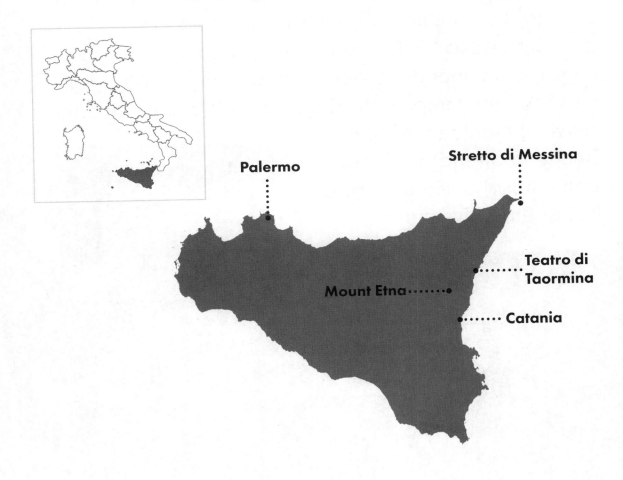

Palermo

Stretto di Messina

Teatro di Taormina

Mount Etna

Catania

NOUNS AND ADJECTIVES / SICILY II

Oggi parliamo della Sicilia. La Sicilia è l'isola più grande dell'Italia e del mare Mediterraneo. È un'isola triangolare. Si chiama anche Trinacria. Ecco la bandiera della Sicilia. La Sicilia ha una storia ricca e lunga, dai tempi dei greci e dei romani fino ad oggi. Ci sono tanti templi antichi a Siracusa. C'è un vulcano attivo: il monte Etna! C'è anche lo Stretto di Messina con i mostri Scilla e Cariddi del poema di Omero!

Today we will speak about Sicily. Sicily is the biggest island in Italy and the Mediterranean Sea. It is a triangular island. It is also called Trinacria. Here is the Sicilian flag. Sicily has a rich and long history from the times of the Greeks and the Romans up until today. There are many ancient temples in Siracusa. There is an active volcano: Mount Etna! There is also the Strait of Messina, with the monsters Scylla and Charybdis from Homer's poem!

il bicchiere	glass (for drinking)	**la bottiglia**	bottle
l'arancino	stuffed rice ball	**il piatto**	plate, dish
la bistecca	steak	**il pesce**	fish
la cassata	traditional Sicilian cake	**la granita**	semi-frozen dessert
il cannolo*	cream-filled pastry	**il biscotto***	cookie
pasta alla Norma	pasta with eggplant, ricotta, and basil	**alla griglia**	grilled
gli occhi	eyes [singular: **l'occhio**]	**i capelli**	hair
basso/a	short (in stature)	**alto/a**	tall
vecchio/a	old	**giovane**	young
magro/a	thin	**grasso/a**	fat
nervoso/a	irritable**	**sensibile**	sensitive**
antipatico/a	mean, rude	**simpatico/a**	nice
triste	sad	**felice**	happy
stanco/a	tired	**calvo/a**	bald
liscio/a	straight (hair)	**riccio/a**	curly (hair)
azzurro/a	blue	**bianco/a**	white
castano/a	brown (hair; *literally*: chestnut)	**grigio/a**	gray
nero/a	black	**verde**	green
americano/a	American	**canadese**	Canadian
cinese	Chinese	**francese**	French
giapponese	Japanese	**inglese**	English
irlandese	Irish	**messicano/a**	Mexican
russo/a	Russian	**spagnolo/a**	Spanish
tedesco/a	German	**coreano/a**	Korean

* Notice that in English, we typically use the plural (*cannoli*, *biscotti*) even for the singular. This is incorrect! *Cannoli* and *biscotti* are the plural forms of these words. Can you think of other Italian words we use incorrectly in the plural? (Hint: sandwiches, ice cream...)

** These are examples of false cognates (also known as "false friends"). Sometimes words in other languages will look very similar to English words but will have completely different meanings. Watch out for them!

RIPASSO GENERALE / GENERAL REVIEW

A. More Notes about Sicily

In the previous lesson, you learned a bit about the rich and diverse history of Sicily, the biggest island in the Mediterranean. Here are some more fun facts:

- Did you know that Mount Etna is one of the most active volcanoes in the world? It is also the tallest in Europe (at 10,900 feet), and it most recently erupted in June 2019. It is also called Mongibello by the Sicilians.
- The Sicilian language is a distinct language from Italian; it is not a dialect, but rather a mix of Italian, Greek, Arabic, Spanish, and Catalan.
- Sicily is home to some of the best orange and lemon trees; in fact, the Sicilian Mafia originally formed to protect the farmers who owned orchards and estates near Palermo.
- Palermo is home to the largest opera house in Italy (the Teatro Massimo). The original Italian sonnet originated in Sicily in the 1200s, when the literary arts flourished under King Federico II. Sicily also boasts a rich history of marionette theater (*l'opera dei pupi*), which traditionally represented tales of chivalry and love.

B. Plural Definite Articles

In the previous lesson, you met singular indefinite and definite articles. While indefinite articles are only singular, definite articles have plural forms. These are very formulaic:

gender	singular	plural
feminine	l' *or* la	le
masculine	l' *or* lo	gli
masculine	il	i

As you can see, there is only one feminine plural form (*le*) and two masculine plural forms (*i* and *gli*). Since *gli* is the plural form of *lo* (and *l'*), it will follow the same rules of use as the singular: It is used with nouns beginning in *s* + consonant, *x, y, z, ps, pn,* and *gn*.

These articles have to match the nouns they modify. But how do we make nouns plural?

C. Pluralizing Italian Nouns

When it comes to making Italian nouns plural, the process is also very formulaic. Aside from irregular nouns and endings, this table shows you how to make a noun plural:

gender	singular	plural
feminine	-a	-e
masculine	-o	-i
feminine or masculine	-e	-i

If you follow these rules, you will be able to form the plural of most Italian words. For example, the plural of *la casa* (the house) is *le case* (the houses); both the article and the noun change to reflect the plural. For a masculine word, you will see *il tavolo* change to *i tavoli* and *lo zaino* change to *gli zaini*. Words that end in *-e* can be either masculine or feminine; regardless, they take an *-i* ending in the plural, and their article also changes. If you remember that words ending in *-ione* are feminine, then you know that the plural of *la stazione* is *le stazioni*.

There are always exceptions, however! Here are some rules for pluralizing irregular nouns (note that while the rules for nouns will change a bit, the rules for the articles will stay the same):

- Accented nouns do not change in the plural. (*il caffè* → *i caffè*; *l'università* → *le università*)
- Foreign nouns do not change in the plural. (*lo sport* → *gli sport*; *il bar* → *i bar*)
- Abbreviated nouns do not change in the plural. (*la moto* → *le moto*; *il film* → *i film*)
- Nouns that end in *-ca*, *-co*, *-ga*, and *-go* need to add an *h* to their plural forms to retain the hard *C* or *G* sound. (*l'amica* → *le amiche*; *il lago* → *i laghi*)
    › This is not true for some words ending in *-ico* (e.g., *medico/medici*, *amico/amici*, *simpatico/simpatici*, *scientifico/scientifici*, etc.).
- Nouns ending in *-io* typically do not double up on the *i* ending in the plural (*lo studio* → *gli studi*; *l'orologio* → *gli orologi*), with very few exceptions (*lo zio* → *gli zii*).
- Nouns ending in *-cia* and *-gia* pluralize differently depending on where the stress falls in the ending. If the ending is split into two syllables (such as in *farmacia*, pronounced "far-ma-CHEE-ah"), then the *i* will be retained in the plural (*le farmacie*, pronounced "far-ma-CHEE-ay"). If, instead, the ending

is contained in one single syllable (such as in the word *valigia*, pronounced "vah-LEE-jah"), it is not necessary to retain the *i*, and the plural form is simply *-ce* or *-ge* (in this case, *le valige*, pronounced "vah-LEE-jay").

- Nouns ending in *-ista* (e.g., *artista*, *barista*, *comunista*, *femminista*, etc.) can be either masculine or feminine in the singular; the article gives away the gender. In the plural, these words change to *-isti* (masculine) and *-iste* (feminine).

- Many body parts, as mentioned in the previous lesson, are very irregular in their plural formations (e.g., *la mano* → *le mani*; *l'orecchio* → *le orecchia*; *il braccio* → *le braccia*). Don't worry about these for now!

D. Numbers from 0 to 20

Here is a list of the numbers from 0 to 20, with a pronunciation guide.

Number	Italian	Pronunciation
0	zero	ZEH-ro
1	uno	OO-noh
2	due	DOO-ay
3	tre	TRAY
4	quattro	QUA-tro
5	cinque	CHEEN-quay
6	sei	SAY
7	sette	SEH-tay
8	otto	OH-toh
9	nove	NO-vay
10	dieci	dee-AY-chee
11	undici	OON-dee-chee
12	dodici	DOH-dee-chee
13	tredici	TRAY-dee-chee
14	quattordici	qua-TOR-dee-chee
15	quindici	QUIN-dee-chee
16	sedici	SAY-dee-chee
17	diciassette	dee-cha-SET-tay
18	diciotto	dee-CHO-toh
19	diciannove	dee-cha-NO-vay
20	venti	VEN-tee

E. Numbers from 20 to 100

The numbers from 20 to 100 are very similar to each other after 20, and they also look similar to their stems.

Number	Italian	Pronunciation
20	venti	VEN-tee
30	trenta	TREYN-tah
40	quaranta	qua-RAHN-tah
50	cinquanta	cheen-QUAN-tah
60	sessanta	seh-SAHN-tah
70	settanta	seh-TAHN-tah
80	ottanta	oh-TAHN-tah
90	novanta	noh-VAHN-tah
100	cento	CHEN-toh

To form the numbers in between these numbers (21, 22, etc.), simply add the cardinal numbers to the end of the stems (*ventuno, ventidue, ventitré, ventiquattro, venticinque, ventisei, ventisette, ventotto, ventinove*). Note that a few of these numbers cut out extra vowels for flow (numbers ending in 1 and 8), and numbers ending in 3 have an accent on them.

> Montalbano è un commissario siciliano. È bello: ha gli occhi castani. Non è né basso né alto, né giovane né vecchio, né grasso né magro. È calvo: non ha capelli. È bravo, responsabile, sensibile, gentile e onesto. Qualche volta è nervoso, antipatico o triste, ma non sempre.

> Montalbano is a Sicilian detective. He is handsome: He has brown eyes. He is neither short nor tall, neither young nor old, neither heavy nor thin. He is bald: He doesn't have any hair [on his head]. He is talented, responsible, sensitive, kind, and honest. Sometimes he is irritable, mean, or sad, but not always.

A. Even Bigger Numbers (Including Dates)

When forming large numbers in Italian, you essentially write out each part of the number, even in dates. Whereas English speakers express the date 1995 as "nineteen-ninety-five," Italians will say "one thousand, nine hundred, and ninety-five"—all one word! It sounds like a mouthful at first, but once you familiarize yourself with the pattern, it will get easier. Here are a few famous dates in Italian:

1492: *millequattrocentonovantadue* (one thousand + four hundred + ninety-two)
1776: *millesettecentosettantasei* (one thousand + seven hundred + seventy-six)
1861: *milleottocentosessantuno* (one thousand + eight hundred + sixty-one)
2018: *due**mila**diciotto* (two thousand + eighteen) [note that the plural of *mille* is *mila*]

> **In quale anno sei nato/a tu? / IN WHAT YEAR WERE YOU BORN?**
>
> Practice writing the year in the Italian format.
> For example: Io sono nata nel millenovecentoottantasei (1986).

A. Descriptive Adjectives (Plus Colors and Nationalities)

There are many adjectives that you can use in Italian to describe yourself or a friend, a few of which are listed in the vocabulary section at the beginning of the lesson. Adjectives are gendered like nouns are and must match the gender of the noun that they modify. They typically go after the noun in an Italian sentence, but not always. They carry the same rules of pluralization: -*a* goes to -*e*, -*o* goes to -*i*, and -*e* goes to -*i*. Here are some difficult examples of phrases that have articles, nouns, and adjectives all together:

- *l'amica americana* / the American female friend
- *la camicia verde* / the green shirt
- *lo studente stressato* / the stressed student
- *il medico tedesco* / the German doctor
- *il caffè costoso* / the expensive coffee

How can we make these phrases plural? Consider each part before you do so, and pay particular attention to the endings of each word.

- *l'amica americana* → *le amiche americane*
- *la camicia verde* → *le camice verdi*
- *lo studente stressato* → *gli studenti stressati*
- *il medico tedesco* → *i medici tedeschi*
- *il caffè costoso* → *i caffè costosi*

Did you notice some of the irregular rules at work? Highlight or underline the irregularities; then, refer back to the rules in section c. if you need clarification.

Ci sono una madre e un bambino. La madre è bella e il bambino è piccolo.
Ci sono due angeli. La madre e il bambino sono tranquilli. La madre ha i
capelli bruni. Il bambino ha i capelli bruni. Un angelo ha un drappo verde.
L'altro angelo ha un drappo rosso. La madre ha le mani belle e graziose.

> There are a mother and a child. The mother is beautiful and the child is small.
> There are two angels. The mother and the child are peaceful. The mother
> has brown hair. The child has brown hair. One angel has a green cloth. The
> other angel has a red cloth. The mother has beautiful and delicate hands.

A. A Brief Note on the Verb *avere*

The verb *avere* means "to have" in Italian. Like *essere*, it is very irregular. You
will learn more about the verb and its idiomatic usages in the following lessons.
For now, look at the conjugation of the verb and familiarize yourself with its
different parts:

Singular	Plural
io **ho**	noi **abbiamo**
tu **hai**	voi **avete**
lui/lei/Lei **ha**	loro **hanno**

Note that the letter *h* is not pronounced.

You can use the verb *avere* to talk about your age or physical characteristics (and
the verb *essere* to talk about your personality traits). For example: *Io ho trentadue
anni. Ho i capelli ricci e castani e gli occhi verdi. Sono allegra e ambiziosa.* (I am
thirty-two years old. I have brown, curly hair and green eyes. I am happy
and ambitious.)

ATTIVITÀ / ACTIVITIES

Tommaso e Giuseppina continuano il loro viaggio a Catania. Si fermano a un
ristorante siciliano e mentre mangiano, fanno appunti sulle cose che vedono in
Piazza del Duomo. (Tommaso and Giuseppina continue their trip in Catania. They
stop at a Sicilian restaurant, and while they eat, they take notes on things that they
see in Piazza del Duomo.)

1. Scrivi la forma plurale delle parole negli spazi vuoti. (Write the correct plurals of
the words given. Don't forget to pluralize the adjectives as well!)

Here's the menu for Caffè del Duomo: http://www.caffedelduomocatania.com/menu.html.

Cameriere: Buona sera, signori. Cosa vogliono da mangiare?

Tommaso: Prendiamo due 1. _____ (bottiglia) di acqua minerale, due 2. _____ (pizza), una margherita e una siciliana, due 3. _____ (insalata mista) e due 4. _____ (piatto) di 5. _____ (patatina fritta).

Cameriere: Certo. Ritorno subito.[1]

Giuseppina: Mamma mia, che bellissima piazza! Stasera[2] ci sono molti 6. _____ (turista) in giro.

Tommaso: Sì, vedo 7. _____ (turista giapponese, spagnolo, irlandese, americano), un po' di tutto![3]

Giuseppina: Ci sono tante belle 8. _____ (cosa) da vedere qui. Ci sono due 9. _____ (palazzo), molte 10. _____ (fontana), e anche molte 11. _____ (chiesa antica).

Tommaso: Facciamo molte 12. _____ (foto)!

Giuseppina: Sì, e voglio comprare anche cinque 13. _____ (cartolina[4]) per i nostri 14. _____ (cugino tedesco).

Tommaso: Perfetto. Ecco il cibo!

Cameriere: Buon appetito!

2. Per ogni parola, scrivi il plurale, sia del sostantivo, sia dell'articolo. (For each word, write its plural form, both for the noun and for the article. Pay attention to irregular rules!)

1. il caffè (*coffee*) _____

2. l'insalata (*salad*) _____

3. l'aeroporto (*airport*) _____

4. il museo (*museum*) _____

---

1 immediately

2 Tonight

3 *un po' di tutto* = a bit of everything

4 postcard

5. la bistecca (*steak*) _____

6. il palazzo (*palace*) _____

7. l'autobus (*city bus*) _____

8. la banca (*bank*) _____

9. lo stadio (*stadium*) _____

10. la tazza (*cup*) _____

3. Scrivi il numero in italiano. (Write out the number in Italian.)

1. 48 _____

2. 52 _____

3. 19 _____

4. 86 _____

5. 27 _____

6. 12 _____

7. 93 _____

8. 34 _____

9. 71 _____

19. 60 _____

4. Scrivi la data in italiano. (Write out the date in Italian.)

1. 1375 _____

2. 1963 _____

3. 2004 _____

4. 1588 _____

5. 1066 _____

5. *Esercizio di scrittura: Come sei tu? Com'è _____?*

Using the vocabulary you learned in this lesson and the verbs *essere* and *avere*, briefly describe yourself in terms of physical appearance and personality traits. Then describe someone else (a relative, friend, stranger—anyone!) in the third person.

ANSWER KEY

1.

1. bottiglie
2. pizze
3. insalate miste
4. piatti
5. patatine fritte
6. turisti
7. turisti giapponesi, spagnoli, irlandesi, americani
8. cose
9. palazzi
10. fontane
11. chiese antiche
12. foto
13. cartoline
14. cugini tedeschi

2.

1. i caffè
2. le insalate
3. gli aeroporti
4. i musei
5. le bistecche
6. i palazzi
7. gli autobus
8. le banche
9. gli stadi
10. le tazze

3.

1. quarantotto
2. cinquantadue
3. diciannove
4. ottantasei
5. ventisette
6. dodici
7. novantatré
8. trentaquattro
9. settantuno
10. sessanta

4.

1. milletrecentosettantacinque
2. millenovecentosessantatré
3. duemilaquattro
4. millecinquecentoottantotto
5. millesessantasei

5. Answers will vary. Example:

Io sono alta, magra e bella. Ho i capelli neri e gli occhi castani. Sono sensibile e simpatica, e non sono nervosa. Mio padre è basso e un po' grasso. Ha gli occhi castani ed è calvo. È vecchio ed è sempre felice!

VERBS ENDING IN -ARE / LOMBARDY

Oggi parliamo della Lombardia. La Lombardia è una regione nella parte nord-ovest dell'Italia. Si trova al confine con la nazione della Svizzera (al nord), il Piemonte (all'ovest), il Veneto (all'est), il Trentino–Alto Adige (ad est), e l'Emilia-Romagna (al sud). La Lombardia è la regione più popolata di tutta l'Italia! Ci sono più persone che abitano in questa regione che in qualsiasi altra regione italiana. Ci sono tante università in questa regione e tante tradizioni culinarie: la polenta, per esempio. La Lombardia è una regione con una lunga storia industriale.

▶ Today we will speak about Lombardy. Lombardy is a region in the northwestern part of Italy. It is located on the border with the nation of Switzerland (to the north), Piedmont (to the west), Veneto (to the east), Trentino–Alto Adige (to the east), and Emilia-Romagna (to the south). Lombardy is the most populated region in all of Italy! There are more people who live in this region than in any other Italian region. There are many universities in this region and many culinary traditions: polenta, for example. Lombardy is a region with a long industrial history.

VOCABOLARIO NUOVO E UTILE / NEW AND USEFUL VOCABULARY

il confine	border	la nazione	nation, country
la tradizione	tradition	l'industria	industry
culinario/a	culinary	popolato/a	populous
abitare	to live (in a place)	amare	to love
arrivare	to arrive	ascoltare	to listen to
aspettare	to wait for	ballare	to dance
cantare	to sing	cercare	to look for
cominciare	to begin	comprare	to buy
desiderare	to desire	dimenticare	to forget
guardare	to look at	imparare	to learn
incontrare	to meet	insegnare	to teach
lavorare	to work	pensare	to think
mangiare	to eat	ricordare	to remember
tornare	to return	trovare	to find
indicare	to indicate, to point	gesticolare	to gesture
andare	to go	dare	to give
fare	to make, to do	stare	to stay, to be
sempre	always	spesso	often
non...mai	never	insieme	together
il ragazzo	boy	la ragazza	girl
l'esame [masc.]	exam	i soldi	money
il posto	employment	l'azienda	company, store
la ricerca	research	la cena	dinner
il letto	bed	la televisione* (la TV)	television
i vestiti	clothing, clothes	sereno/a	calm
preoccupato/a	worried	portare	to wear, to bring
rosa**	pink	marrone	brown

* This noun refers to the shows and programs you watch. The word for a television set is *il televisore*. *TV*, the shortened form of *televisione*, is pronounced "tee-voo."

** This adjective is invariable, meaning that it stays the same in all forms, no matter the gender or number of the noun it modifies (e.g., *i pantaloni rosa, la camicia rosa, il cappello rosa*).

A. Notes on Lombardy

Lombardy (Lombardia) is the most populated region of Italy. It boasts a rich cultural history that extends from ancient Roman times to the Renaissance, and its heritage is well preserved. The northern regions of Italy—especially those that border the countries of Austria, Switzerland, and France—are very different than the southern regions, in terms of not only everyday life but also industries, culinary traditions, and language. Lombardy is a land of wine, cheese, risotto, and polenta. Its provinces and principal cities are world renowned. With its *capoluogo* of Milan, famous lakes and national parks, and countless museums and churches (one of which houses the famous *Last Supper* fresco by Leonardo da Vinci), there is no mistaking the global fascination of this region.

B. Verbs Ending in -*are* (First Conjugation)

You have already learned how to conjugate three verbs—*essere*, *stare*, and *avere*—which belong to two categories of verbs in Italian: the first and second conjugations (out of three major conjugations; there are other verbs that fall outside of these three groupings). Verbs that belong to the first conjugation end in -*are* and are, for the most part, fairly regular in their formula and easy to conjugate.

Let's start from what you already know from lesson 1: the conjugation of the verb *stare*.

io **sto**	noi **stiamo**
tu **stai**	voi **state**
lui/lei/Lei **sta**	loro/Loro **stanno**

Regular -*are* verbs will have almost the exact same endings as *stare*. Memorize this formula:

-o	-iamo
-i	-ate
-a	-ano

Now that you know the appropriate endings for each person of the verb, you can conjugate almost any verb ending in -*are*!

However, there are a few tiny exceptions in the spelling of some -are verbs that you need to know.

- Verbs ending in -care and -gare (e.g., cercare, pagare) have the same endings but need an *h* added in persons that feature an *i* in their conjugation (namely, the *tu* and *noi* forms). So the conjugations look like this:

io **cerco**	noi **cerchiamo**
tu **cerchi**	voi **cercate**
lui/lei/Lei **cerca**	loro/Loro **cercano**

- Verbs that end in -ciare and -giare (e.g., cominciare, mangiare) conjugate as usual and retain the *i* in their stems, but they do not need an extra *i* in the *tu* and *noi* forms. Their conjugations are as follows:

io **mangio**	noi **mangiamo**
tu **mangi**	voi **mangiate**
lui/lei/Lei **mangia**	loro/Loro **mangiano**

C. Irregular -are Verbs: *Andare, dare, fare,* and *stare* (Plus Idiomatic Usages)

There are many irregular verbs in every conjugation, but the following four are the most commonly used in the first conjugation. Since they are so irregular, it is best to memorize their forms. Take notice of the similarities between them:

	andare	dare	fare	stare
io	vado	do	faccio	sto
tu	vai	dai	fai	stai
lui/lei/Lei	va	dà	fa	sta
noi	andiamo	diamo	facciamo	stiamo
voi	andate	date	fate	state
loro/Loro	vanno	danno	fanno	stanno

Each of these verbs has a variety of idiomatic usages. You'll notice that their translations include many different verbs in English. Here are a few:

ANDARE
andare bene/male (to go well/badly)
andare d'accordo (to get along)
andare a piedi (to go by foot)
andare in _____ (to go by train, plane, etc.)

STARE
stare bene/male (to be well/unwell)
stare attento/a (to pay attention)
stare zitto/a (to be quiet)

DARE
darsi la mano (to hold/shake hands)
dare una mano (to lend a hand/to help)
dare del tu/Lei (to address someone informally/formally)
dare un esame (to take an exam)

FARE
fare freddo/caldo/bel tempo (to be hot/cold/nice weather)
fare una passeggiata (to take a walk)
fare una foto (to take a picture)
fare una domanda (to ask a question)
fare attenzione (to pay attention)

E tu? Try to use some of these idiomatic phrases to answer the following questions:

- *Come vai al lavoro?* (How do you get to work?)
- *Fai una domanda quando non capisci qualcosa? o stai zitto/a?* (Do you ask a question when you don't understand something? Or do you remain quiet?)
- *Dai una mano a tua nonna qualche volta?* (Do you help your grandmother out sometimes?)

D. Adverbs of Frequency

In this lesson, you meet a few adverbs: *sempre* (always), *spesso* (often), and *non... mai* (never). Adverbs typically come after the verb in an Italian sentence, whereas they can be a bit more flexible in English syntax:

- *Parli al telefono? Sì, parlo **sempre** al telefono.* (Do you talk on the phone? Yes, I **always** talk on the phone.)
- *Guardi la TV? Sì, guardo **spesso** la TV.* (Do you watch TV? Yes, I **often** watch TV / I watch TV **often**.)

You might be wondering why *non...mai* has an ellipsis in it. The word *mai* can be used by itself to mean *never*, but in general, sentences that have a negative verbal or adverbial phrase in them must be accompanied by *non* to indicate that they are negative. You'll see this in more detail in a later lesson, but here are a few examples:

- *Parli al telefono? No, **non** parlo **mai** al telefono.* (Do you talk on the phone? No, I **never** talk on the phone.)
- *Guardi la TV? No, **non** guardo **mai** la TV.* (Do you watch TV? No, I **never** watch TV.)

Note that the word *non* almost always begins a negative sentence. It comes before a verb and after a personal pronoun (if one is included). Adverbial phrases including *non* sandwich a verb.

Questo film parla di un ragazzo che si chiama Domenico. Domenico è un ragazzo giovane. Non frequenta più la scuola perché la sua famiglia ha bisogno di soldi. Lui va a Milano per cercare lavoro. Dà tanti esami per avere il posto. Trova un posto in un'azienda grande. Nell'azienda incontra Antonietta, una ragazza giovane e bella. Domenico e Antonietta vanno a tanti posti insieme. Ad una festa dell'azienda, Domenico balla.

> This film is about (*literally*: speaks about) a boy who is called Domenico. Domenico is a young boy. He doesn't go to school any longer because his family needs money. He goes to Milan to look for work. He takes many tests to have this job. He finds a job in a big company. He meets Antonietta, a young and beautiful girl, at the company. Domenico and Antonietta go to many places together. Domenico dances at a company party.

ATTIVITÀ / ACTIVITIES

Due amici, Elena e Nino, si preparano a viaggiare a Milano questo fine settimana. Parlano delle cose che vogliono fare, dove vogliono stare, e come vanno alla città da Brescia. (Two friends, Elena and Nino, are preparing to travel to Milan this weekend. They are talking about the things they want to do, where they want to stay, and how they will get to the city from Brescia.)

1. Scrivi le parole giuste negli spazi vuoti. (Write the correct words in the spaces given.)

Elena:	Nino, che 1. _____ (fare, tu) questo fine settimana? 2. _____ (stare, tu) a casa o 3. _____ (avere, tu) intenzioni[1] di viaggiare?

Elena: Nino, che 1. _____ (fare, tu) questo fine settimana? 2. _____ (stare, tu) a casa o 3. _____ (avere, tu) intenzioni[1] di viaggiare?

Nino: Certamente non 4. _____ (stare, io) a casa! 5. _____ (fare, noi) qualcosa di divertente.[2] Perché non 6. _____ (andare, noi) a Milano? Non è molto lontano da qui.

Elena: Buon'idea! Come 7. _____ (arrivare, noi) alla città? 8. _____ (andare, noi) in treno o in macchina?

Nino: Il treno è molto costoso. Ti 9. _____ (dare, io) un passaggio in macchina.

Elena: Benissimo, grazie! 10. _____ (visitare, io) tutti i musei e il Duomo di Milano, e poi 11. _____ (fare, io) una bellissima passeggiata nei giardini. Poi 12. _____ (andare, io) a visitare la mia amica Lauretta, che certamente ci 13. _____ (dare, lei) ospitalità a casa sua. Ci stai?[3]

Nino: Va bene. Ti 14. _____ (aspettare, io) di fronte a casa tua domani mattina dopo che 15. _____ (fare, io) colazione.[4] Ciao!

Elena: Arrivederci!

2. Inserisci le coniugazioni mancanti nella tabella. (Write the correct missing verb conjugations in the chart. Watch out for verbs that require different spelling!)

	lavare	mancare	ordinare	salvare	studiare
io	lavo	4.	7.	salvo	13.
tu	1.	5.	ordini	salvi	14.
lui/lei/Lei	2.	manca	ordina	10.	studia
noi	laviamo	manchiamo	8.	salviamo	15.
voi	lavate	6.	ordinate	11.	studiate
loro/Loro	3.	mancano	9.	12.	studiano

....

1 *avere intenzioni di* = to intend to

2 fun, entertaining

3 *Ci stai?* = from the pronominal verb *starci*, essentially meaning "Are you interested?"

4 breakfast

3. Scegli la forma giusta del verbo. (Choose the correct form of the verb.)

1. Valentina, mi _____ (dare) una mano per favore?
   a. dio   b. dia   c. dai   d. d

2. Nella classe di biologia io non _____ (fare) mai attenzione!
   a. faccio   b. fanno   c. foccaccia   d. fai

3. Ciao ragazzi, come _____ (stare) oggi?
   a. stai   b. state   c. stano   d. stanno

4. Mio fratello e io non _____ (andare) d'accordo spesso.
   a. andiamo   b. andamo   c. viamo   d. andate

5. Loro non hanno una macchina; _____ (andare) sempre a piedi a scuola.
   a. andano   b. andate   c. vado   d. vanno

4. Scrivi la forma giusta del verbo nella frase. (Write the correct form of the verb in the sentence.)

1. Laura e Stefano _____ (mangiare) insieme al parco.

2. Asuka _____ (parlare) giapponese ma _____ (imparare) l'italiano a scuola.

3. Non ho molti soldi, ma _____ (pagare) per tutti stasera.

4. Mia sorella e io _____ (amare) gli sport. _____ (giocare) a calcio[1] insieme ogni fine settimana.

5. Mireille, quando _____ (tornare) in Francia?

6. Ad agosto mia madre _____ (cominciare) a prendere lezioni di danza all'università. Lei _____ (ballare) bene, ma _____ (cantare) male!

7. Quando esci[2] con gli amici, tu _____ (incontrare) loro in centro[3] o a casa?

8. Dove _____ (abitare) tu e la tua famiglia?

....

1 soccer (from the verb *calciare*, which means "to kick")

2 the *tu* form of the verb *uscire* ("to go out")

3 *in centro* = downtown

5. *Esercizio di scrittura: Cosa fai questo fine settimana?*

Using the verbs and idiomatic phrases you learned in this lesson, list five activities you plan to complete this weekend. To practice with different forms of the verbs, redo the exercise for a different person or ask another person (or people) what his or her (or their) plans are.

_____

_____

_____

_____

ANSWER KEY

1.

1. fai
2. Stai
3. hai
4. sto
5. Facciamo
6. andiamo
7. arriviamo
8. Andiamo
9. do
10. Visito
11. faccio
12. vado
13. dà
14. aspetto
15. faccio

2.

1. lavi
2. lava
3. lavano
4. manco
5. manchi
6. mancate
7. ordino
8. ordiniamo
9. ordinano
10. salva
11. salvate
12. salvano
13. studio
14. studi
15. studiamo

3.

1. c.
2. a.
3. b.
4. a.
5. d.

4.

1. mangiano
2. parla, impara
3. pago
4. amiamo, Giochiamo
5. torni
6. comincia, balla, canta
7. incontri
8. abitate

5. Answers will vary. Example:

Questo fine settimana faccio molte cose. Faccio colazione con Maria, e poi facciamo una passeggiata in centro. Andiamo al museo d'arte, e dopo, Maria va a casa e io vado a trovare un altro amico, Davide. Davide e io mangiamo una pizza e poi...

NAMES OF PROVINCES AND FAMOUS LANDMARKS IN LOMBARDY

Province	Famous Landmark(s)
Milano (capoluogo)	Duomo di Milano; Teatro alla Scala; Biblioteca Ambrosiana; Santa Maria delle Grazie (site of Leonardo's *Last Supper* fresco)
Bergamo	Funicular to Città Alta (walled medieval city); Piazza Vecchia; Accademia Carrara
Brescia	Lago di Garda; Museo di Santa Giulia; Castello di Brescia
Como	Lago di Como; Museo della Seta (Educational Silk Museum); Villa Olmo
Cremona	Museo del Violino (Violin Museum); Piazza Antonio Stradiveri; Torrazzo di Cremona (decorated bell tower)
Lecco	Palazzo delle Paure (art museum named Palace of Fears); Monte Barro; Museo Manzoniano (museum dedicated to author Alessandro Manzoni)
Lodi	Parco Regionale dell'Adda Sud (South Adda Regional Park); Museo della Stampa e Stampa d'Arte (Museum of Printing); Tempio Civico della Beata Vergine Incoronata
Mantova (Mantua)	Museo del Risorgimento (museum dedicated to the Italian Unification movement); Galleria Storica Nazionale dei Vigili di Fuoco (National Historical Gallery of Firemen); Palazzo Ducale
Monza e Brianza	Villa Reale di Monza; Acquaworld (water park); Roseto Niso Fumagalli (rose garden)
Pavia	Castello Visconteo; Ponte Coperto (Covered Bridge); Orto Botanico dell'Università di Pavia (botanical garden)
Sondrio	Museo Valtellinese di Storia e Arte; Palazzo Pretorio; Cantina ARPEPE (family winery)
Varese	Sacro Monte di Varese; Villa Panza; Palazzo Estense

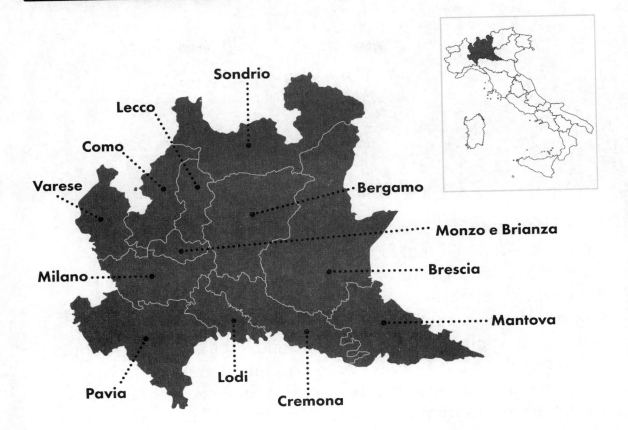

Sondrio
Lecco
Como
Varese
Bergamo
Monzo e Brianza
Milano
Brescia
Mantova
Pavia
Lodi
Cremona

VERBS ENDING IN -ERE / LAZIO

Oggi parliamo del Lazio. Il Lazio è una regione nella parte centro-ovest dell'Italia. Si trova al confine con la Toscana e l'Umbria (al nord), l'Abruzzo e il Molise (all'est), e la Campania (al sud). Il Mar Tirreno bagna la costa occidentale della regione. Il Lazio contiene la capitale della nazione: Roma! Ci sono quattro province: Frosinone, Latina, Rieti e Viterbo. Segue direttamente la Lombardia in due cose: ha una popolazione grande e un'economia molto forte. C'è tanta storia antica, particolarmente romana, in questa regione. Ci sono tante cose da fare e da vedere per i turisti. La Città del Vaticano si trova in questa regione, anche se non fa parte della nazione italiana.

Today we will speak about Lazio. Lazio is a region in the central-western part of Italy. It borders with Tuscany and Umbria (to the north), Abruzzo and Molise (to the east), and Campania (to the south). The Tyrrhenian Sea washes its western shore. Lazio contains the nation's capital: Rome! There are four provinces: Frosinone, Latina, Rieti, and Viterbo. It directly follows Lombardy in two things: It has a large population and a very strong economy. There is a lot of ancient history, particularly Roman history, in this region. There are many things for tourists to do and to see. Vatican City is located in this region, even if it is not part of the Italian nation.

VOCABOLARIO NUOVO E UTILE / NEW AND USEFUL VOCABULARY

la parte	part	**la costa**	coast
occidentale	western	**orientale**	eastern
la provincia	province	**l'economia**	economy
lavare	to wash	**visitare**	to visit (a place)
andare a trovare	to visit (a person)	**conoscere**	to be familiar with
volare	to fly	**dormire**	to sleep
cadere	to fall	**sapere**	to know
chiedere	to ask	**chiudere**	to close
correre	to run	**decidere**	to decide
dipingere	to paint	**discutere**	to discuss
leggere	to read	**mettere**	to put, to place
perdere	to lose	**prendere**	to take
ricevere	to receive	**rispondere**	to respond
scrivere	to write	**spendere**	to spend
vedere	to see	**vendere**	to sell
vincere	to win	**vivere**	to live
dovere	to need to, to owe	**potere**	to be able to
volere	to want to	**bere**	to drink
rimanere	to remain	**scegliere**	to choose
spegnere	to turn off	**tenere**	to hold
avere caldo	to be hot/warm	**avere freddo**	to be cold
avere fame	to be hungry	**avere sete**	to be thirsty
avere ragione	to be right	**avere torto**	to be wrong
avere sonno	to be sleepy	**avere...anni**	to be...years old
avere bisogno di	to have need of	**avere voglia di**	to have want of

RIPASSO GENERALE / GENERAL REVIEW

A. **Notes about Lazio (Latium)**

The region of Latium—or, as the Italians call it, Lazio—is not the most populous region of Italy but is certainly the most famous and historic. Home to the Eternal City (Rome), Vatican City,[1] and countless other breathtaking sites and sights, this region captivates tourists from all over the world. Lazio's western edge makes up a big part of the Italian coastline, which has been important for international trade for centuries. Almost everyone is familiar with the history of the ancient Romans and their many emperors, but the region's name comes from the Latini tribe, who preceded the Romans and spoke Latin. Before the Romans, there were also the Etruscans, whose culture and art remains visible even today. These peoples might not be as well known as the Romans but are equally fascinating. In this lesson, you will learn more about verbs; the avid Latin scholar may find many recognizable structures in their conjugations.

B. **Verbs Ending in *-ere* and *-ire* (Second and Third Conjugations)**

In the previous lesson, you learned how to conjugate regular and irregular first conjugation verbs, which end in *-are*. Let's review that conjugation:

[io] -o	[noi] -iamo
[tu] -i	[voi] -ate
[lei, lui, Lei] -a	[loro] -ano

Now let's take a look at the (regular) endings for second and third conjugation (*-ere* and *-ire*) verbs:

[io] -o	[noi] -iamo
[tu] -i	[voi] **-ete**
[lei, lui, Lei] **-e**	[loro] **-ono**

[io] -o	[noi] -iamo
[tu] -i	[voi] **-ite**
[lei, lui, Lei] **-e**	[loro] **-ono**

....

1 Vatican City, though not a part of the country of Italy, can be found in this particular region.

You'll notice that the endings only differ slightly from each other among the three principal conjugations; in fact, the *io, tu,* and *noi* forms all look exactly the same. The third person conjugations are the same between *-ere* and *-ire* verbs. Really, the only person that varies the most is the *voi* form, which merely switches the *r* in the infinitive to a *t*.

Sounds easy, right? Unfortunately, there are many more irregular verbs in these two conjugations than there are in the first conjugation. What follows is a table containing some of the most common irregular second conjugation verbs and their forms. Note that some verbs that seem to have added wildly random letters are actually using Latin stems that have been discarded over the years but have been retained within the verb conjugations. Circle or underline the most irregular parts and commit them to memory:

bere (to drink)	rimanere (to remain)	sapere (to know)	dovere (to need to, to owe)	potere (to be able to)
bevo	rimango	so	devo	posso
bevi	rimani	sai	devi	puoi
beve	rimane	sa	deve	può
beviamo	rimaniamo	sappiamo	dobbiamo	possiamo
bevete	rimanete	sapete	dovete	potete
bevono	rimangono	sanno	devono	possono

volere (to want to)	scegliere (to choose)	spegnere (to turn off)	tenere (to hold)
voglio	scelgo	spengo	tengo
vuoi	scegli	spegni	tieni
vuole	sceglie	spegne	tiene
vogliamo	scegliamo	spegniamo	teniamo
volete	scegliete	spegnete	tenete
vogliono	scelgono	spengono	tengono

You'll learn more about regular and irregular *-ire* verbs in lesson 6.

C. A Note on Pronunciation of Various Second Conjugation Verbs

Look at the verbs in the table previous that have the syllable *go* in them (e.g., *rimanere, scegliere, spegnere, tenere*). Do you remember how to pronounce *G* sounds in Italian? If you're having trouble recalling which sounds take a hard *G* and which take a soft *G*, review <u>lesson 1</u>. Don't forget that *GA/GO/GU* are hard *G* sounds and *GE/GI* are soft; the same pattern holds for *C* sounds (*CA/CO/CU* are all hard *C* sounds while *CE/CI* are soft).

Keeping this in mind, how will you pronounce the following verb conjugations? Say each one out loud, practicing the differences between hard and soft *C* and *G* sounds. It may help to put a square around hard sounds and a circle around soft ones. Then, make a rule about the patterns that emerge:

vincere (to win)	**conoscere** (to know)	**leggere** (to read)	**spingere** (to push)
vinco	conosco	leggo	spingo
vinci	conosci	leggi	spingi
vince	conosce	legge	spinge
vinciamo	conosciamo	leggiamo	spingiamo
vincete	conoscete	leggete	spingete
vincono	conoscono	leggono	spingono

D. The Verb *avere* and Its Idiomatic Usages

Let's review the conjugation of the verb *avere*, which is technically a second conjugation verb but is very irregular in its forms:

[io] **ho**	[noi] **abbiamo**
[tu] **hai**	[voi] **avete**
[lei, lui, Lei] **ha**	[loro] **hanno**

Marcello è alto e bruno. Ha i capelli corti. Porta una giacca nera e dei pantaloni neri. Lui tiene il polso di Sylvia con la mano destra. Sylvia è alta. Ha dei capelli lunghi e biondi. Porta un abito da sera nero.

▸ Marcello is tall and has brown hair. He has short hair. He carries a black jacket and black pants. He holds Sylvia's wrist with his right hand. Sylvia is tall. She has long blonde hair. She wears a black evening dress.

Avere is used in many idiomatic expressions. These may be difficult to learn at first, considering that we typically use "to be" (which would be *essere*) for quite a few of them in their English equivalents:

Italian Expression	English Translation	Sample Sentence
avere caldo	to feel warm/hot	Oggi ho caldo e non posso dormire. (Today I feel hot and cannot sleep.)
avere freddo	to feel cold	Se hai freddo, porti una sciarpa. (If you feel cold, you wear a scarf.)
avere fame	to be hungry	Luigi ha fame e mangia un panino. (Luigi is hungry and eats a sandwich.)
avere sete	to be thirsty	I cammelli non hanno mai sete! (Camels are never thirsty!)
avere ragione	to be correct	Ah, avete ragione, i dragoni non sono veri. (Ah, you're right; dragons aren't real.)
avere torto	to be incorrect	Mario dice che 2 + 2 = 5, ma ha torto. (Mario says that 2 + 2 = 5, but he is incorrect.)
avere sonno	to be sleepy	Se hai sonno, vai a letto! (If you're tired, go to bed!)
avere ... anni	to be ... years old	Oggi è il compleanno di mia madre. Ha 60 anni. (Today is my mother's birthday. She is 60 years old.)
avere bisogno (di)	to need	Ho bisogno di studiare per quest'esame. (I need to study for this exam.)
avere voglia (di)	to want	Hanno voglia di uscire stasera. (They want to go out tonight.)
avere paura (di)	to be afraid (of)	Hai paura dei ragni? (Are you afraid of spiders?)
avere fretta	to be in a rush	Non posso fermarmi, ho fretta! (I can't stop; I'm in a rush!)

Marcello è un giornalista che vive a Roma. Scrive articoli per una rivista di pettegolezzi. Nella prima scena del film, Marcello fa un giro in elicottero. C'è un altro elicottero che porta una statua di Gesù Cristo. Volano sopra un aquedotto romano e vanno in città. Vediamo Marcello che segue la statua fino alla Basilica di San Pietro. In un'altra scena del film, vediamo Marcello con un'attrice svedese-americana, Sylvia (che è la famosa Anita Ekberg). Marcello chiede a Sylvia di fare una gita alla Basilica di San Pietro. Lei risponde di sì. Loro discutono poco. Loro entrano nella Fontana dei Trevi.

Marcello is a journalist who lives in Rome, writing articles for a gossip magazine. In the first scene of the film, Marcello takes a helicopter ride. There is another helicopter that carries a statue of Jesus Christ. They fly over a Roman aqueduct and go to the city. We see Marcello, who follows the statue until St. Peter's Basilica. In another scene of the film, we see Marcello with a Swedish American actress, Sylvia (who is played by the famous Anita Ekberg). Marcello asks Sylvia to go on a trip to St. Peter's Basilica. She answers yes. They speak very little. They go into the Trevi Fountain.

ATTIVITÀ / ACTIVITIES

Grazia e Rossana sono sorelle gemelle, ma sono molto diverse e a volte hanno opinioni che si contraddicono. Oggi sono a Viterbo. Grazia vuole vedere le necropoli etrusche[1] e Rossana vuole visitare il Parco dei Mostri[2]. Non hanno abbastanza tempo per fare tutte e due cose e non possono arrivare a una decisione. (Grazia and Rossana are twin sisters, but they are very different and sometimes have opinions that contradict each other. Today they are in Viterbo. Grazia wants to see the Etruscan necropolises, and Rossana wants to visit the Park of the Monsters. They don't have enough time to do both of these things, and they cannot arrive at a decision.)

1. Scegli le parole giuste e scrivile negli spazi vuoti. (Choose the correct words from the word bank and write them in the spaces given.)

bisogno   caldo   chiedere   conosci

voglia   perdere   provincia

1 A necropolis is a "city of the dead," where you can find remains of tombs and sacred burial grounds that were (in this case) built by the Etruscans. Many of these tombs have well-preserved artwork and objects, including "furniture" carved into the rock walls that the inhabitants could make use of in the afterlife, and some even resemble the inside of Egyptian pyramids. Learn more about the necropolises in Cerveteri and Tarquinia here: https://whc.unesco.org/en/list/1158/.

2 The Park of the Monsters (also known as the Sacro Bosco, or Sacred Forest, and the Gardens of Bomarzo) is a fun tourist attraction in Bomarzo, in the province of Viterbo. It was built in the 16th century and features many odd sculptures and statues, a leaning house, and various "traps" within the gardens. Learn more here: http://www.bomarzo.net/.

Rossana:	Che bella giornata oggi! Che cosa vogliamo fare? Ci sono tante buone cose da fare in questa 1. _____.
Grazia:	Bella? Oggi fa brutto tempo. Fa 32 gradi³ e ho un 2. _____ terribile!
Rossana:	Forse hai 3. _____ di un po' di acqua?
Grazia:	Non mi piace l'acqua. Ho 4. _____ di un caffè.
Rossana:	Va bene. Io voglio andare al Parco dei Mostri a Bomarzo.
Grazia:	Io invece⁴ voglio visitare la Necropoli Etrusca a Cerveteri. 5. _____ la storia degli Etruschi?
Rossana:	No, ma voglio stare fuori, sotto il sole⁵. Non è un'opportunità da 6. _____!
Grazia:	E io invece voglio stare in un posto sottoterreno, più freddo.
Rossana:	Forse dobbiamo 7. _____ consiglio⁶ a qualcun'altro.

2. Inserisci le coniugazioni mancanti nella lista. (Write the correct missing verb conjugations in the list. Watch out for irregular verbs!)

1. **bere:** bevo, bevi, _____, _____, bevete, _____

2. **prendere:** _____, prendi, prende, _____, _____, prendono

3. **avere:** _____, _____, ha, abbiamo, _____, hanno

4. **leggere:** leggo, leggi, _____, _____, leggete, _____

5. **chiudere:** chiudo, _____, chiude, chiudiamo, _____, _____

6. **decidere:** _____, decidi, _____, _____, decidete, decidono

7. **mettere:** metto, _____, mette, _____, mettete, _____

8. **vivere:** _____, _____, _____, viviamo, vivete, vivono

9. **rimanere:** rimango, rimani, rimane, _____, _____, _____

10. **scegliere:** _____, _____, sceglie, scegliamo, _____, scelgono

---

3 *Fa 32 gradi* = It is 32 degrees Celsius [equivalent to about 90 degrees Fahrenheit].

4 instead

5 *fuori, sotto il sole* = outside, under the sun

6 advice

3. Come si pronuncia? Scegli l'opzione giusta. (How do you pronounce it? Choose the correct option.)

1. Riman**g**o
   a. Hard *G* ("go")   b. Soft *G* ("jo")   c. *Y* sound ("yo")

2. Vin**ci**
   a. Hard *C* ("key")   b. Soft *C* ("chee")   c. *S* sound ("see")

3. Le**gg**iamo
   a. Hard *G* ("ghee")   b. Soft *G* ("jee")   c. *Y* sound ("yee")

4. Sce**gl**ie
   a. Hard *G* ("glee")   b. Soft *G* ("jee")   c. *Y* sound ("lyee")

5. Spe**gn**ete
   a. Hard *G* ("g-ne")   b. Soft *G* ("j-ne")   c. *Y* sound ("nyeh")

4. Abbina le parole nella lista B alle frasi nella lista A. (Match the words in column B to the sentences in column A.)

Column A	**Column B**
1. Franca ha _____ e così mangia una pizza.	a. fretta
2. Piero ha _____ e così prende il treno veloce.	b. paura
3. Mariangela ha _____ del buio.	c. fame
4. Emma ha _____ e così fa un pisolino.	d. freddo
5. Anna ha _____ e così si mette una maglia.	e. sonno

5. *Esercizio di scrittura: Hai bisogno di...?*

Using the idiomatic phrase *avere bisogno di* that you learned in this lesson, list five things that you (or other people) need right now. You can add to the sentences by using other idiomatic phrases with *avere*. After you list five things that you need, list five things that you want (*avere voglia di*).

_____

_____

_____

_____

_____

_____

_____

_____

_____

_____

_____

ANSWER KEY

1.

1. provincia
2. caldo
3. bisogno
4. voglia
5. Conosci
6. perdere
7. chiedere

2.

1. beve, beviamo, bevono
2. prendo, prendiamo, prendete
3. ho, hai, avete
4. legge, leggiamo, leggono
5. chiudi, chiudete, chiudono
6. decido, decide, decidiamo
7. metti, mettiamo, mettono
8. vivo, vivi, vive
9. rimaniamo, rimanete, rimangono
10. scelgo, scegli, scegliete

3.

1. a.
2. b.
3. b.
4. c.
5. c.

4.

1. c.
2. a.
3. b.
4. e.
5. d.

5. Answers will vary. Example:

Ho sete. Ho bisogno di acqua. / Ho sonno. Ho bisogno di dormire.

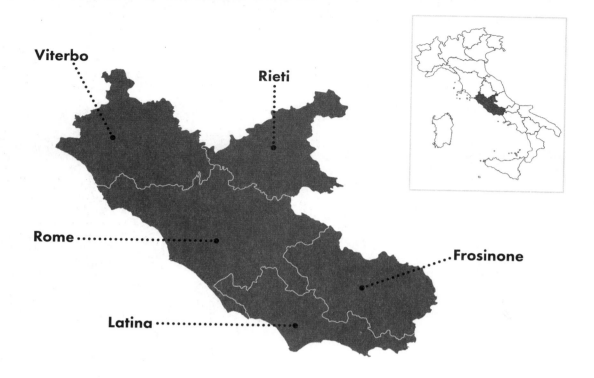

VERBS ENDING IN -*IRE* / AOSTA AND TRENTINO-ALTO ADIGE

Oggi parliamo di due regioni: la Valle d'Aosta e Trentino–Alto Adige. Sono regioni molto montagnose. Sono luoghi perfetti per sciare e passeggiare all'aria aperta. Si trovano nell'Italia settentrionale. La Valle d'Aosta confina con la regione del Piemonte (a sud) e anche con la Francia (ad ovest) e la Svizzera (a nord). Qui, l'italiano e il francese sono le due lingue officiali. È la regione più piccola e meno popolata di tutta l'Italia. Il suo capoluogo è Aosta. Contiene alcuni dei monti più alti delle Alpi, come il monte Bianco, il monte più alto di tutta l'Europa! Il Parco Nazionale del Gran Paradiso è in questa regione.

Il Trentino–Alto Adige è anche una regione con un paesaggio molto bello. Questa regione confina con la Lombardia e il Veneto. Il suo capoluogo è Trento, una città famosa per la storia medievale e rinascimentale (come il Concilio di Trento). Le Dolomiti, una catena montuosa spettacolare che fa parte delle Alpi, si trovano in questa regione. Le Dolomiti sono perfette per fare alpinismo e altre attività sportive. Sono due regioni che offrono tantissimo per chi ama la natura e l'attività sportiva!

Today we will speak about two regions: Valle d'Aosta and Trentino–Alto Adige. They are very mountainous regions. They are the perfect places for skiing and walking in the outdoors. They are located in northern Italy. Valle d'Aosta borders with the region of Piedmont (to the south) and also with France (to the west) and Switzerland (to the north). Italian and French are the two official languages here. It is the smallest and least populated region in all of Italy. Its capital is Aosta. It contains some of the tallest mountains of the Alps, like Monte Bianco, the tallest mountain in all of Europe! The Parco Nazionale del Gran Paradiso is in this region.

Trentino–Alto Adige is also a region with a very beautiful landscape. This region borders with Lombardy and Veneto. Its capital is Trent, a city famous for its medieval and Renaissance history (such as the Council of Trent). The Dolomites, a spectacular mountain range that is part of the Alps, are in this region. The Dolomites are perfect for mountain climbing and other athletic activities. They are two regions that offer so much for those who love nature and sports!

VOCABOLARIO NUOVO E UTILE / NEW AND USEFUL VOCABULARY

sciare	to ski	passeggiare	to walk
nuotare	to swim	fare sollevamento pesi	to lift weights
andare in palestra	to go to the gym	fare aerobica	to work out
prendere lezioni di...	to take lessons in...	correre	to run
la primavera	spring	l'estate	summer
l'autunno	fall	l'inverno	winter
estivo	summer [adj.]	invernale	winter [adj.]
confinare	to border	trovare	to find
vedere	to see	contenere	to contain
possedere	to possess	cambiare	to change
offrire	to offer	fare	to do, to make
seguire	to follow	sedere	to sit
aprire	to open	coprire	to cover
dormire	to sleep	partire	to leave
sentire	to smell, to hear	servire	to serve
vestire	to dress	venire	to come
morire	to die	uscire	to go out
salire	to go up	dire	to say
capire	to understand	finire	to finish
preferire	to prefer	pulire	to clean
la pallacanestro	basketball	le Olimpiadi	the Olympics
il calcio	soccer	le arti marziali	martial arts
la scherma	fencing	il canottaggio	rowing
l'equitazione	equestrian sports	la ginnastica	gymnastics
il nuoto	swimming	il pallanuoto	water polo
il pallavolo	volleyball	la vela	sailing
lo sci	skiing	il pattinaggio	skating
l'hockey	hockey	il ghiaccio	ice
la piscina	pool	la pista	course (skiing)

A. Notes about la Valle d'Aosta and Trentino–Alto Adige

The two beautiful regions in this lesson, la Valle d'Aosta and Trentino–Alto Adige, are sorely underrepresented in the tourism industry. Many tourists flock to the popular cities of Rome, Florence, and Venice, but much fewer get to see the extreme south or north of Italy. Valle d'Aosta (or Val d'Aosta, as it is more commonly called) is about as north as you can get in the country. The region borders both France and Switzerland, as well as the Italian region of Piemonte. While it has two official languages (Italian and French), there are also various dialects spoken here, such as Valdôtain, a Franco-Provençal dialect. With the Italian Alps—including Monte Bianco, Monte Rosa, Gran Paradiso, and the Matterhorn—as a backdrop, skiing is very popular here.

Trentino–Alto Adige, otherwise known as Südtirol, is another region found at the very north of Italy, abutting Switzerland, Austria, and the Italian regions of Lombardia and Veneto. Like Valle d'Aosta, it is a mountainous region, but this one includes the Dolomites as well as the Alps. While this region has suffered considerable poverty in the past, it is now one of the wealthiest parts of Italy (and of Europe). Its main exports include wine, fruit, timber, and hydroelectric power.

In this lesson, you will continue learning about verbs and their conjugations, specifically in the third conjugation (*-ire*). You will also meet some irregular *-ire* verbs (*dire*, *venire*, and *uscire*) and use them to talk about a trip to the north of Italy!

B. Present Tense of Third Conjugation (*-ire*) Verbs

In the previous lesson, you encountered a lot of irregular verbs in the second and third conjugations. Most of these verbs still follow the general pattern of regular verbs in these conjugations but have slight spelling variations. In this lesson, you'll look at a few more irregular third conjugation (*-ire*) verbs, as well as a special category of *-ire* verbs.

Let's review the regular verb forms for the third conjugation:

[io] -o	[noi] -iamo
[tu] -i	[voi] **-ite**
[lei, lui, Lei] **-e**	[loro] **-ono**

Now let's look at a special category of third conjugation verbs that have the same endings but a few extra letters in four of the forms:

[io] **-isc**o	[noi] -iamo
[tu] -**isc**i	[voi] -ite
[lei, lui, Lei] -**isc**e	[loro] -**isc**ono

How can you tell which -*ire* verbs have this special conjugation? Teachers of Italian have come up with many tricks and tactics over the years, but none is 100% reliable. You might come across this trick: "If, counting five letters backward from the end of the verb, there is a vowel, it will have this conjugation." However, this doesn't apply to all verbs with that formula (see, for example, *morire* or *salire*). It might be easier to simply memorize a list of the most common verbs in this category, since there aren't very many of them.

Here are some of the more common "special" -*ire* verbs, with their definitions and conjugations listed:

Verb	Definition	Conjugation
capire	to understand	capisco, capisci, capisce, capiamo, capite, capiscono
colpire	to hit	colpisco, colpisci, colpisce, colpiamo, colpite, colpiscono
costruire	to construct/build	costruisco, costruisci, costruisce, costruiamo, costruite, costruiscono
distribuire	to distribute	distribuisco, distribuisci, distribuisce, distribuiamo, distribuite, distribuiscono
finire	to finish	finisco, finisci, finisce, finiamo, finite, finiscono
riunire	to reunite	riunisco, riunisci, riunisce, riuniamo, riunite, riuniscono
preferire	to prefer	preferisco, preferisci, preferisce, preferiamo, preferite, preferiscono
pulire	to clean	pulisco, pulisci, pulisce, puliamo, pulite, puliscono
punire	to punish	punisco, punisci, punisce, puniamo, punite, puniscono
scolpire	to sculpt	scolpisco, scolpisci, scolpisce, scolpiamo, scolpite, scolpiscono
spedire	to send	spedisco, spedisci, spedisce, spediamo, spedite, spediscono

Notice that the *noi* and *voi* forms always revert back to the regular conjugation and are closer to the original infinitive. Also notice that the conjugation will change slightly between the *io* and *loro* forms (hard *C* sound = "SKO," "SKONO") and the *tu* and *lui/lei* forms (soft *C* sound = "SHEE," "SHAY").

C. Irregular *-ire* Verbs: *Dire, venire, uscire*

As always, each category of verbs has its irregular forms. Here are three that will be used in this lesson in particular: *dire* ("to say"), *venire* ("to come") and *uscire* ("to go out"). *Uscire* can be used in a few different ways: to exit a place, to go out with friends, and to date someone.

The conjugations are listed in the following table. Can you find the changes in spelling and pronunciation within the same verb?

dire	venire	uscire
dico	vengo	esco
dici	vieni	esci
dice	viene	esce
diciamo	veniamo	usciamo
dite	venite	uscite
dicono	vengono	escono

In the verb *dire*, there are *C*s in the conjugation (a vestige of the Latin verb *dicere*), and the *io* and *loro* forms have a hard *C*, while the *tu*, *lui/lei*, and *noi* forms have a soft *C* sound. In *venire*, there are *G*s in the *io* and *loro* forms, and the *tu* and *lui/lei* have *vie-* stems. Finally, in *uscire*, the forms switch back and forth between *E* and *U* beginnings, as well as having both hard and soft *C* sounds.

> Ma, nella regione della Valle d'Aosta, c'è uno sport particolare: lo tsan! Lo tsan è un gioco di squadre che si gioca con il pallino e la mazza. È simile al baseball ma è un gioco molto complesso.

▶ But in the region of Valle d'Aosta, there is a special sport: tsan!
Tsan is a team sport that is played with a small ball and a club.
It is similar to baseball, but it is a very complex game.

Mirko e Raffaella sono amici dall'infanzia e sono in montagna per andare a sciare. Hanno viaggiato da Roma e sono finalmente arrivati alla loro chalet, che ha un bellissimo panorama delle piste di Monte Rosa. Mentre disfanno le loro valige, parlano dei loro programmi per il fine settimana. (Mirko and Raffaella are childhood friends, and they are in the mountains to go skiing. They have traveled from Rome and are finally arriving at their chalet, which has a beautiful panoramic view of the slopes of Monte Rosa. While they are unpacking their bags, they are talking about their plans for the weekend.)

1. Scegli le parole giuste e scrivile negli spazi vuoti. (Choose the correct words from the word bank and write them in the spaces given.)

invernali   sciare   prendere lezioni

piste   salire

Mirko: Siamo finalmente arrivati in montagna! Guarda, Raffa, abbiamo una bella vista delle 1. _____ di Monte Rosa.

Raffaella: Proprio bella! Dove hai trovato[1] questa chalet?

Mirko: L'ho trovata in Internet, su un sito di turismo.

Raffaella: Fantastico! È difficile trovare un posto in questa stagione?

Mirko: Non molto difficile, dato che quest'anno non ci sono le Olimpiadi 2. _____. Però, ci sono molte persone che vengono qui per 3. _____.

Raffaella: Anch'io voglio farlo[2], ma non sono brava!

Mirko: Dunque possiamo 4. _____ con un istruttore!

Raffaella: Sarebbe[3] bellissimo. Ho molto freddo, vuoi bere un cioccolato caldo con me?

Mirko: Certo! Poi, andiamo a 5. _____ la montagna. Non è una competizione, ma...

Raffaella: Con te, tutta è una competizione!

Check out this Italian website to start putting your vocabulary to use! Don't worry if you don't understand everything; it's simply good practice to start seeing full sentences in Italian and matching them up with pictures and videos. https://www.vialattea.it/

....
1 *Dove hai trovato...?* = Where did you find...?

2 *Anch'io voglio farlo* = I also want to do it

3 *Sarebbe* = It would be

1. Di questi verbi, scegli quali hanno una coniugazione regolare (-*o*, -*i*, -*e*...) e quali sono irregolari (-*isco*, -*isci*, -*isce*...). Poi, scrivi le loro coniugazioni nella tabella. (From the verbs given, choose which ones have a regular conjugation (-*o*, -*i*, -*e*...) and which ones are irregular (-*isco*, -*isci*, -*isce*...). Then, write their conjugations in the table.)

1. capire   **regolare**   **irregolare**

2. dormire   **regolare**   **irregolare**

3. finire   **regolare**   **irregolare**

4. pulire   **regolare**   **irregolare**

5. offrire   **regolare**   **irregolare**

capire	dormire	finire	pulire	offrire

2. Abbina gli atleti famosi nella lista A agli sport nella lista B. (Match the famous athletes in column A to the sports vocabulary in column B.)

Column A	Column B
1. Wayne Gretzky	a. il calcio
2. Lionel Messi	b. il pattinaggio su ghiaccio
3. Katie Ledecky	c. il nuoto
4. Michelle Kwan	d. l'hockey su ghiaccio
5. Michael Jordan	e. la pallacanestro

3. *Esercizio di scrittura: Ti va di...?*

Using the vocabulary that you learned in this lesson—especially infinitive verbs and sports terminology—ask a friend if he or she would like to play a sport with you this weekend (*Ti va di* + [*infinitive verb*]?). Try to use as many vocabulary words as possible.

_____

_____

_____

_____

_____

ANSWER KEY

1.

1. piste
2. invernali
3. sciare
4. prendere lezioni
5. salire

2.

1. irregolare
2. regolare
3. irregolare
4. irregolare
5. regolare

capire	dormire	finire	pulire	offrire
capisco	dormo	finisco	pulisco	offro
capisci	dormi	finisci	pulisci	offri
capisce	dorme	finisce	pulisce	offre
capiamo	dormiamo	finiamo	puliamo	offriamo
capite	dormite	finite	pulite	offrite
capiscono	dormono	finiscono	puliscono	offrono

3.

1. d.
2. a.
3. c.
4. b.
5. e.

4. Answers will vary. Example:

Ti va di sciare questo fine settimana? (*Would you like to ski this weekend?*) Ti va di giocare a pallacanestro questo fine settimana?

MAP OF VALLE D'AOSTA AND TRENTINO–ALTO ADIGE

WHERE ARE YOU NOW?

Congratulations! You've made it through the first quarter of the workbook. By now, you should be familiar with the following topics in vocabulary:

1. greetings and goodbyes

2. geographical terms

3. adjectives

4. nationalities

5. numbers 0 to 10,000

6. colors

7. seasons

8. sports

You have also covered quite a bit of grammar:

1. subject pronouns

2. *essere* vs. *stare*

3. the formal and informal voice

4. genders of nouns (regular and irregular)

5. indefinite articles

6. definite articles

7. *ecco*, *c'è*, and *ci sono*

8. plurals of nouns

9. descriptive adjectives

10. the verb *avere*

11. verbs ending in *-are*

12. adverbs of frequency

13. verbs ending in *-ere*

14. verbs ending in *-ire*

15. idiomatic expressions with *avere*

Next to each topic, rate your comfort level from 1 to 5, with 1 being the least comfortable and 5 being the most. What can you work on more?

Here are some helpful tools and methods:

EXERCISES

A. Redo the exercises at the end of each lesson.

B. Look online for sample exercises that automatically check your answers. (Here are some good websites: http://italienencounter.com/en/free-italian-exercises/, http://www.oneworlditaliano.com/english/italian/italian-exercises-free-online.htm, http://www.impariamoitaliano.com/.)

METHODS

A. Study with a friend or family member.

B. Make physical or computer-generated flashcards (e.g., https://quizlet.com/create-set, https://www.cram.com/flashcards/create, https://www.canva.com/create/flashcards/). [Hint: Be sure to make flashcards that go from English to Italian as well as from Italian to English!]

C. Repeat verb conjugations while doing various activities (walking, singing, exercising, rapping, with your eyes closed, with your nose pinched, etc.).

D. Create a visual design of the grammar and vocabulary that works for you, with various colors, shapes, and layouts.

POSSESSIVE ADJECTIVES AND PRONOUNS / PUGLIA

Oggi parliamo della Puglia. La Puglia è una regione nella parte sud-est della penisola italiana: infatti, è la regione più orientale di tutta l'Italia. È il tacco dello stivale italiano! Confina con le regioni del Molise al nord-ovest e della Campania e della Basilicata ad ovest. Il Mar Adriatico bagna la costa orientale della regione e il Mar Ionio bagna la costa meridionale. Il suo capoluogo è Bari. Tante città pugliesi, come Bari e Lecce (chiamata "la Firenze del sud"), sono importanti per la loro storia antica.

Le province sono sei: Bari, Foggia, Barletta-Andria-Trani, Taranto, Brindisi e Lecce. La topografia di questa regione è più piatta che montagnosa: ci sono tante pianure che la percorrono. Ci sono tante cose da fare e da vedere per i turisti. Le sue coste sono bellissime: ci sono tante spiagge e bellezze naturali, soprattutto sul promontorio del Gargano ("lo sperone"). I trulli di Alberobello sono case circolari fatte con pietre bianche. I loro tetti sono a forma di cono. Alcuni di queste case adesso sono alberghi!

▶ Today we will speak about Puglia. Puglia is a region in the southeastern part of the Italian peninsula. In fact, it is the most eastern region in all of Italy. It is the "heel" of the Italian "boot"! It borders with the regions of Molise to the northwest and Campania and Basilicata to the west. The Adriatic Sea bathes the eastern coast of the region and the Ionian Sea bathes the southern coast. Its capital is Bari. Many Apulian cities, such as Bari and Lecce (called "the Florence of the south"), are important for their ancient history.

Its provinces are six: Bari, Foggia, Barletta-Andria-Trani, Taranto, Brindisi, and Lecce. The topography of this region is more flat than mountainous: There are many plains that run throughout it. Its coasts are beautiful: There are many beaches and places of natural beauty, most of all on the Gargano promontory (known as "the spur"). The trulli in Alberbello are circular homes made with white stones. Their roofs are conical. Some of these houses are now hotels!

il tacco	heel	**lo stivale**	boot
la costa	coast	**il tetto**	roof
l'albergo	hotel	**la bellezza**	beauty
il panzerotto	"pizza pouch"[1]	**i trulli**	domed houses[1]
la spiaggia	beach	**il duomo**	main church[2]
la basilica	basilica	**la grotta**	grotto
il castello	castle	**la camera**	room
i parenti	relatives	**i genitori**	parents
il padre	father	**la madre**	mother
il figlio	son	**la figlia**	daughter
il fratello	brother	**la sorella**	sister
il marito	husband	**la moglie**	wife
lo zio	uncle	**la zia**	aunt
il nonno	grandfather	**la nonna**	grandmother
il cugino	cousin (m.)	**la cugina**	cousin (f.)
il nipote	nephew[3]	**la nipote**	niece[3]
il suocero	father-in-law	**la suocera**	mother-in-law
il genero	son-in-law	**la nuora**	daughter-in-law
il cognato	brother-in-law	**la cognata**	sister-in-law
il patrigno	stepfather	**la matrigna**	stepmother
il fratellastro	stepbrother	**la sorellastra**	stepsister
il figliastro	stepson	**la figliastra**	stepdaughter
i bisnonni	great-grandparents	**il/la fidanzato/a**	fiancé(e)[4]
questo	this	**quello**	that
numeroso	numerous	**unico**	unique, only

1 *il panzerotto/i trulli* = These are things that are culturally particular to Puglia.

2 *il duomo* = Although many famous churches in Italy have domes (think of the Cattedrale di Santa Maria del Fiore in Florence), the word *duomo* derives from the Latin word *domus*, or *house* (of God).

3 *il/la nipote* = This is also the word for *grandson/granddaughter*. To distinguish these from *niece/nephew*, grandchildren will often be expressed with a diminutive ending (*nipotino/nipotina*).

4 *il/la fidanzato/a* = This is also used for serious relationships, not necessarily for someone to whom one is engaged.

RIPASSO GENERALE / GENERAL REVIEW

A. **Notes about Puglia**

Puglia—also commonly spelled Apulia, after its Latin name—is a fascinating region that forms the "heel" of the Italian boot. Like other southern regions of Italy, many impoverished immigrants came to the United States in the late 19th and early 20th centuries in search of the so-called American dream. Surrounded on three sides by water, Puglia boasts a long coastline—the longest in Italy, in fact—of breathtakingly beautiful beaches. Some of its most famous cities include Brindisi, Ostuni, Taranto, and the beach town Bari. Unlike the regions in the previous lesson, Puglia rarely experiences snowfall. Its Mediterranean climate contributes to a large production of olive oil, from an estimated 50 to 60 million olive trees!

In this lesson, you will continue to learn how to use present tense verbs. You will meet possessive adjectives and pronouns, which are a bit more complicated in Italian than in French or Spanish, as well as the demonstrative adjectives *questo* and *quello* (*this/these* and *that/those*).

B. **Possessive Adjectives and Pronouns**

Possessive adjectives are quite complicated in Italian and hold different rules for usage with family members. First, let's concentrate on their regular usage—with all nouns except for those regarding relatives.

When expressing ownership or possession in Italian, you must take two things into account: who the possessor is and what is being possessed. Three things are required to shape a possessive phrase: the definite article pertaining to the thing possessed; the possessive adjective pertaining both to the possessor and the gender of the possessed; and the thing possessed. The beginning stem of the possessive adjectives (everything but the final letter) will tell you who possesses the thing, and everything else (the definite article, the ending letter of the possessive adjective, and the noun) will tell you what is being possessed.

Look at this chart to understand the first two parts:

	Singular Subjects Singular Objects	Singular Subjects Plural Objects	Plural Subjects Singular Objects	Plural Subjects Plural Objects
first person	il mio la mia	i miei le mie	il nostro la nostra	i nostri le nostre
second person	il tuo la tua	i tuoi le tue	il vostro la vostra	i vostri le vostre
third person	il suo la sua	i suoi le sue	il **loro** la **loro**	i **loro** le **loro**

What would fit into the first box? A singular possessor with a singular thing being possessed (masculine or feminine) would go there. For example: *il mio cane* (*my dog*: singular possessor and singular masculine possessed thing) or *la mia amica* (*my female friend*: singular possessor and singular feminine possessed thing).

Notice that the six stems (which convey the possessor) correspond to the six personal pronouns that are used to conjugate verbs, so it might be helpful to think of them that way: *mi-, ti-, su-, nostr-, vostr-,* and *loro* match up to *I* (*my*), *you* (*your*), *he/she* (*his/her*), *we* (*our*), *you* [pl.] (*your*), and *they* (*their*).

> Il protagonista di questo film è Tommaso Cantone, uno scrittore che abita a Roma. Tommaso torna a casa, a Lecce, per trovare la sua famiglia. La famiglia abita in una villa grande con due domestiche. Tommaso ha due genitori, Vincenzo e Stefania. Vincenzo è suo padre e Stefania è sua madre. Vincenzo e Stefania hanno tre figli. Tommaso ha due fratelli: un fratello, Antonio, e una sorella, Elena. Elena è sposata con Salvatore: Salvatore è suo marito. Ci sono altri parenti che abitano nella villa. Luciana è sua zia. C'è anche la nonna, che è la madre di Vincenzo e la suocera di Stefania. Il fidanzato di Tommaso si chiama Marco.

▶ The protagonist of this film is Tommaso Cantone, a writer who lives in Rome. Tommaso returns home to Lecce to visit his family. His family lives in a large villa with two maids. Tommaso has two parents, Vincenzo and Stefania. Vincenzo is his father and Stefania is his mother. Vincenzo and Stefania have three children. Tommaso has two siblings: one brother, Antonio, and one sister, Elena. Elena is married to Salvatore: Salvatore is her husband. There are other relatives who live in the villa. Luciana is his aunt. There is also the grandmother, who is Vincenzo's mother and Stefania's mother-in-law. Tommaso's boyfriend is Marco.

A. Possessive Pronouns

While possessive adjectives typically have the three parts to them, possessive pronouns can omit the noun if you have already established it in previous conversation. Instead of answering the question *"Are these your shoes?"* with *"Yes, they are my shoes,"* you could simply answer *"Yes, they are **mine**."* In Italian, you'd omit the final noun, so the conversation would go like this: *"Sono le tue scarpe?"* *"Sì, sono **le mie**."* Now the six forms are (in English): *mine, yours, his/hers, ours, yours,* and *theirs.*

B. Possessive Adjectives with Family Members

The rules for expressing possession with family members are a bit different than the normal forms seen previously, but only in certain instances. In general, there are two rules you must memorize: Singular family members do not use the definite article in possessive phrases (except with *loro*), and plural family members always use the article.

However, there are (of course) exceptions to these rules, especially for singular family members. If you modify the noun in any way—such as adding a suffix or an adjective—you need to put the article back in. So you would say *mia sorella* (my sister) but *la mia sorellina* (my little sister) or *la mia cara sorella* (my dear sister). Terms of endearment, such as *babbo* (daddy) or *papà* (papa) and *mamma* (mama), also use articles.

Questo film è ambientato in Puglia: specificamente ad Altamura, Cassano delle Murge e Gravina in Puglia. C'è una madre che muore e suo marito, Donato, chiama i tre figli a casa. Questi tre fratelli si chiamano Raffaele, Nicola e Rocco. Raffaele è un giudice che abita a Roma e processa i mafiosi, una vita molto pericolosa! Ma quell'uomo non ha paura. Nicola è un operaio a Torino che partecipa alle manifestazioni per i diritti lavorativi, numerose a quell'epoca. Rocco, invece, è un terapista che lavora con i ragazzi giovani in prigione. I tre fratelli pensano al passato e al futuro. Questo pensa alla sua morte. Quest'altro pensa alla sua ex-moglie. Quest'ultimo pensa invece a trovare una vita migliore per i giovani napoletani. Il nonno e sua nipote, la figlia di Nicola, passano il tempo insieme alla fattoria in mezzo della natura.

▶ This film is set in Puglia: specifically at Altamura, Cassano delle Murge, and Gravina in Puglia. A mother dies and her husband, Donato, calls the three sons home. These three brothers are called Raffaele, Nicola, and Rocco. Raffaele is a judge who lives in Rome and prosecutes mafiosi: a very dangerous profession! But that man isn't afraid. Nicola is a worker in Turin who participates in demonstrations for workers' rights, which were numerous in those times, the 1970s. Rocco, instead, is a therapist who works with young boys in prison. All three brothers think about the past and the future. This one thinks about his death. This other one thinks about his ex-wife. This last one thinks instead about finding a new life for the Neapolitan youth. The grandfather and his granddaughter, Nicola's daughter, spend their time together on the farm in the midst of nature.

A. Demonstrative Adjectives: *Questo* and *quello*

Demonstrative adjectives are so called because they clearly demonstrate *this/these* or *that/those*. The first category (*questo*) is very simple, since it only has the four typical forms for adjectives: *-o*, *-a*, *-i*, and *-e* (in addition to *quest'* for nouns beginning with a vowel). The second is a bit more challenging, with eight forms instead of just four, but you might notice a pattern:

	singolare	plurale	singolare	plurale
maschile	**questo** fratello (**quest'**uomo)	**questi** fratelli (**questi** uomini)	**quel** fratello **quell'**uomo **quello** zio	**quei** fratelli **quegli** uomini **quegli** zii
femminile	**questa** sorella (**quest'**amica)	**queste** sorelle (**queste** amiche)	**quella** sorella **quell'**amica	**quelle** sorelle **quelle** amiche

If you noticed that the forms for *quello* correspond to the definite articles you'd need for those nouns, good eye! (Side note: the forms for the adjective *bello*, or *beautiful*, will follow the same patterns.)

ATTIVITÀ / ACTIVITIES

Claudia e Alessandro sono nuovi colleghi a una compagnia finanziaria. Sono a pranzo a un ristorante nel centro di Bari e parlano delle loro famiglie per imparare più dell'uno l'altro. (Claudia and Alessandro are new colleagues at a finance company. They are at lunch at a restaurant in the center of Bari and are talking about their families to get to know each other better.)

1. Scrivi gli aggettivi possessivi corretti negli spazi vuoti, usando gli articoli determinativi quando necessario. Attenzione alle regole per i possessivi con la famiglia! (Write the correct possessive adjectives in the blank spaces, using definite articles when necessary. Don't forget the rules for possessives with family members!)

Claudia:	Alessandro, com'è 1. _____ famiglia? È grande o piccola?
Alessandro:	2. _____ famiglia è grandissima! Ho un padre, una madre, tre sorelle e un fratello, e tre nipoti. Abbiamo anche due cani e un gatto. 3. _____ casa è un po' affollata,[1] ma tutti vanno d'accordo.[2] Mi piace molto avere tutta la famiglia sotto un tetto.[3]
Claudia:	Che bello! Come si chiamano tutte queste persone? Come sono?
Alessandro:	4. _____ genitori sono vecchi e tranquilli. 5. _____ madre si chiama Francesca e 6. _____ padre si chiama Gianluca. 7. _____ sorelle sono Anna, Lisa, e Paola e sono molto diverse. Anna è l'unica persona della famiglia che ha figli. 8. _____ marito si chiama Andrea e 9. _____ figli si chiamano Lorenzo e Antonia. 10. _____ fratello, Giovanni, ha solo tredici anni.
Claudia:	E gli animali?
Alessandro:	11. _____ animali si chiamano Beppe e Lilo. Sono cattivelli[4] ma carini! E tu, Claudia, hai una grande famiglia come 12. _____?
Claudia:	No, 13. _____ famiglia è piccolissima, solo io, 14. _____ nonna e 15. _____ genitori. Sono figlia unica.
Alessandro:	È anche bello avere una famiglia piccola! 16. _____ feste sono anche piccole?
Claudia:	No – infatti, invitiamo tutti 17. _____ vicini! A Natale siamo ospiti a quattro altre famiglie.
Alessandro:	Wow, impressionante!

2. Per ogni frase, scrivi l'opzione giusta per gli aggettivi dimostrativi. Il primo spazio è una forma di *questo* e il secondo è una forma di *quello*. (For every sentence, write the correct demonstrative adjective. The first blank will be a form of *questo*, and the second will be a form of *quello*.)

1. _____ studente si chiama Edoardo e _____ studente si chiama Ugo.

2. _____ ragazza è più intelligente di _____ ragazza.

....
1 crowded

2 *andare d'accordo* = to get along

3 *sotto un tetto* = under one roof

4 naughty

3. _____ uomini non sanno parlare l'italiano così bene come

_____ uomini.

4. _____ libri sono francesi e _____ libri sono russi.

5. _____ banane sono buone ma _____ banane sono marce![5] Puah!

3. *Esercizio di scrittura: Com'è la tua famiglia?*

Using the vocabulary that you learned in this lesson, write a paragraph about the members of your family (or of a famous family). Try to use as many possessive adjectives as possible.

_____

_____

_____

_____

_____

_____

_____

_____

_____

_____

ANSWER KEY

1.

1. la tua
2. La mia
3. La nostra (*or* La mia)
4. I miei
5. Mia
6. mio
7. Le mie
8. Suo
9. i suoi (*or* i loro)
10. Mio
11. I nostri
12. la mia
13. la mia
14. mia
15. i miei
16. Le vostre
17. i nostri

2.

1. Questo, quello
2. Questa, quella
3. Questi, quegli
4. Questi, quei
5. Queste, quelle

---

5 rotten

3. Answers will vary. Example:

La mia famiglia è molto italiana! I miei nonni sono siciliani e abbruzzesi, e ho molti zii e cugini. I loro nomi sono...

MAP OF PUGLIA BY PROVINCES

LEZIONE 8

PREPOSITIONS / ABRUZZO AND MOLISE

Oggi parliamo di due regioni: l'Abruzzo e il Molise, nell'Italia centrale. Sono regioni molto montagnose, come il Trentino—Alto Adige e la Valle d'Aosta. Queste regioni, però, non hanno soltanto i monti più alti degli Appennini ma anche una gran parte della costa orientale d'Italia. Queste regioni sono perfette per chi ama la natura e la storia.

L'Abruzzo (o "gli Abruzzi") confina con la regione delle Marche (a nord), con il Lazio (ad ovest), e con il Molise (a sud). Ci sono tre monti importanti: quello del Gran Sasso (con la cima più alta degli Appennini!), quello della Majella e quello di Velino-Sirente. Questa regione si chiama "la regione dei parchi" e anche "la regione verde d'Europa"! Il suo capoluogo è l'Aquila, una città che è stata distrutta da un terremoto nel 2009. Pescara, una città industriale sul mare, ha anche una vita culturale molto vivace. Tanti autori importanti sono dell'Abruzzo, come il gran poeta latino Ovidio (di Sulmona), Gabriele D'Annunzio (di Pescara), e Benedetto Croce (di Pescasseroli).

Il Molise era parte della regione abruzzese fino al 1963 ma adesso è autonomo. È anche una regione con un paesaggio molto bello. Questa regione confina con l'Abruzzo, il Lazio, la Campania e la Puglia. Il suo capoluogo è Campobasso. L'agricoltura e la pastorizia sono molto importanti per la sua economia. Ci sono solo due province: Isernia, una zona importantissima per la preistoria, e la provincia di Campobasso. A Campobasso ci sono processioni e cerimonie religiose durante la Settimana santa.

Sono due regioni che offrono tantissimo per chi ama la cultura e la storia, o la montagna e il mare!

▶ Today let's speak about two regions: Abruzzo and Molise, in central Italy. These are very mountains regions, like Trentino—Alto Adige and Valle d'Aosta. These regions, however, not only have the highest mountains of the Apennines but also a large part of the eastern coast. These regions are perfect for those who love nature and history.

Abruzzo (or "gli Abruzzi") borders with the region of the Marches (to the north), Lazio (to the west), and Molise (to the south). There are three important mountains here: that of the Gran Sasso (with the highest summit of the Apennines!), that of the Majella, and that of Velino-Sirente. This region is called "the park region" as well as "the green region of Europe"! Its capital is L'Aquila, a city that was destroyed by an earthquake in 2009. Pescara, an industrial city on the sea, has a very lively cultural life. Many important authors come from Abruzzo, such as the great Latin poet Ovid (from Sulmona), Gabrielle D'Annunzio (from Pescara), and Benedetto Croce (from Pescasseroli).

Molise was part of the Abruzzese region until 1963 but now is autonomous. It is also a region with a very beautiful landscape. This region borders with Abruzzo, Lazio, Campania, and Puglia. Its capital is Campobasso. Agriculture and livestock rearing are very important to its economy. There are two provinces: Isernia, an important area for prehistory, and the province of Campobasso. The city of Campobasso is home to many religious festivals and processions around the Christian Holy Week.

They are two regions that offer much for those who love culture and history, mountains and the sea!

VOCABOLARIO NUOVO E UTILE / NEW AND USEFUL VOCABULARY

montagnoso	mountainous	**particolare**	particular, unique
l'orso	bear	**il lupo**	wolf
l'industria	industry	**l'agricoltura**	agriculture
la pastorizia	pastoralism	**la processione**	procession
a	at, to, in	**in**	in, to, at
con	with	**per**	for
di	of	**su**	on
da	from, by	**tra/fra**	between, among
l'arrosticino	lamb skewer	**la porchetta**	pork roast
il timballo	molded casserole	**le scrippelle**	crepes in broth
la chitarra	pasta-cutting machine	**la pastuccia**	pork flan
la caciotta	semisoft cheese	**i confetti**	Italian candies
la ciambella	doughnut	**la bomba**	cream-filled sweet
le pizzelle	waffle cookies	**il parrozzo**	Abruzzese cake
fa fresco	it's brisk	**fa freddo**	it's cold
fa caldo	it's hot	**fa bel tempo**	it's nice weather
fa brutto tempo	it's bad weather	**c'è sole**	there's sun
nevica	it's snowing	**piove**	it's raining
tira il vento	it's windy	**il terremoto**	earthquake
la tempesta	storm	**la grandine**	hail
il tornado	tornado	**l'uragano**	hurricane
avere caldo	to feel hot	**avere freddo**	to feel cold

RIPASSO GENERALE / GENERAL REVIEW

A. Notes about Abruzzo and Molise

The provinces of Abruzzo and Molise were, until fairly recently, only one region. The two formally split in 1970, making Molise the "newest" region of Italy. The geography of these regions is varied: The western edges hit the Apennines, the mountains in the middle of the country (including the famous Gran Sasso d'Italia), and the Adriatic Sea forms the eastern border. Abruzzo is home to numerous national parks and nature reserves, where the unsuspecting tourist might find bears, wolves, wild dogs, sheep, and goats roaming freely. Molise may be the second smallest region of Italy (after la Valle d'Aosta), but there are many things to do and see there, too, including factories, museums, medieval fortresses, cathedrals, and archaeological sites.

This lesson introduces you to one of the most difficult grammatical concepts: prepositions. Prepositions are tough in any language and are typically not used in the same way as English speakers are accustomed to seeing them used in English. Let's go through the basics together.

B. Prepositions

The Italian language has many prepositions—far many more than will be covered here, in fact—but this lesson concentrates on just eight.

Notice in the vocabulary section that many of these eight prepositions have more than one definition. That is because these words might be used in different ways in English but are all encompassed within the same preposition in Italian. Read through each of these prepositions and learn about the different ways they can be translated into English. As you go through, try to think of the Italian first—that way, you won't be constantly confused. See sections **VII** and **VIII** at the end of this lesson for lists of verbs that are linked by certain prepositions and section **IX** for some examples of the verb *andare* used with the prepositions *a* and *in*.

A – at, to, in

The preposition *a* has the aforementioned three different basic meanings, but it is mostly used in terms of location. It is used literally as "at" in most senses where you'd use it in English (e.g., *Passo le vacanze **al** mare* = I spend my vacations **at** the seaside). It is used in the sense of "to" or "in" when referring to a city or town (*Abito **a** Fairfax* = I live **in** Fairfax; *Vado **a** Fairfax* = I'm going **to** Fairfax). It can also be used in other idiomatic phrases, such as *Guardo un programma **alla** televisione* (I'm watching a show **on** TV) and *Vado **a** piedi* (I'm going **by** foot).

DA – from, by, at the house/workplace of

The preposition *da* usually signifies either "from" or the passive "by," but it can also have some other particular usages. First, it can be used to mean "at someone's house or office," much like the preposition *chez* is used in French. If you're invited to a party "*da Marco*," the party will be at Marco's house. If you are going "*dal dottore*," you are going to see a doctor at his or her office. *Da* can also be used with expressions of time, when used with present tense verbs. In English, speakers use the past tense with these expressions, so this can be tricky. In Italian, you would say, "*Non ti vedo **da** un anno!*" but the English equivalent would be, "I haven't seen you for a year!" Finally, *da* can indicate the function of something, such as a soccer field (*un campo **da** calcio*), sunglasses (*occhiali **da** sole*), or a snowsuit (*tuta **da** neve*).

DI – of

Di is a very common preposition in Italian. It can be used to indicate possession ("***Di** chi sono questi occhiali?*" "*Sono **di** Antonia*" = "**Whose** glasses are these?" "They are Antonia's [glasses].*"). *Di* is also used to say what material or texture something is made of (e.g., *una maglietta **di** cotone* = a cotton t-shirt). *Di* can also be used to make comparisons, which you'll learn in lesson 24. You have previously seen this preposition in saying where you hail from (*Sono **di** Filadelfia*). Finally, you can use *di* when making time-related phrases, such as ***di** mattina*, ***di** sera*, and ***di** notte* (in the mornings, in the evenings, and at night), and adverbial phrases, such as ***di** solito* (usually), ***di** nuovo* (again), and ***di** rado* (rarely).

IN – in, to

In can be used in a similar fashion to "a" when referring to where you are currently or where you are going—but for countries, states, regions, and continents instead of cities and towns (*Vado **a** Roma* but *Vado **in** Italia*; *Sono **a** Parigi* but *Sono **in** Francia*). *In* is used with methods of transportation by vehicle (***in** macchina*, ***in** treno*, ***in** aereo*, ***in** bicicletta*). *In* can also be used to indicate "going **to**" or "being **at/in**" certain places, if the place is vague enough not to be named explicitly (e.g., ***in** banca*, ***in** centro*, ***in** chiesa*, ***in** vacanza*).

SU – on, over, above, about

Su is almost always used as the equivalent of "on" in English, but it can also be used if you are talking about something as a subject matter (e.g., *Leggo un articolo **sulla** politica* = I'm reading an article **on/about** politics). Another example of usage is "over" or "onto," such as in the phrase *dare **su*** ("to look out over," as from a window). This preposition can also be used as an exhortative exclamation meaning "Come on!" (e.g., ***Su**, forza!*).

PER – for, through, throughout

Thankfully, the preposition *per* is relatively simple. It usually means "for," as in "This coffee is **for** you" (*Questo caffè è **per** te*). It can also be used in your travels as you go all over (= **throughout**) the country (*Viaggio **per** tutta l'Italia!*).

CON – with

Here's an even simpler one: *Con* really only means "with," in almost all the ways that English speakers use the same preposition in English.

TRA/FRA – among, between, within

These two prepositions are interchangeable—they mean the same thing. They can be used to mean "among" or "between" in terms of location or "within" when speaking of the time it will take to do something (I will have it done **within** five minutes = *Lo faccio **tra/fra** cinque minuti*). The only reason you would need to choose one or the other would be when the following word begins with the same letter. For instance, phrases like ***tra tre** minuti* and ***fra fratelli*** don't quite flow off the tongue, so you'd use the alternate lettering instead.

C. Articulated Prepositions

Italian is a unique Romance language in that, where you come across a preposition and a definite article together, with the exception of *con, per*, and *tra/fra*, they must combine to form what is called an articulated preposition. The combinations are seen in this table:

+	il	lo	l'	la	i	gli	le
a	al	allo	all'	alla	ai	agli	alle
da	dal	dallo	dall'	dalla	dai	dagli	dalle
di → de	del	dello	dell'	della	dei	degli	delle
in → ne	nel	nello	nell'	nella	nei	negli	nelle
su	sul	sullo	sull'	sulla	sui	sugli	sulle

These are fairly easy to form if you understand the following two patterns: Anytime an article begins with the letter *l*, it will be doubled; and the prepositions *di* and *in* change their stems to *de* and *ne*, respectively.

These combinations translate to phrases such as "to the," "from the," "of the," etc. So, "of the girls" is *delle ragazze*. As you continue learning, reading, and speaking the language, these will become easier to use, and eventually, hearing something like "*di le ragazze*" will sound terrible!

D. Partitives/Adjectives of Quantity (*di*)

A subset of the previous chart—the combinations formed from the preposition *di* and the definite articles—can be used to form what is known as the partitive, or a part of the whole. In English, we use the equivalent word *some*. In Spanish, you would use *unos* or *unas*. But in Italian, the indefinite articles are only used in the singular. Let's look at the combinations: What could we say we have "some of"? Hint: Think of a grocery trip.

+	il	lo	l'	la	i	gli	le
di → de	del	dello	dell'	della	dei	degli	delle

If you were going to the grocery store, you could buy *some milk* (*il latte*), *some bananas* (*le banane*), and *some spaghetti*. You would express that in Italian as follows: *Vado al supermercato e compro **del** latte, **delle** banane e **degli** spaghetti.*

E. Seasons and Weather

To talk about the weather in Italian, there are many phrases and verbs at your disposal. The most common verb used for expressing the enjoyability of the weather is *fare*, used with an adjective (e.g., *Fa bel tempo! Fa brutto tempo!*). Other phrases can be found in the vocabulary section of this lesson. For a review of the verb *fare*, see lesson 3; here, you'll only need to use it in the third person.

ATTIVITÀ / ACTIVITIES

Domenico è il nonno di Giulia, una ragazza americana che viene in Abruzzo per la prima volta a vedere la città natale di suo nonno. La città si chiama Colledimacine ed è un piccolo paese nella regione di Chieti. Non c'è molto da fare, ma c'è molta storia da sapere. (Domenico is the grandfather of Giulia, an American girl who is coming to Abruzzo for the first time to see her grandfather's hometown. The place is called Colledimacine, and it's a very small town in the Chieti region. There's not much to do, but there is a lot of history to learn.)

1. Nel dialogo, scrivi la preposizione (semplice) giusta negli spazi vuoti. (In the dialogue, write the correct simple preposition in the empty spaces.)

Domenico: Giulia, cara mia, benvenuta 1. _____ Colledimacine! È la tua prima volta 2. _____ Abruzzo, vero?

Giulia: Grazie, nonno! Sì, anzi,[1] è la mia prima volta 3. _____ Italia. Ecco, questi fiori sono 4. _____ te e nonna.

Domenico: Ah, bellissimi! Il giglio[2] è il fiore preferito 5. _____ tua nonna, grazie.

Giulia: Cosa facciamo oggi? Ho molta fame, non mangio 6. _____ quattro ore.

....
1 actually/rather

2 lily

Domenico: Senti, andiamo 7. _____ centro e pranziamo 8. _____ nostro cugino Benedetto. Poi andiamo 9. _____ Benedetto per un dolce. Ti va bene? Lui e sua moglie hanno due figlie giovani come te.

Giulia: Mi va benissimo. È possibile anche andare 10. _____ Gran Sasso? Tutti dicono che è un bel posto!

Domenico: Certo, cara. Il parco nazionale è anche bellissimo. Compriamo i biglietti e possiamo andarci[3] 11. _____ tre giorni.

Giulia: Che emozione! Ho una gran voglia 12. _____ vedere gli orsi marsicani![4]

Domenico: Eh, magari[5] non da molto vicino!!

2. Preposizione semplice o articolata? Scegli l'opzione giusta per ogni frase. (Simple or articulated preposition? Choose the correct option for each sentence.)

1. Metto lo zucchero _____ (in / nel) mio caffè.

2. Facciamo colazione _____ (da / dalla) mia nonna ogni sabato.

3. Per il mio compleanno quest'anno, vado _____ (a / al) mare con i miei amici.

4. La nostra trattoria preferita è _____ (in / nel) centro.

5. La professoressa assegna i compiti (a / agli) studenti.

3. Scegli la combinazione giusta per ogni domanda per formare una preposizione articolata. (Choose the correct combination for each question to form an articulated preposition.)

1. a + gli	a. alli	b. agli	c. ai
2. in + lo	a. nello	b. nelo	c. in lo
3. di + l'	a. del	b. dell'	c. dill'
4. da + la	a. dala	b. dall'	c. dalla
5. su + le	a. sulle	b. su le	c. sull'

---

3 to go there

4 *orso marsicano* = Marsican brown bears, who live in the Abruzzo National Park

5 if only/I wish/hopefully

4. Scrivi il partitivo (di + articolo determinativo) per ogni sostantivo. (Write the partitive form that goes with each noun.)

1. le mele _____

2. il tè _____

3. lo zucchero _____

4. gli amici _____

5. l'aranciata _____

5. *Esercizio di scrittura: Cosa devo comprare al supermercato, amore?*

Using the partitive (the preposition *di* + definite articles), talk about things that you need to buy at the supermarket today. It's OK if you don't know all the words to complete the paragraph; focus on the partitive first and foremost.

_____

_____

_____

_____

_____

_____

_____

ANSWER KEY

1.

1. a
2. in
3. in
4. per
5. di
6. da
7. in
8. con
9. da
10. a
11. fra
12. di

2.

1. nel
2. da
3. al
4. in
5. agli

3.

1. b.
2. a.

3. b.
4. c.

5. a.

4.

1. delle
2. del

3. dello
4. degli

5. dell'

5. Answers will vary. Example:

Oggi vado al supermercato e devo comprare (*I need to buy*) **del** latte, **delle** mele, **delle** banane, **degli** spaghetti...

MAP OF ABRUZZO AND MOLISE

VERBS LINKED TO OTHER VERBS BY THE PREPOSITION A

Note: This is not an exhaustive list.

andare a...	to go to...[1]
aiutare a...	to help to...
cominciare a...	to start/begin to...
imparare a...	to learn to...
incoraggiare a...	to encourage to...
insegnare a...	to teach to...
mettersi a...	to start/begin to...
pensare a...	to think about...
provare a...	to try to...
riuscire a...	to manage to...
venire a...	to come to...

VERBS LINKED TO OTHER VERBS BY THE PREPOSITION *DI*

Note: This is not an exhaustive list.

avere bisogno di...	to have need of...
avere intenzione di...	to intend to...
avere paura di...	to be afraid of...
avere voglia di...	to want to...
cercare di...	to try to...
chiedere di...	to ask to...
credere di...	to believe to...
decidere di...	to decide to...
dimenticare di...	to forget to...
dire di...	to say to...
finire di...	to finish to...
pensare di...	to think of...
permettere di...	to allow to...
promettere di...	to promise to...
ricordare di...	to remember to...
smettere di...	to cease to...
sperare di...	to hope to...

1 Be aware that this is a way of expressing a change in geographic location to engage in a specified activity. This is not a way of speaking about future events.

USAGE OF THE PREPOSITIONS A AND *IN* WITH THE VERB *ANDARE*

●●●●●●●●●
Andare a

Vado a Barcellona.	Vado al bar.
Vado a casa.	Vado al cinema.
Vado a Cipro.	**Vado al lavoro.**
Vado a Cuba.	Vado al mare.
Vado a letto.	Vado al mercato.
Vado a messa.	Vado al pronto soccorso.
Vado a passeggio.	Vado al ristorante.
Vado a Palazzo Pitti.	**Vado alla Banca Nazionale.**
Vado a Puerto Rico.	**Vado alla biblioteca comunale.**
Vado a scuola.	Vado alla stazione.
Vado a spasso.	Vado all'aeroporto.
Vado a Sud.	Vado all'ambasciata.
Vado a teatro.	Vado all'edicola.
Vado a Villa Medici.	Vado allo stadio.
Vado a zonzo.	**Vado allo studio.**
	Vado all'ufficio turistico.

●●●●●●●●●
Andare in

Vado in aereo.	Vado in giardino.
Vado in America.	Vado in libreria.
Vado in banca.	Vado in macchina.
Vado in biblioteca.	Vado in montagna.
Vado in bicicletta.	Vado in panetteria.
Vado in birreria.	Vado in piscina.
Vado in Brasile.	Vado in questura.
Vado in California.	**Vado in Sicilia.**
Vado in campagna.	**Vado in Sardegna.**
Vado in Corsica.	Vado in strada.
Vado in centro.	**Vado in Toscana.**
Vado in chiesa.	Vado in treno.
Vado in cucina.	Vado in ufficio.
Vado in discoteca.	Vado in un museo
Vado in farmacia.	Vado in un'agenzia di viaggi.
Vado in Germania.	Vado in vacanza.

MODAL VERBS, SAPERE, AND CONOSCERE / LIGURIA

Conosci già la Liguria? Forse! La Liguria è una regione molto bella nella parte nordovest dell'Italia, conosciuta da tanti turisti. Sembra una striscia lunga sulla costa. Confina con il paese della Francia (ad ovest), e con le regioni del Piemonte (a nord) e quelle dell'Emilia-Romagna e la Toscana (ad est). Il capoluogo della Liguria è Genova, una città situata tra il mare e le colline. È una città molto importante per la sua storia, per le figure storiche e per la sua funzione di un porto sul mare Mediterraneo. Sai chi è Cristoforo Colombo, per esempio? Certo! Lui è nato a Genova nel 1451. Sai che la parola *jeans* viene dal nome della città di Genova? Forse sì o forse no!

La parte del mare Mediterraneo che è vicina alla costa si chiama Mar Ligure. Altre città importanti sono Savona, Rapallo, Sestri Levante e La Spezia. La Liguria è una regione multicolore per l'abbondanza di fiori e piante che possono crescere in questo clima. Devi assolutamente andare a vedere il Parco Nazionale delle Cinque Terre, che sono cinque paesi pittoreschi—Riomaggiore, Manarola, Corniglia, Vernazza e Monterosso—dove il paesaggio naturale è davvero bellissimo da vedere, con tanti terrazzi e viti sui muri. Nella Liguria, crescono l'olivo, gli agrumi e le nocciole. Voglio spesso mangiare il pesto alla Genovese, una specialità ligure!

La Liguria è anche nota per i suoi spettacoli teatrali e musicali. Conosci San Remo? Il festival della canzone italiana si svolge ogni anno a San Remo, dove tanti musicisti, quelli famosi e soprattutto quelli nuovi, esibiscono i loro talenti. Sai che ci sono tantissimi teatri a Genova, più che in ogni altra città italiana? È un fatto interessante!

▶ Are you already familiar with Liguria? Perhaps! Liguria is a very beautiful region in the northwestern part of Italy, known by many tourists. It looks like a long stripe on the shore. It borders with France (to the west) and with the regions of Piedmont (to the north) and those of Emilia-Romagna and Tuscany (to the east). The capital of Liguria is Genoa, a city that is situated between the ocean and the hills. It is very important for its history and its historical figures, and for its function as a port on the Mediterranean. Do you know who Christopher Columbus is, for example? Of course! He was born in Genoa in 1451. Do you know that the word *jeans* comes from the city name of Genova? Perhaps, or maybe not!

The part of the Mediterranean Sea that is close to the coast is called the Ligurian Sea. Other important cities are Savona, Rapallo, Sestri Levante, and La Spezia. Liguria is a multicolored region with its abundance of flowers and plants that can grow in this climate. You absolutely have to go and see the National Park of the Cinque Terre, which is five picturesque towns—Riomaggiore, Manarola, Corniglia, Vernazza, and Monterosso—where the natural landscape is truly very beautiful to see, with many terraces and vines on the walls. In Liguria, olives, citrus, and nuts grow. I often want to eat Genoese pesto, a Ligurian specialty!

Liguria is also known for its theatrical and musical performances. Do you know San Remo? The festival of Italian music takes place every year at San Remo, where many musicians, those who are famous and most of all those who are new, exhibit their talent. Do you know that there are so many theaters in Genoa, more than in any other Italian city? It's an interesting fact!

VOCABOLARIO NUOVO E UTILE / NEW AND USEFUL VOCABULARY

dovere	to need (to), to owe	**potere**	to be able (to)
volere	to want (to)	**sapere**	to know (a fact)
conoscere	to be familiar	**esibire**	to exhibit
il dovere	need [noun]	**il potere**	power
la volontà	will	**la sapienza**	wisdom
la conoscenza	knowledge		
la striscia	strip, stripe	**la collina**	hill
la funzione	function, use	**l'abbondanza**	abundance
il fiore	flower	**la pianta**	plant
il clima	climate, clime	**il terrazzo**	terrace
la vite	vine	**il muro**	wall
l'olivo	olive tree	**l'agrume**	citrus tree
la nocciola	hazelnut	**il pesto**	pesto spread
l'acciuga	anchovy	**il cioccolato**	chocolate
teatrale	theatrical	**musicale**	musical
pittoresco	picturesque	**ligure**	Ligurian
distrutto	destroyed	**ridisegnato**	redesigned
entrambi	both	**assaggiare**	to taste, to try
il sentiero	path	**il vicino**	neighbor*
la struttura	structure	**la gru**	crane
il porto	port	**il panorama**	panorama, view
il concerto	concert	**lo spettacolo**	show, play
l'acquario	aquarium	**il viadotto**	viaduct (arched bridge)

* *Il vicino* is the noun form, meaning "neighbor." The adjective *vicino* means "close"/"near."

RIPASSO GENERALE / GENERAL REVIEW

A. **Notes about Liguria**

If you've traveled to Italy and have already seen Rome, Florence, and Venice, typically your next biggest tourist destination will probably be the region of Liguria. Liguria is a coastal region in the northwest of Italy whose claim to fame is the Italian Riviera, Genoa, and the Cinque Terre ("Five Lands"). These places are so popular, in fact, that this lesson's theme is travel and tourism. Liguria is bordered by the Italian regions Piemonte, Emilia-Romagna, and Tuscany, and it also shares a border with France. It is also bordered by the Ligurian Sea and the Alpine and Apennine mountain ranges, making it another region with a varied landscape and many interesting things to do and see. Due to its sea border, seafood is the main cuisine. But did you know that the delicious pesto sauce was invented in this region? Now you do!

In this lesson, you'll also learn about modal verbs (*dovere*, *potere*, and *volere*) and the very important verbs *conoscere* and *sapere*, which both mean "to know" but have different connotations.

B. **Present Tense of Modal Verbs:** *Dovere, potere, volere*

Three of the new verbs you are meeting in this lesson are the modal verbs *dovere*, *potere*, and *volere*, which mean, respectively, "to need to"/"must", "to be able to"/ "can," and "to want to." You've already met their conjugations in <ins>lesson 5</ins>, but let's review them here:

dovere	potere	volere
devo	posso	voglio
devi	puoi	vuoi
deve	può	vuole
dobbiamo	possiamo	vogliamo
dovete	potete	volete
devono	possono	vogliono

As you may have noticed, the definitions of each of these verbs ends in *to*; this is because these three verbs are typically (but not always) followed by another verb in the infinitive, just like in English. In English, you'd say, "*I need **to study**" or "I am able **to go out** tonight*"—it's the same in Italian. These two sentences would translate to "*Devo **studiare**" and "Posso **uscire** stasera.*"

A good way to practice the (very irregular) conjugations of these three verbs is to get used to seeing all three in the same sentence. You'll do this in the *Esercizio di scrittura* at the end of this lesson's Activities section.

C. *Conoscere* and *sapere* ("To Be Familiar With" and "To Know")

In English, sometimes we use the verb "to know" in contexts where Italians would use two separate verbs. The difference in meaning can be subtle, but generally *conoscere* is used with people and concepts with which you are familiar, and *sapere* is used with verbs and things that you know as factual. At times, you will need to choose between the two if you change the sentence slightly. For example, you would say, "*Conosco l'italiano*" ("*I am familiar with Italian as a language*"), but you would say, "*So parlare l'italiano*" ("*I know how to speak Italian*").

Let's review their conjugations. *Conoscere* is a regular *-ere* verb, but its pronunciation varies among its forms. *Sapere* is very irregular, but by now you might recognize its pattern from other irregular verbs you've encountered.

conoscere	sapere
conosco	so
conosci	sai
conosce	sa
conosciamo	sappiamo
conoscete	sapete
conoscono	sanno

Sai chi è Renzo Piano? Renzo Piano è un famoso architetto genovese. È nato a Genova nel settembre 1947. Ha disegnato tantissimi edifici famosi per tutto il mondo. Conosci le sue creazioni? A Genova ha ridisegnato il porto principale, che si chiama il Porto Antico, perché era stato distrutto dalla guerra. Ha creato una struttura che si chiama Bigo, che assomiglia ad una gru che si usa al porto, con delle braccia lunghe. Puoi salire il Bigo per vedere il panorama del porto! Lui ha creato anche uno spazio dove si possono tenere concerti e spettacoli teatrali e un nuovo acquario che si chiama La Bolla. Lui vuole anche ricostruire il viadotto Morandi sul Polcevera, che è crollato nel 2018. Non deve farlo, ma vuole ricostruirlo gratis.

▶ Do you know who Renzo Piano is? Renzo Piano is a famous Genoese architect. He was born in Genoa in September 1947. He designed many famous buildings all over the world. Are you familiar with his creations? He redesigned the main port at Genova, which is called the Porto Antico, because it had been destroyed by the war. He created a structure that is called Bigo, which resembles a crane with long arms used at a port. You can go up the Bigo to see the panorama of the port! He also created a space where concerts and theatrical shows can be held, and a new aquarium that is called La Bolla ("The Bubble"). He also wants to rebuild the Morandi viaduct on the Polcevera, which collapsed in 2018. He doesn't have to do it, but he wants to rebuild it for free.

Cristoforo e Isabella sono cugini italiani. Cristoforo sta per andare negli Stati Uniti per la prima volta ed è nervoso. Isabella gli dà qualche consiglio su cosa lui deve fare prima del viaggio per prepararsi per la sua nuova avventura. (Cristoforo and Isabella are Italian cousins. Cristoforo is about to go to the United States for the first time, and he is nervous. Isabella is giving him some suggestions as to what he must do before his trip to prepare for his new adventure.)

1. Nel dialogo, scrivi la forma corretta del verbo giusto negli spazi vuoti. (In the dialogue, write the correct form of the appropriate verb in the empty spaces. Note: Some verbs may be used more than once.)

dovere   **potere**   **volere**

sapere   **conoscere**

Isabella: Cristoforo, cosa stai facendo?

Cristoforo: Mi preparo per un viaggio americano! Sono un po' nervoso e non 1. _____ cosa mettere nella valigia.

Isabella: Io ti 2. _____ aiutare perché ci sono stata[1] due anni fa e 3. _____ bene il paese.

Cristoforo: Allora cosa 4. _____ portare?

Isabella: Hmm, non devi portare una giacca così grande. Non fa molto freddo in questa stagione.

Cristoforo: Bene. 5. _____ portare il mio computer?

Isabella: Sì che puoi portarlo ma forse non è necessario, ed è possibile che sarà rubato.[2]

Cristoforo: Non 6. _____ perdere il computer! È molto costoso.

Isabella: Certo. È più importante portare le cose non preziose. 7. _____ che è difficile ricuperarle.[3]

Cristoforo: Capito.[4] Grazie, cugina!

....

1 *ci sono stata* = I have been there

2 *sarà rubato* = it will be stolen

3 *ricuperare* = to recover/recuperate

4 Understood

2. Per ogni frase, scegli il verbo giusto tra *sapere* e *conoscere*. (For every sentence, decide whether *sapere* or *conoscere* is the correct verb to use.)

1. Ignazio (sa / conosce) parlare l'inglese.

2. Scusi, dottore, mi (sa / conosce) dire come arrivare alla stazione?

3. Professoressa Rossi? No, io non la (so / conosco) molto bene.

4. Ilaria, (sai / conosci) la storia di Genova?

5. Ilaria, (sai / conosci) chi è il Presidente degli Stati Uniti?

3. Scrivi la forma giusta del verbo modale tra parentesi. (Write the correct form of the modal verb given in parentheses.)

1. Stasera io _____ (dovere) andare da mia nonna per aiutarla a preparare per una festa.

2. Ragazzi, cosa _____ (volere) fare questo fine settimana? _____ (dovere) lavorare o _____ (potere) venire al cinema con noi?

3. Asuka è giapponese e non _____ (potere) parlare l'italiano, ma _____ (volere) studiarlo all'università.

4. Io e i miei amici _____ (dovere) studiare per l'esame di matematica, ma _____ (volere) dormire invece!

5. Jennifer ed Elena non _____ (potere) andare al bar perché non si sentono bene.

4. *Esercizio di scrittura: Cosa vuoi fare? Cosa devi fare? Cosa puoi fare?*

Using the three modal verbs that you learned in this lesson, talk about things that you want to do (*volere*), things that you need to do (*dovere*), and things that you can do (*potere*). For extra practice, switch to the negative, or try to include all three in the same sentence (e.g., "I want to do _____, but I can't, because I have to _____.").

_____

_____

_____

_____

_____

_____

1.

1. so
2. posso
3. conosco

4. devo
5. Posso
6. voglio

7. So

2.

1. sa
2. sa

3. conosco
4. conosci

5. sai

3.

1. devo
2. volete, Dovete, potete

3. può, vuole
4. dobbiamo, vogliamo
5. possono

4. Answers will vary. Example:

Voglio sciare questo weekend, ma non posso, perché devo studiare. Non voglio studiare!

MAP OF LIGURIA BY PROVINCES

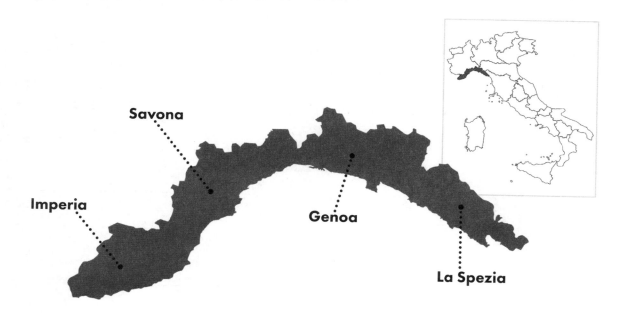

Savona

Imperia

Genoa

La Spezia

THE IMPERATIVE MOOD / CAMPANIA

"Vedi Napoli e poi muori!" Forse conosci questa frase? Napoli è una bella città sulla baia e la sua bellezza è famosa e conosciuta al mondo. È il capoluogo della regione della Campania, una regione meridionale dell'Italia. La Campania è la regione più popolata del Sud. Confina con le regioni del Lazio (a nordovest), del Molise (a nord) e la Puglia e la Basilicata (ad est). Ad ovest c'è il mar Tirreno. La Campania ha quattro golfi sulle sue coste.

La Campania è una regione nota per la sua storia che risale ai tempi prima dei greci e dei romani. Ci sono sei siti che fanno parte del Patrimonio dell'Umanità dell'UNESCO in questa regione. Includono il centro storico di Napoli, gli Scavi di Pompei ed Ercolano e la Costiera Amalfitana. La Campania è tra le tre regioni più visitate d'Italia, e tra quelle zone più visitate d'Europa. È una regione con tante montagne e colline ed anche con quattro vulcani come Vesuvio! Ci sono anche delle isole molto belle, come Capri, Ischia e Procida.

Napoli è famosa per il panorama della baia, per le sue chiese barocche, per la pizza margherita, per i suoi attori e i suoi cantanti. Conosci Totò, il grande attore comico? O Enrico Caruso, il tenore napoletano? Ci sono anche grandi filosofi che sono nati o vissuti a Napoli: Giambattista Vico e Benedetto Croce sono degli ottimi esempi.

C'è tanto da dire su Napoli e sulla regione della Campania. Forse hai parenti che vengono da questa zona!

▶ "See Naples and then die!" Perhaps you know this phrase? Naples is a beautiful city on the bay and its beauty is famous and known throughout the world. It is the capital of the Campania region, a southern region in Italy. Campania is the most populated region of the South. It borders with the regions of Lazio (to the northwest), Molise (to the north), and Puglia and Basilicata (to the east). To the west is also the Tyrrhenian Sea. Campania has four gulfs on its coasts.

Campania is a region known for its history that hearkens back to the times before the Greeks and the Romans. There are six sites that are part of UNESCO's Patrimony of Humanity in this region. They include the historic center of Naples, the sites of Pompei and Ercolano, and the Amalfi Coast. Campania is among the most visited regions in Italy, and one of the most visited in all of Europe! It's a region with many mountains and hills, and even four volcanos, such as Vesuvius! There are also many beautiful islands, such as Capri, Ischia, and Procida.

Naples is also famous for the panorama of the bay, for its baroque churches, for *pizza margherita*, for its actors and its singers. Are you familiar with Totò, the great comic actor? Or with Enrico Caruso, the Neapolitan tenor? There are also many great philosophers who were born or who lived in Naples: Giambattista Vico and Benedetto Croce are some excellent examples.

There is much to say about Naples and the Campania region. Perhaps you have relatives who come from this area!

la baia	bay	gli scavi	excavations
il golfo	gulf	il sito	site
il centro storico	historical center	la costiera	coast
barocco	baroque	comico	comical, funny
noto	noted, noteworthy	visitato	visited
il/la cantante	singer	il baritono	baritone
il filosofo	philosopher	l'esempio	example
la frase	sentence	la parte	part
risalire a	to hark back (to)	fare parte di	to be a part (of)
vedere	to see	morire	to die
ripetere	to repeat	raggiungere	to reach, to get to
poi	then	insieme	together
Vorrei...	I would like...	Le dispiacerebbe...?	Would you like...? [formal]

RIPASSO GENERALE / GENERAL REVIEW

A. Notes about Campania

The region of Campania is home to many cities, coastlines, and islands that have enjoyed more and more tourism in the past decades. From ancient archaeological sites, such as Paestum, Pompeii, and Herculaneum; to the Amalfi Coast; to the islands of Ischia and Capri; and finally to the beautiful cities of Sorrento, Salerno, and Naples, this region is rich in history. It is also rich in culinary history: Naples is the birthplace of *pizza margherita* (named for a queen), and the region has an abundance of orange and lemon trees, which are used to make limoncello and other tasty treats.

In this lesson, you will learn how to use informal and formal imperatives (commands). The forms are quite similar to regular verb conjugations, with a few exceptions.

B. The Informal Imperative

The informal imperative is used in the same situations and with the same people you would use informal speech: friends, family, children—in other words, those with whom you are familiar. This form of speech can only be used in the *tu*, *noi*, and *voi* forms, since you can't command someone to whom you are not directly speaking. Here are the affirmative, or positive ("do this!"), forms for almost all verbs:

	-are	-ere	-ire	-ire (-isc)
tu	-a	-i	-i	-isci
noi	-iamo	-iamo	-iamo	-iamo
voi	-ate	-ete	-ite	-ite

Essentially, you conjugate the verbs as you normally would, with the exception of the *tu* form of *-are* verbs (which end in *-a*). Here are examples of verbs in usage:

	parlare	mettere	aprire	finire
tu	parla!	metti!	apri!	finisci!
noi	parliamo!	mettiamo!	apriamo!	finiamo!
voi	parlate!	mettete!	aprite!	finite!

As for the negative ("don't do this!") forms, only the *tu* form will change slightly (to *non* + the infinitive). The other forms (*noi* and *voi*) simply tack a *non* in front.

	-are	-ere	-ire	-ire (-isc)
tu = non +	-are	-ere	-ire	-ire
noi = non +	-iamo	-iamo	-iamo	-iamo
voi = non +	-ate	-ete	-ite	-ite

Here are examples of usage:

	parlare	mettere	aprire	finire
tu	Non parlare!	Non mettere!	Non aprire!	Non finire!
noi	Non parliamo!	Non mettiamo!	Non apriamo!	Non finiamo!
voi	Non parlate!	Non mettete!	Non aprite!	Non finite!

There are, of course, irregular verbs, but not many. Their most irregular forms are in the affirmative *tu* conjugation; the other forms follow all of the other forms in the previous charts. Conjugations with two forms are interchangeable:

	andare	dare	fare	stare	dire
tu	va'/vai	da'/dai	fa'/fai	sta'/stai	di'
noi	andiamo	diamo	facciamo	stiamo	diciamo
voi	andate	date	fate	state	dite

So, remember that the *tu* form—in both the affirmative and the negative—is the irregular one here.

Two other very irregular imperatives are the usual suspects *essere* and *avere*. Here are their forms:

	avere	essere
tu	abbi	sii
noi	abbiamo	siamo
voi	abbiate	siate

C. The Formal Imperative

The formal imperative is used in situations where you'd use the formal tense (i.e., with elders, strangers, and authority figures). There are also three forms for the formal, and they correspond to the *tu*, *noi*, and *voi* (singular *you*, *us*, and *you all*), but now they are *Lei*, *noi*, and *Loro*. These forms are flipped around from the informal: Where in the informal (*tu*) there is -*a*, -*i*, -*i*, -*isci*, there is -*i*, -*a*, -*a*, -*isca* in the formal (*Lei*). The *noi* stays exactly the same, and the *Loro* simply adds *no* to the end of the *Lei* forms.

	-are	-ere	-ire	-ire (-isc)
Lei	-i	-a	-a	-isca
noi	-iamo	-iamo	-iamo	-iamo
Loro	-ino	-ano	-ano	-iscano

In usage:

	parlare	mettere	aprire	finire
Lei	parli!	metta!	apra!	finisca!
noi	parliamo!	mettiamo!	apriamo!	finiamo!
Loro	parlino!	mettano!	aprano!	finiscano!

Negative forms of the formal do not change at all; they just add *non* in front of them.

While the formal is a bit easier to form than the informal, there are many more irregular forms for the formal. Here are the irregular *Lei* forms (remember that to form the *Loro*, you simply add *no* to the end).

Infinitive Verb	Irregular Form
andare	vada
avere	abbia
bere	beva
dare	dia
dire	dica
essere	sia
fare	faccia
sapere	sappia
stare	stia
uscire	esca
venire	venga

There are more irregular verbs in this tense, but these are the most common.

ATTIVITÀ / ACTIVITIES

Giovanni e Anna sono nuovamente sposati e fanno il loro viaggio di nozze a Capri. I due si amano molto e stanno bene insieme, ma hanno gusti e preferenze diversi. Mentre vanno in giro, Giovanni suggerisce una cosa e Anna dice sempre qualcosa di differente. (Giovanni and Anna are newlyweds and are taking their honeymoon trip to Capri. The two love each other very much and are a good match, but they have different tastes and preferences. While they walk around, Giovanni suggests one thing and Anna always says something different.)

1. Scrivi la forma giusta dell'imperativo negli spazi vuoti nel dialogo. (Write the correct form of the imperative in the blanks in the dialogue.)

Giovanni: Finalmente siamo arrivati a Capri. È una bellissima giornata – perché non 1. _____ (noi, andare) a prendere una pizza napoletana?

Anna: Amore, tu sai bene che sono a dieta! Non 2. _____ (tu, dire) sciocchezze![1] 3. _____ (noi, prendere) una bella insalata nizzarda[2] e 4. _____ (noi, rilassare) alla spiaggia.

....
1 trifles, stupid things

2 *insalata nizzarda* = salade Niçoise

Giovanni:	Va bene, 5. _____ (tu, prendere) un'insalata e io prendo una pizza. E poi 6. _____ (noi, andare) a vedere la Grotta Azzurra!
Anna:	Ehh, non mi va. È troppo freddo dentro. 7. _____ (noi, visitare) il Museo Ignazio Cerio!
Giovanni:	Okay, ma almeno 8. _____ (tu, andare) alla Chiesa di Santo Stefano con me?
Anna:	Io invece voglio vedere la Chiesa di Santa Sofia.
Giovanni:	Ho deciso:[1] 9. _____ (tu, fare) quello che vuoi tu e io faccio le mie cose, e poi 10. _____ (noi, incontrare) all'hotel?
Anna:	Perfetto, adesso siamo d'accordo. 11. _____ (tu, avere) una bella giornata!

2. Decidi se l'imperativo è formale o informale. (Decide whether the command is formal or informal.)

1. Signore, <u>parlino</u> più piano, per favore!

2. Ragazzi, <u>non correte</u> in casa!

3. Marcello, ti prego, <u>non dire</u> niente ad Alessia – la festa è una sorpresa!

4. Professoressa Olson, mi <u>dia</u> un bel voto in questo corso!

5. Signore Alighieri, <u>scriva</u> un'altra poesia d'amore!

3. Scrivi la forma giusta dell'imperativo informale. (Write the correct form of the informal imperative.)

1. tu, dormire _____

2. voi, alzare _____

3. voi, avere _____

4. noi, prendere _____

5. tu, andare _____

....
1 *ho deciso* = I've decided

4. Scrivi la forma giusta dell'imperativo formale. Attenzione: ogni verbo è irregolare. (Write the correct form of the formal imperative. Be careful: Every verb is irregular.)

1. Lei, andare   _____

2. Lei, venire   _____

3. Loro, dire   _____

4. Lei, essere   _____

5. Loro, uscire   _____

5. *Esercizio di scrittura: Andiamo!*

Use the imperative to convince a friend or family member to visit Capri (or another place in Campania) with you. Hopefully he or she will be more agreeable than the couple in the dialogue! Google Maps (www.google.com/maps) is a good source if you'd like to see the sites in Street View first.

_____

_____

_____

_____

_____

_____

ANSWER KEY

1.

1. andiamo
2. dire
3. Prendiamo
4. rilassiamo
5. prendi
6. andiamo
7. Visitiamo
8. va'/vai
9. fa'/fai
10. incontriamo
11. Abbi

2.

1. formale
2. informale
3. informale
4. formale
5. formale

3.

1. Dormi!
2. Alzate!
3. Abbiate!
4. Prendiamo!
5. Va'/Vai!

4.

1. Vada!
2. Venga!
3. Dicano!
4. Sia!
5. Escano!

5. Answers will vary. Example:

Quest'estate andiamo a Napoli! Vediamo la baia e visitiamo il Museo Archeologico Nazionale, poi mangiamo una pizza margherita.

MAP OF CAMPANIA

LEZIONE 11

DIRECT OBJECTS / EMILIA-ROMAGNA

Conosci la bellissima regione dell'Emilia-Romagna? Forse sì o forse no, ma sicuramente conosci i buonissimi prodotti alimentari di questa regione, per esempio il prosciutto di Parma, l'aceto balsamico di Modena e il formaggio di Parma, che si chiama il parmiggiano. L'Emilia-Romagna è tra le mie regioni preferite perché lì si mangia bene!

L'Emilia-Romagna è composta da due regioni: L'Emilia, dove si trovano le città di Parma, Modena e Ferrara, e la Romagna, dove si trovano le città di Ravenna, Forlì, Rimini e Bologna. Bologna è il capoluogo dell'Emilia-Romagna. Questa doppia regione confina con le regioni della Lombardia e del Piemonte (ad ovest), e le regioni della Liguria, della Toscana, delle Marche e della Repubblica di San Marino (ad est). Ad est, c'è il bel mare Adriatico e le bellissime spiagge di Rimini sono attrazioni locali soprattutto durante l'estate.

Ci sono tante città stupende in questa regione, ma la mia preferita è Bologna, una bella città medievale e rinascimentale. C'è l'università più antica di tutta l'Europa, che risale al 1088! Tutte le belle facciate ed i tetti degli edifici sono rossi e offrono un bel panorama. Poi ci sono le due torri. Le vedi in questa foto? Ci sono anche i portici che continuano per quasi tutta la città. Li vedi in questa foto? Puoi camminare per la città senza un ombrello!

Bologna è famosa per la sua mortadella. La mangi spesso? È buona! Bologna è anche famosa per le sue tagliatelle al ragù bolognese. Le prepari ogni tanto? Sono buone! Modena è famosa per l'aceto balsamico. Lo metti sull'insalata? È buono! Questa regione è anche famosa per la piadina romagnola, un panino fatto di formaggio, mortadella e salsicce. Puoi comprare tanti buoni prodotti alimentari di questa regione in giro per il mondo. Forse li puoi trovare nel tuo supermercato!

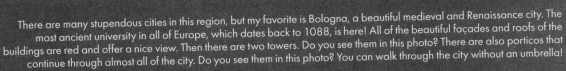

••••▶ Are you familiar with the beautiful region of Emilia-Romagna? Maybe yes or maybe no, but certainly you are familiar with the most delicious food products from this region, such as prosciutto from Parma, balsamic vinegar from Modena, and cheese from Parma, which is called Parmesan. Emilia-Romagna is among my favorite regions because one eats well there!

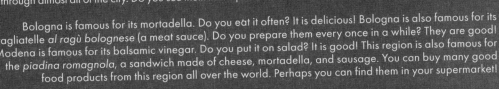

Emilia-Romagna is composed of two regions: Emilia, where the cities of Parma, Modena, and Ferrara are found; and Romagna, where the cities of Ravenna, Forlì, Rimini, and Bologna are found. Bologna is the capital of Emilia-Romagna. This double region borders with the regions of Lombardy, Piedmont, and Liguria (to the west) and the regions of Tuscany, the Marches, and the Republic of San Marino (to the east). The beautiful Adriatic Sea is to the east, and the beautiful beaches of Rimini are local attractions especially during the summer.

There are many stupendous cities in this region, but my favorite is Bologna, a beautiful medieval and Renaissance city. The most ancient university in all of Europe, which dates back to 1088, is here! All of the beautiful façades and roofs of the buildings are red and offer a nice view. Then there are two towers. Do you see them in this photo? There are also porticos that continue through almost all of the city. Do you see them in this photo? You can walk through the city without an umbrella!

Bologna is famous for its mortadella. Do you eat it often? It is delicious! Bologna is also famous for its tagliatelle *al ragù bolognese* (a meat sauce). Do you prepare them every once in a while? They are good! Modena is famous for its balsamic vinegar. Do you put it on salad? It is good! This region is also famous for the *piadina romagnola*, a sandwich made of cheese, mortadella, and sausage. You can buy many good food products from this region all over the world. Perhaps you can find them in your supermarket!

Italian	English	Italian	English
sicuramente	surely	**per esempio**	for example
soprattutto	above all	**dappertutto**	everywhere
senza	without	**migliore**	better
risalire*	to date back to	**si trova(no)****	to find
composto/a (di)	composed (of)	**doppio/a**	double
stupendo/a	stupendous	**medievale**	medieval
rinascimentale	renaissance [adj.]	**l'attrazione locale**	local attraction
la facciata	façade	**l'edificio**	building
il tetto	roof	**il portico**	portico
la torre	tower	**l'abbazia**	abbey
il prosciutto	ham	**l'aceto balsamico**	balsamic vinegar
il formaggio	cheese	**il parmiggiano**	Parmesan cheese
la mortadella	sliced salami	**le tagliatelle**	thin, broad noodles
l'insalata	salad	**la piadina**	flatbread sandwich
la salsiccia	sausage	**il prodotto alimentare**	food product
buono/a	good	**bello/a**	beautiful, good
bravo/a	good (talented)	**nuovo/a**	new
vecchio/a	old	**brutto/a**	ugly
quello/a/i/e	that/those	**Ecco!**	Here (it is/they are)!

* This is a verb that can take on many different idiomatic meanings: It can also mean "to return," "to revisit," "to go back," and "to discover," among other definitions. In this lesson, it is used to mean "to date back to," in terms of the University of Bologna.

** *Si trova/si trovano* are the singular and plural forms of *trovare* ("to find") with the impersonal *si*. They essentially mean "one finds this/these" in a certain location. For example: *Si trova la Torre Eiffel a Parigi* [singular]; *Si trovano molti gatti a Roma* [plural].

RIPASSO GENERALE / GENERAL REVIEW

A. Notes about Emilia-Romagna

The region of Emilia-Romagna is home to some of the best food in Italy—perhaps even the world! That's because the capital, Bologna, is famous for its mouthwatering cuisine, such as its cheese, prosciutto, vinegar, and many other treats. The region also boasts stunning and historically fascinating cities, such as Parma, Modena, and Ravenna.

As you go through the grammar for this lesson, you can talk about the best things to eat using vocabulary to indicate things (“*Ecco!*”), direct object pronouns (e.g., “*Do you eat prosciutto?*” “*Yes, I eat **it**.*”), and the correct forms of *buono* and *bello* (which mean “good” and “beautiful,” respectively). *Impariamo e mangiamo!*

B. Direct Object Pronouns

Direct objects are things that take the direct action of the verb; that is, if, while using a verb, the verb can act directly on something, that something is the direct object. If you kick a ball, the ball is the direct object. If you read a book, the book is the direct object. What if someone gives a gift to you? There are two recipients in this sentence, but one is direct and the other is indirect. If you guessed that the gift is the direct object, you'd be right; *you* in this sentence is an indirect object, which you'll learn about soon.

Direct objects correspond to subject pronouns, some in both number and gender. Let's review subject pronouns:

io	noi
tu	voi
lui/lei/Lei	loro/Loro

And let's look at the direct objects that correspond to them:

mi	ci
ti	vi
lo, la, La	li/le, Li/Le

Notice that *mi*, *ti*, *ci*, and *vi* don't change, but the third person pronouns must agree with gender. Remember how to tell the gender of an Italian noun? If you're unsure, look at its article (*il*, *lo*, *la*, etc.)—that will help you decide which direct object pronoun to use in its place, especially with irregular nouns like *la mano*. Even though *mano* ends in an *-o* and appears masculine, its article is *la*, which means that it is feminine and should be replaced by the direct object *la*.

Where do direct objects go in a sentence? English has what is called an S-V-O syntax (subject-object-verb): English speakers say things like "*I eat bananas. I eat **them**.*" In Italian, typical sentences are still S-V-O ("*Io mangio le banane*"), but when you replace the direct object with a pronoun, the pronoun must go between the subject and the verb, making it S-O-V ("*Io le mangio*"). Even when a subject or subject pronoun is not present, the pronoun goes before the verb (and always after *non*).

Direct object pronouns can be tacked onto the ends of infinitive verbs, informal imperatives, and the word *ecco*:

> *Ti piace mangiare le mele? / Sì, mi piace mangiarle!*
>
> *Mangia le mele! / Mangiale!*
>
> *Dove sono le mele? / Ah, eccole!*

C. The Adjectives *buono* and *bello*

The adjectives *buono* and *bello* are very common in Italian and have quite a few different forms. *Buono* is easier than *bello*, but only because it has fewer forms.

Do you remember learning indefinite and definite articles in lesson 2? If not, let's review them here; you might recognize a pattern later.

Indefinite Articles
un
uno
una
un'

Definite Articles	
il	i
lo	gli
l'	gli
la	le
l'	le

Now let's look at the forms of the adjectives *buono* and *bello*.

buono
buon
buono
buona
buon'

bello	
bel	bei
bello	begli
bell'	begli
bella	belle
bell'	belle
X	belli

Notice any similarities between these and the articles in the previous charts? The forms of *buono* are exactly the same as how you would use an indefinite article before a noun, and the forms of *bello* correspond to the usage of definite articles (with the exception of *belli*, which must stand alone).

Here are some examples. Note how the forms change before and after nouns:

*Il tavolo è **buono**. Che **buon** tavolo!*
*Lo zaino è **buono**. Che **buono** zaino!*

*Il tavolo è **bello**. Che **bel** tavolo!*
*Lo zaino è **bello**. Che **bello** zaino!*

*La torta è **buona**. Che **buona** torta!*
*L'amica è **buona**. Che **buon'**amica!*

*La torta è **bella**. Che **bella** torta!*
*L'amica è **bella**. Che **bell'**amica!*

*Gli amici sono **buoni**. Che **buoni** amici!*

*Gli amici sono **belli**. Che **begli** amici!*

ATTIVITÀ / ACTIVITIES

Vittoria e Matteo sono sposati e vogliono andare in vacanza in Emilia-Romagna, specificamente a Bologna. Oggi vanno all'agenzia di viaggi per prenotare il volo, l'albergo, e altre cose importanti. (Vittoria and Matteo are married and want to go on vacation in Emilia-Romagna, specifically to Bologna. Today they are going to the travel agency to book a flight, a hotel, and other important things.)

1. Scrivi il pronome diretto corretto negli spazi vuoti. (Write the correct direct object pronoun in the blank spaces.)

Agente: Buon giorno, Signori, come posso aiutar 1. _____?

Vittoria: Buon giorno. Vogliamo fare una vacanza in Emilia-Romagna. Lei cosa 2. _____ suggerisce[1]?

Matteo: Abbiamo cugini a Bologna e vogliamo andare a trovar 3. _____[2].

Agente: Certo. Anche il cibo a Bologna è fantastico! Gli piace la mortadella? Si possono[3] anche mangiare le tagliatelle, le piadine, il prosciutto, il parmiggiano...gnam[4]!

Vittoria: La mortadella? Non 4. _____ posso mangiare perché sono vegetariana. Le tagliatelle? 5. _____ mangio ogni giorno se possibile!

....

1 What do you suggest? [formal]

2 *andare a trovare* = to visit (people)

3 *Si possono* = One can .

4 yum!

Agente:	Quanto mi piace l'aceto balsamico bolognese! 6. _____ metto spesso sull'insalata.
Matteo:	...è questo un ristorante o un'agenzia di viaggi? Dobbiamo prenotare anche il volo e l'albergo.
Vittoria:	Non importa! Se parliamo del cibo, sono felice. Il volo e l'albergo saranno[1] sempre lì; 7. _____ possiamo prenotare dopo.

2. Scrivi il pronome diretto corretto nella nuova frase. (Write the correct direct object pronoun in the new sentence. Look out for prepositional phrases!)

1. Mangio sempre **le mele.**   _____ mangio sempre.

2. Mangiamo sempre **il tiramisù.**   _____ mangiamo sempre.

3. Adoro **gli spaghetti alle vongole.**   _____ adoro.

4. Mangi **la torta al cioccolato**?   _____ mangi?

5. Non cucinare **il prosciutto crudo.**   Non _____ cucinare. / Non cucinar_____.

6. L'agente vede **noi.**   L'agente _____ vede.

7. Non mangio mai **i pomodori.**   Non _____ mangio mai.

3. Scrivi la forma giusta di *buono* e *bello* negli spazi vuoti. (Write the correct form of *buono* and *bello* in the blank spaces. Note: *Buono* comes first; *bello* is second.)

1. Che _____ tavolo!   Che _____ tavolo!

2. Che _____ torta!   Che _____ torta!

3. Che _____ amici!   Che _____ amici!

4. Che _____ zoo!   Che _____ zoo!

5. Che _____ alunna!   Che _____ alunna!

6. Che _____ libri!   Che _____ libri!

7. Che _____ studentesse!   Che _____ studentesse!

8. **(Bonus)** I miei amici sono _____.   I miei amici sono _____.

---

1 They will be

4. *Esercizio di scrittura: Non la mangio!*

Use direct object pronouns to talk about things that you do or do not eat. You can pretend to be on a certain diet, or just be picky, for some variation and extra practice.

_____

_____

_____

_____

_____

_____

ANSWER KEY

1.

1. aiutar<u>li</u>/vi
2. ci
3. trovar<u>li</u>
4. la
5. Le
6. Lo
7. li

2.

1. Le
2. Lo
3. Li
4. La
5. lo / cucinar<u>lo</u>.
6. ci
7. li

3.

1. buon, bel
2. buona, bella
3. buoni, begli
4. buono, bello
5. buon', bell'
6. buoni, bei
7. buone, belle
8. buoni, belli

4. Answers will vary. Example:

Non mi piacciono le mele. Non le mangio. Mangio sempre gli spaghetti perché li adoro.

MAP OF EMILIA-ROMAGNA BY PROVINCES

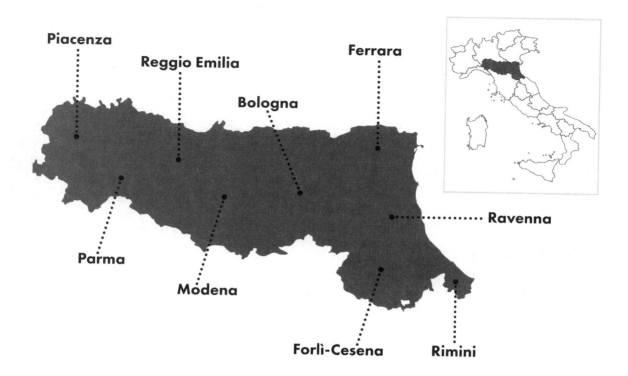

Piacenza

Reggio Emilia

Bologna

Ferrara

Ravenna

Parma

Modena

Forlì-Cesena

Rimini

INDIRECT OBJECTS / FRIULI–VENEZIA GIULIA

La regione del Friuli–Venezia Giulia si trova nel nord d'Italia. Confina con due altri paesi: con l'Austria a nord e con la Slovenia ad est. Confina anche con il mare Adriatico a sud e con la regione del Veneto ad ovest. Sì, la città di Venezia non si trova in questa regione anche se il nome della regione è Friuli–Venezia Giulia! La città di Venezia si trova nella regione del Veneto.

Conosci questa regione? Forse sì, forse no. Sai che in questa regione tante persone parlano più di una lingua? Le lingue ufficiali di questa regione sono quattro: l'italiano, il friulano, lo sloveno e il tedesco. Sai parlare queste lingue? Se vai in Friuli–Venezia Giulia, puoi parlarle lì. Se qualcuno ti parla in italiano, forse gli puoi rispondere in tedesco! Questa regione ti dà l'impressione di essere al centro dell'Europa! L'Italia è un paese multilingue.

Questa regione ha tante bellezze naturali come il mare e la montagna. Ti piace l'alpinismo? Mi piace l'alpinismo. Ci sono le Alpi in questa regione. Ma ci sono anche tante colline e pianure, per esempio la pianura friulana ed anche tantissimi laghi. Ci sono anche delle grotte da esplorare in questa regione, per esempio la Grotta Gigante! Ci sono dei fiumi sotterranei come il fiume Timavo! Mi piace la Grotta Gigante, anche se non mi piace essere sottoterra. La Grotta Gigante è la grotta più grande in tutta l'Europa! Essere nella grotta ti dà la sensazione di essere davvero sottoterra!

Il capoluogo di questa regione è una città bellissima e molto particolare, la città di Trieste. L'architettura della città riflette la sua storia austriaca, quando era parte dell'impero austriaco. I colori dei palazzi di Trieste sono molto belli: sono colori chiari, come il rosa e il celeste. Si riflettono nel Canal Grande. Ti piacciono i colori chiari? Mi piacciono. Ti piacciono la cultura italiana, tedesca e austriaca? Forse ti piace Trieste! Piaceva a James Joyce, l'autore irlandese che ha vissuto per molto tempo a Trieste!

Ti consiglio di visitare il Friuli–Venezia Giulia. È una regione che ti regala un'esperienza ricca e diversa dell'Italia.

• • • ▶ The region of Friuli–Venezia Giulia is located in northern Italy. It borders with two other countries: with Austria to the north and with Slovenia to the east. It also borders with the Adriatic Sea to the south and with the Veneto region to the west. Yes, the city of Venice is not located in this region, even if the name of the region is Friuli–Venezia Giulia! The city of Venice is located in the Veneto region.

Are you familiar with this region? Maybe, or maybe not. Do you know that in this region, many people speak more than one language? There are four official languages in this region: Italian, Friulian, Slovenian, and German. Do you know how to speak these languages? If you go to Friuli–Venezia Giulia, you can speak them there. If someone speaks to you in Italian, maybe you can respond to him/to her in German! This region gives you the impression of being at the center of Europe! Italy is a multilingual country.

This region has much natural beauty, such as the sea and the mountains. Do you like mountain hiking? I like mountain hiking. The Alps are in this region. One part of these mountains are the Carnic Alps. But there are also many hills and plains—for example, the Friulian plain—and also many lakes. There are also caves to explore in this region, such as the Grotta Gigante ("The Gigantic Cave")! There are underground rivers, such as the Timavo River! I like the Grotta Gigante, even if I don't like being underground. The Grotta Gigante is the largest cave in all of Europe! Being in the cave gives you the sensation of truly being underground!

The capital of this region is a beautiful and very special city, the city of Trieste. The city's architecture reflects its Austrian history, when it was part of the Austrian Empire. The colors of the buildings in Trieste are very pretty: They are pale colors, such as pink and baby blue. They are reflected in the Canal Grande. Do you like pale colors? I like them. Do you like Italian, German, and Austrian culture? Perhaps you will like Trieste! James Joyce, the Irish author who lived a long time in Trieste, liked it.

I recommend that you visit Friuli–Venezia Giulia. It is a region that gives you a rich and diverse experience of Italy.

VOCABOLARIO NUOVO E UTILE / NEW AND USEFUL VOCABULARY

anche se	even though	**Sai che...?**	Do you know that...?
forse	maybe	**davvero**	really, truly
dare l'impressione	to give the impression	**dare la sensazione**	to give the sensation
consigliare	to advise	**regalare**	to gift
riflettere	to reflect	**mostrare**	to show
l'alpinismo	mountain climbing	**la bellezza**	beauty
la collina	hill	**la pianura**	plain (nature)
la grotta	grotto	**il fiume**	river
gigante	giant	**sotterraneo/a**	underground [adj.]
chiaro/a	clear, bright	**austriaco/a**	Austrian
rosa	pink	**azzurro/a**	light blue
celeste	sky blue	**sottoterra**	underground [loc.]
piace*	it pleases [sing.]	**piacciono**	they please [pl.]
piaceva	it pleased [sing.]	**piacevano**	they pleased [pl.]

* As you'll see in this lesson, the verb *piacere* ("to please") is used in a different way than how English speakers say "to like (something)."

RIPASSO GENERALE / GENERAL REVIEW

A. Notes about Friuli–Venezia Giulia

Even though the region of Friuli–Venezia Giulia has the name *Venezia* in it, the city of Venice is not in this region. In fact, this is one of the smallest regions of Italy and is largely missed by tourists. Being right on the border with Austria and Slovenia, the region is a delightful mix of cultures and dialects. Here you can find the cities of Trieste, where many famous authors have stayed and written masterpieces, and Udine, which boasts incredible views of the Alps. There are many geographical wonders to see here!

In this lesson, you'll cover different types of pronouns and the verb *piacere*. By the end, you'll be able to say exactly what you like about Friuli–Venezia Giulia and why!

B. Indirect Object Pronouns

In the previous lesson, you learned about direct object pronouns, which replace direct objects, which take the direct action of a verb. In the example "I give the book to her," *the book* is the direct object, and *her* is the indirect object. The indirect object is the indirect recipient of a verb and answers the question "to/for whom?" So, you'll typically see it used with the prepositions *a* and *per* (*to* and *for*).[1]

Be careful because the indirect object pronouns are largely very similar to the direct object pronouns. Let's review the direct object pronouns:

mi	ci
ti	vi
lo/la/La	li/le/Loro

And here are the indirect object pronouns:

mi	ci
ti	vi
gli/le/Le	gli/...loro/...Loro

Like direct object pronouns, indirect object pronouns go before the verb in a new sentence. For the third person plural, however, you have two options: Place *gli* before the verb to signify "to them" or place *loro* directly after the verb. However, *loro* as an indirect object pronoun is slowly fading out of linguistic usage. They can also attach to the end of infinitives. If you were to rephrase the sentence "I give the book to her," you would write "***Le do il libro***." If you give the book to a male person, you would write "***Gli do il libro***." Don't worry about replacing both the direct and indirect object in the same subject just yet; it's coming up later in the course.

1 Verbs that frequently take indirect objects are the following: *chiedere* ("to ask"), *consigliare* ("to advise"), *dare* ("to give"), *dire* ("to say"), *domandare* ("to ask"), *insegnare* ("to teach"), *mandare* ("to send"), *mostrare* ("to show"), *offrire* ("to offer"), *parlare* ("to speak"), *portare* ("to bring"), *regalare* ("to gift"), *rispondere* ("to respond"), *scrivere* ("to write"), and *telefonare* ("to call").

C. Tonic Pronouns

Two types of pronouns you'll learn about in Italian are *pronomi tonici* and *pronomi atoni*—*stressed pronouns* and *unstressed pronouns*, respectively. You've already seen the unstressed pronouns in play; they're the forms that come before the verb in a sentence, such as "**Le do il libro.**"

Stressed pronouns still give the same meaning to the sentence but have more emphasis on them. They are typically placed after a verb instead of before them, but not always. They almost always follow a preposition (*a, per, con*, etc.). Many verbs in Italian don't require subject pronouns to accompany them because the conjugations are very clearly designated. However, if you're in a conversation and you want to repeat a pronoun for emphasis, this is when you'd use a *pronome tonico*.

Here are the tonic pronouns in Italian:

me	noi
te	voi
lui/lei/Lei	loro/Loro

For instance, you could say, "**Mi** *piace l'italiano!*" Or you could say, "*L'italiano piace a* **me**; *e a* **te**?" Both sentences mean the same thing, but note the difference in the placement and the emphasis.

D. The Verb *piacere*

The verb *piacere* means "to please" or "to be pleasing to" in Italian and is used to indicate things that someone likes. However, differently from English, the person liking a thing is not the subject; rather, the thing that pleases is the subject, and the person to whom it is pleasing is the indirect object. That's why the indirect object pronouns are important for this lesson!

In Italian, you would say, "The book is pleasing to me" rather than "I like the book." That would translate to "*Il libro piace a* **me**" (using the stressed pronouns you just learned) or "**Mi** *piace il libro*" (using the indirect object pronouns). Unlike in Spanish, you wouldn't say, "*A me mi piace*"—although some regions of Italy do use this construction colloquially.

As a reminder, here are the two forms of *piacere* that are used the most (although it does have six forms like all other verbs):

piace	piacciono

The singular form, *piace*, is used for singular nouns that please, and *piacciono* is used for plural. So, you would say, "*Mi piace il libro*" (because *libro* is singular) but "*Mi piacciono i libri.*" This verb is almost always used in the third person singular and plural for all verb tenses.[1]

ATTIVITÀ / ACTIVITIES

Judith è una donna austriaca che parla l'italiano molto bene, essendo cresciuta a Trieste. Il suo amico Giacomo vive ad Udine e ospita Judith questo fine settimana. A Judith non piacciono molte cose; ha i gusti molto raffinati. D'altro canto, a Giacomo piace tutto. I due amici cercano di trovare qualcosa che piace a lui e a lei ugualmente. (Judith is an Austrian woman who speaks Italian very well, having grown up in Trieste. Her friend Giacomo lives in Udine and is hosting Judith this weekend. Judith does not like many things; she has very refined tastes. On the other hand, Giacomo likes everything. The two friends try to find something that pleases them both equally.)

1. Scrivi la forma corretta del verbo *piacere* (o *piace* o *piacciono*) negli spazi vuoti. (Write the correct form of the verb *piacere* (either *piace* or *piacciono*) in the spaces.)

Judith:	Giacomo, che piacere vederti! Cosa ti 1. _____ fare questo fine settimana?
Giacomo:	Veramente mi 2. _____ tante cose. Ti 3. _____ sciare?
Judith:	No, non mi 4. _____ sciare perché non mi 5. _____ il freddo. Ti 6. _____ lo schnitzel? Ce l'ho[2] nella valigia.
Giacomo:	No, mi 7. _____ solo i cibi italiani. A proposito del[3] cibo italiano, a me 8. _____ molto le tagliatelle, e a te?
Judith:	No, le tagliatelle non 9. _____ a me. Ti 10. _____ invece il vino bianco?
Giacomo:	No, mi 11. _____ il vino rosso.
Judith:	Allora cosa facciamo?? Cosa mangiamo?
Giacomo:	A me 12. _____ fare shopping, e a te?!
Judith:	A me sì! Mi 13. _____ i negozi italiani. Andiamo!

....
1 The verbs *mancare* ("to be missing"/"to be lacking") and *dispiacere* ("to displease") behave the same as *piacere*.

2 *Ce l'ho* = I have it

3 *A proposito di* = Speaking of

2. Scrivi il pronome indiretto corretto negli spazi vuoti. (Write the correct indirect object pronoun in the blank spaces.)

1. Il cibo italiano piace **a me**. Il cibo italiano _____ piace.

2. Le fettuccine piacciono **a Davide**. Le fettuccine _____ piacciono.

3. **A Daniele e Alice** piace la pizza. _____ piace la pizza.

4. **A te e Fabio** piace leggere? _____ piace leggere?

5. Questa sedia non piace **a mia madre**. Questa sedia non _____ piace.

3. Abbina le parole alla sinistra ai pronomi indiretti alla destra che le corrispondono. (Match the words on the left to the indirect object pronouns on the right that correspond to them.)

1. a voi   a. ci

2. a Lei   b. vi

3. a Luigi   c. mi

4. a me   d. Le

5. a me ed Emilio   e. gli

4. *Esercizio di scrittura: Mi piace!*

Write to your imaginary foreign pen pal about things that you like about your hometown and things that you do not like as much. For extra practice, list the reasons why you do or do not like these things.

_____

_____

_____

_____

_____

_____

ANSWER KEY

1.

1. piace   2. piacciono   3. piace

4. piace
5. piace
6. piace
7. piacciono

8. piacciono
9. piacciono
10. piace
11. piace

12. piace
13. piacciono

2.

1. mi
2. gli

3. Gli piace/Piace loro
4. Vi

5. le

3.

1. b.
2. d.

3. e.
4. c.

5. a.

4. Answers will vary. Example:

Di Baltimora, mi piace l'Inner Harbor. Mi piace l'acquario perché mi piacciono i pesci. Non mi piace il traffico!

MAP OF FRIULI–VENEZIA GIULIA BY PROVINCES

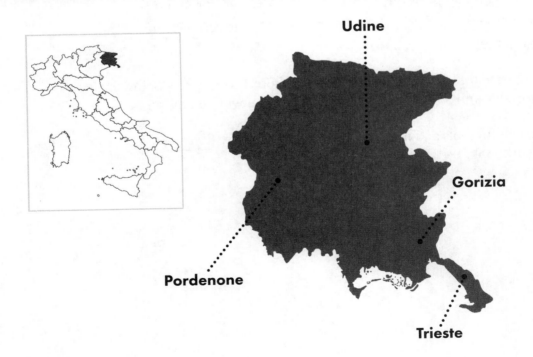

Udine

Gorizia

Pordenone

Trieste

WHERE ARE YOU NOW?

Congratulations! You've made it through the first half of the workbook. By now, you should be familiar with the following topics in vocabulary:

1. family members

2. weather terms

You have also covered quite a bit of grammar:

1. possessive adjectives and pronouns

2. possessives with family members

3. *questo* and *quello* (demonstrative adjectives)

4. prepositions

5. articulated prepositions

6. partitives

7. modal verbs (*dovere, potere, volere*)

8. *conoscere* and *sapere*

9. informal and formal imperatives

10. direct object pronouns

11. *buono* and *bello*

12. indirect object pronouns

13. tonic pronouns

14. the verb *piacere*

Next to each topic, rate your comfort level from 1 to 5, with 1 being the least comfortable and 5 being the most. What can you work on more?

Some helpful tools and methods are listed in the first *Where Are You Now?* section in this workbook.

LEZIONE 13

IRREGULAR NOUNS / BASILICATA

La regione della Basilicata si trova nel sud dell'Italia. Infatti, è la regione più piccola del sud. Confina con tre altre regioni: con la Calabria a sud, con la Campania a nord-ovest e con la Puglia a nord-est. Confina anche con il mare Tirreno a sud e con il golfo di Taranto. Se la regione della Calabria è il punto dello stivale e la Puglia è il tacco dello stivale, la Basilicata è il collo del piede!

Conosci questa regione? Forse sì, forse no. La Basilicata si chiama anche Lucania, il suo nome romano antico. Infatti, le persone in questa regione si chiamano lucani. È una regione che è molto isolata dal resto della penisola. Il capoluogo è Potenza e ci sono due province: Potenza e Matera.

Matera, infatti, è il nome della città che adesso è un'attrazione turistica molto importante e un sito UNESCO dal 1993 per il suo patrimonio culturale. Quest'attrazione sono "i Sassi" ("the Rocks"). Matera era la capitale della cultura europea nel 2019! I Sassi sono case scavate nelle rocce fino dall'epoca paleolitica. La regione era sempre molto povera e così i Sassi erano anche le abitazioni della gente povera della regione. Adesso alcune di queste case sono alberghi, negozi e bar! Ci sono anche delle chiese scavate nei Sassi.

Il panorama di questa regione è affascinante, come i Sassi. Ci sono delle montagne bianche, e il terreno è arido. Sembra lunare o come il deserto! Qui l'agricoltura è l'industria principale, ma la terra non è molto fertile. Adesso l'industria in ascesa è il petrolio, che c'è in questa zona.

La Basilicata assomiglia molto a Gerusalemme. Quindi anche se non la conosci, puoi vederla in tanti film: *The Gospel According to St. Matthew* (Pier Paolo Pasolini, 1964), *The Passion of the Christ* (Mel Gibson, 2004), *The Nativity Story* (Catherine Hardwicke, 2006) e *Ben-Hur* (Timur Bekmambetov, 2016). La puoi anche vedere nel film di *Wonder Woman*! Ti suggerisco di andare a visitare la Basilicata. È una regione che ti offre un'esperienza unica dell'Italia.

The Basilicata region is located in the Italian south. In fact, it is the smallest region in the south. It borders with three other regions: with Calabria to the south, with Campania to the northwest, and with Puglia to the northeast. It also borders with the Tyrrhenian Sea to the south and with the Gulf of Taranto. If the Calabria region is the tip of the boot and Puglia is the heel of the boot, then Basilicata is the arch of the foot!

Are you familiar with the region? Maybe, or maybe not. Basilicata is also called Luciania, its ancient Roman name. In fact, the people in this region are called Lucanians. It is a region that is very isolated from the rest of the peninsula. The capital is Potenza and there are two provinces: Potenza and Matera.

Matera, in fact, is the name of the city, which is now a very important tourist attraction and a UNESCO site since 1993 for its cultural heritage. This attraction is the Sassi ("the Rocks"). Matera was the European Capital of Culture in 2019! The Sassi are homes dug into rocky cliffs from the Paleolithic era. The region was always very poor, and so the Sassi were also the dwellings of poor people in the region. Now some of these homes are hotels, stores, and cafès! There are also churches dug into the Sassi.

The panorama of this region, like the Sassi, is fascinating. There are white mountains, and the terrain is arid. It looks like the moon, or like the desert! Here agriculture is the main industry, but the ground is not very fertile. Now the industry on the rise is petroleum, which is in this area.

Basilicata truly resembles Jerusalem. Therefore, even if you don't know it, you can see it in many films: *The Gospel According to St. Matthew* (Pier Paolo Pasolini, 1964), *The Passion of the Christ* (Mel Gibson, 2004), *The Nativity Story* (Catherine Hardwicke, 2006), and *Ben-Hur* (Timur Bekmambetov, 2016). You can also see it in the film *Wonder Woman*! I recommend that you go to visit Basilicata. It is a region that gives you a unique experience of Italy.

VOCABOLARIO NUOVO E UTILE / NEW AND USEFUL VOCABULARY

infatti	in fact	**in salita**	rising
il tacco	heel	**lo stivale**	boot
il collo	neck	**il piede**	foot
il collo del piede	arch of the foot (idiomatic expression)		
il patrimonio	patrimony	**la roccia**	rock
l'epoca	epoch, era	**la povertà**	poverty
l'abitazione	inhabitation	**l'albergo**	hotel
il negozio	store	**la chiesa**	church
il tufo	tuff (type of rock)	**la calcarenite**	calcarenite (type of limestone)
scavato/a	excavated, dug	**paleolitico/a**	paleolithic
drammatico/a	dramatic	**affascinante**	fascinating
bianco/a	white	**arido/a**	dry, arid
lunare	lunar	**principale**	principal, main
assomigliare	to resemble	**suggerire**	to suggest

RIPASSO GENERALE / GENERAL REVIEW

A. Notes about Basilicata

While Basilicata is the smallest southern region of Italy, making up the "arch" of the boot, it boasts a large history and itinerary of places to see and things to do. One of the most fascinating cities in Basilicata is surely Matera, named a UNESCO World Heritage site in 1993. Matera is also known as *la città dei Sassi* because the houses there are carved into the rock of the hillside, which dates back to the paleolithic era. Don't miss it!

This lesson covers more nouns—these will be irregular nouns, with difficult endings and plurals. It also covers interrogative words: *How* will we get to Matera? *What* will we see there? *Why* should everyone visit? You'll be able to answer these questions, and more, by the end of the lesson.

B. Nouns (Irregular, Difficult Plural Endings)

When you first learned nouns, you discovered that they fall into three major categories: masculine (typically ending in *-o*), feminine (typically ending in *-a*), and nouns that end in *-e*, which must be memorized. Sometimes, nouns that end in *-e* are easy to categorize; for example, nouns that end in *-ione* are feminine. Other times it's not so easy. What about nouns that end in *-ista*? That ending looks feminine, right?

A noun that ends in *-ista* can actually be feminine or masculine, depending on the article that is used with it. So, you can have *il turista* (a male tourist) or *la turista* (a female tourist). The plural has the same *-i* and *-e* endings you're used to having for masculine and feminine: *i turisti* (male tourists, or a group of male and female tourists) and *le turiste* (female tourists). Adjectives ending in *-ista* behave the same way (e.g., *ottimista*, *pessimista*, *socialista*, etc.).

> Remember: *-ista* nouns have three forms: *-ista*, *-isti*, and *-iste*.

Nouns of Greek origin that end in *-pa* (*il papa*), *-ta* (*il poeta*), and *-ma* (*il clima*) are also irregular—they are masculine, even though they end in *-a*. Here are a few more: *il panorama*, *il problema*, *il dilemma*, *il tema*, *il sistema*, *il programma*. These have an *-i* ending in the plural (*i papi*, *i poeti*, *i climi*, etc.).

> Remember: *-pa*, *-ta*, and *-ma* nouns in this list are masculine and have an *-i* plural ending.

In the same vein, nouns that end in *-si* (*l'analisi*, *la crisi*, *la tesi*) are also Greek, and are feminine. Only the article changes in the plural (*le analisi*, *le crisi*, *le tesi*).

Enough about Greek loan words—what about difficult Italian plurals?

You've learned about how words that end in *-co/-ca* and *-go/-ga* need to add an *h* in the plural to maintain their hard *G* and *C* sounds (e.g., *lago* → *laghi*; *amica* → *amiche*), but some nouns and adjectives—such as *medico*, *simpatico*, *amico*, *greco*, and *energico*—only have *-ci* in the ending. What about nouns and adjectives that end in *-cio/-cia* and *-gio/-gia*?

The rule for this is dependent on where the accent falls in the ending. If there's a stress on the *-ci* or *-gi* part of the ending, the *i* is retained in the plural (e.g., *farmaCIa* → *farmaCIe*; *bioloGIa* → *bioloGIe*). If the ending is all one syllable, then the plural drops the *i* (e.g., *RIccio* → *RIcci*; *GRIgio* → *GRIge*).

Sounds confusing, right? It'll get easier with time and practice. Every time you meet a word whose plural you are unsure of, type the word into Google Translate and then listen to it being spoken. This will help with both pronunciation and memorization of the sounds and rhythms of Italian words.

C. Interrogative Nouns and Pronouns

Let's look at a list of Italian interrogative (question) words and consider the distinction between a few of them. Surprisingly, Italians have more than one way to ask what a thing is!

Italian Interrogative	English Translation
che / cosa / che cosa	what
quale/i	what, which
come	how
quando	when
quanto/a/i/e	how much/many
chi	who
perché	why

As you can see, many of these words are cut and dry and only have one meaning. Others, however, have either two meanings or two (or even three) options in Italian.

The three phrases *che/cosa/che cosa* are relatively interchangeable. They are not interchangeable with *quale*, however. In Italian, *quale* is used mainly to mean "which," but Italians also use it to ask what your phone number is or what the capital of a region is. Generally, if you are asking for the definition of something (What is a butterfly?), you would use *che/cosa/che cosa*, and if you are asking for something that exists in the realm of all possibilities (Which of the thousands of phone numbers is yours?), you would use *quale*.

These generally appear at the beginning of a sentence. They can also follow a preposition (*con chi, per quanto tempo, a che cosa*). *Chi* is used only at the beginning of a sentence, or with a preposition, to mean "who" (and also in proverbial phrases like "He who does this..."). Where in English you would say, "He is the person *who* studies Italian," that would be *che*, not *chi*.

Perché can be used to mean both "why" and "because," but if you want to say "because of...," you would use *a causa di*. If you'd like to say "since," it's *siccome*.

Your hard work is paying off! These are the minute rules and distinctions in Italian that will make a big difference when you go to Italy and begin using your Italian with a native speaker.

Ti piace la storia? Se ti piace la storia lucana, devi leggere *Cristo si è fermato a Eboli* di Carlo Levi! Parliamo di questo autore e di questo libro. La regione della Basilicata adesso è conosciuta e famosa grazie a questo libro che Carlo Levi ha scritto durante gli anni Quaranta.

In questo libro, Levi parla della gente lucana, del clima, del paesaggio, e del terreno arido, particolarmente di Aliano. Ci dimostra le abitudini della gente lucana, le loro superstizioni e il tessuto sociale. Durante gli anni del fascismo, e anche prima, la malaria era molto comune in questa regione. Levi è un medico che non esercita da molto tempo, ma la gente viene a trovarlo per curarsi. Levi anche è un pittore e dipinge tanti quadri della gente e del paesaggio, come vediamo in questi esempi. I colori dell'argilla e delle montagne di questo paesaggio arido ma bellissimo sembrano lunari. Ad Aliano c'è un museo dedicato a Carlo Levi.

▶ Do you like history? If you like Lucanian history, you must read *Christ Stopped at Eboli* by Carlo Levi! Let's speak about this author and this book. The Basilicata region is now known and famous thanks to this book that Carlo Levi wrote during the 1940s.

In this book, Levi talks about the Lucanian people, the climate, the landscape, and the arid terrain, especially in Aliano. It demonstrates to us the habits of the Lucanian people, their superstitions, and the social fabric. During the years of Fascism, and even earlier, malaria was very common in this region. Levi is a doctor who has not practiced for a long time, but people come to him to be cured. Levi is also a painter and paints many paintings of the people and the landscape, such as we see in these examples. The colors of the clay and the mountains of this dry but beautiful landscape seem moonlike. There is a museum dedicated to Carlo Levi in Aliano.

ATTIVITÀ / ACTIVITIES

Ivano ed Emilia sono fratello e sorella. Sono in Basilicata per vedere i loro cugini e sono completamente persi. Devono fare domande alle persone di Matera per arrivare a casa in tempo per cena. (Ivano and Emilia are brother and sister. They are in Basilicata to see their cousins and they are completely lost. They must ask questions of the people in Matera in order to arrive home in time for dinner.)

1. Scegli la parola interrogativa giusta. (Choose the correct question word.)

   Emilia: Ivano, siamo persi! Veramente non so 1. _____ (perché / come) arrivare da zia Laura.

Ivano:	2. _____ (quale / perché) non hai portato una mappa con te?
Emilia:	Perché ho dimenticato![1] Forse dobbiamo chiedere a qualcuno 3. _____ (quale / che cosa) strada prendere.
Ivano:	Certo, ecco un bar. Buon giorno, 4. _____ (cosa / come) sta?
Barista:	Sto bene, grazie. 5. _____ (quale / cosa) volete da mangiare oggi?
Emilia:	Non siamo qui per mangiare. Dobbiamo andare a via Casalnuovo 28, la casa di nostra zia.
Barista:	Mi dispiace, signori, non sono di qui e non vi posso aiutare. 6. _____ (chi / perché) non chiedere a qualcun altro?
Ivano:	Veramente? Che interessante, di 7. _____ (dove / come) è Lei?
Emilia:	Ivano, dai, dobbiamo andare!

2. Trasforma le frasi dal singolare al plurale. (Change the phrases from singular to plural.)

1. la barista italiana _____

2. l'artista tedesco _____

3. il socialista giapponese _____

4. la femminista americana _____

5. l'economista russo _____

3. Decidi se le seguenti parole sono maschili o femminili. (Decide whether the following words are masculine or feminine.)

1. panorama   M   F

2. tema   M   F

3. patata   M   F

4. papa   M   F

5. sistema   M   F

6. mamma   M   F

7. problema   M   F

....

1 *ho dimenticato* = I forgot

4. Inserisci l'interrogativo corretto nello spazio. (Insert the correct question word in the blank space.)

1. _____ è la ragazza bionda nella foto?

2. Di _____ sei, Enrico?

3. _____ è il tuo numero di telefono?

4. _____ non mi dai il tuo numero di telefono? Sei arrabbiato con me?

5. _____ stai oggi?

5. Esercizio di scrittura: Perché?

Write to your friend and ask about his or her dream vacation. Then ask them why they want to go to that particular place, what they want to see there, and how they plan to get there.

_____

_____

_____

_____

_____

_____

_____

_____

_____

ANSWER KEY

1.

1. come
2. Perché
3. quale
4. come
5. Cosa
6. Perché
7. dove

2.

1. le bariste italiane
2. gli artisti tedeschi
3. i socialisti giapponesi
4. le femministe americane
5. gli economisti russi

3.

1. M
2. M
3. F

4. M
5. M
6. F

7. M

4.

1. Chi
2. dove

3. Qual
4. Perché

5. Come

5. Answers will vary. Example:

Dove vuoi andare in vacanza? Perché? Cosa vuoi vedere a/in _____ ?

MAP OF BASILICATA BY PROVINCES

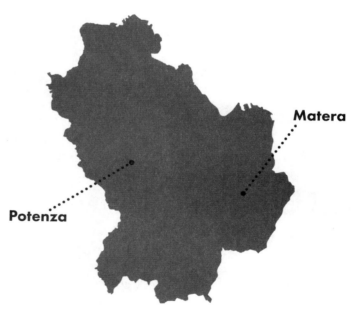

LEZIONE 14

REFLEXIVE PRONOUNS AND VERBS / THE MARCHES

Dov'è la regione delle Marche? La regione delle Marche si trova nel centro dell'Italia. Con quali altre regioni confina? Confina con cinque altre regioni: con l'Emilia-Romagna a nord, con la Toscana all'ovest, con l'Umbria al sud-ovest e con l'Abruzzo e il Lazio al sud. Confina anche con la Repubblica di San Marino al nord e con il mare Adriatico all'est.

Qual è il capoluogo delle Marche? Il capoluogo è Ancona, una città sul mare e un porto. Com'è il suo clima? Il suo clima è simile a quello della Basilicata: vicino al mare il clima è mediterraneo, ma nell'entroterra e nelle montagne il clima è continentale. Qual è la topografia di questa zona? La topografia di questa regione è simile a quella dell'Abruzzo. Entrambe hanno gli Appennini ad est. Ma le montagne delle Marche non sono così alte come quelle dell'Abruzzo. Nelle Marche ci sono montagne più basse e colline che scendono verso la costa. Ci sono anche delle pianure molto belle e fertili e tanti campi di girasoli. Quali sono alcuni parchi nazionali di questa zona? Sono due: il Parco Nazionale dei monti Sibillini e il Parco del Monte Conero. Come si chiamano le province marchigiane? Ci sono cinque province: Ancona, Ascoli Piceno, Fermo, Macerata e Pesaro e Urbino. Ad Urbino c'è il Palazzo dei Montefeltro dove puoi vedere le opere d'arte.

Chi è un marchigiano famoso nell'arte e nella letteratura? Ci sono tante figure storiche che vengono dalle Marche! La regione delle Marche è anche la terra del Rinascimento, perché Rafaello Sanzio, conosciuto come Raffaello, è nato qui nel 1483. Puoi vedere i suoi quadri nel Palazzo dei Montefeltro. Ci sono tante città e tanti paesi che hanno ancora dei castelli e delle torri medievali e rinascimentali come ad Ascoli Piceno, Cingoli, Recanati e Urbino. Giacomo Leopardi, un grande poeta italiano, è nato a Recanati. Quando? Nel 1798. Gioacchino Rossini è nato a Pesaro. Quando? Nel 1792. Qui c'è il festival della musica dedicato a lui. Quando? Il Rossini Opera Festival si svolge ogni anno.

L'industria primaria è l'agricoltura ma le Marche sono anche famose per i prodotti di cuoio, come le scarpe. Ci sono delle ditte famose che hanno sedi principali in questa regione: Todds, per esempio. Ma le Marche sono famose anche per le scienze della salute. Ci sono delle terme dove puoi curare tante malattie. La medicina è un pregio di questa regione.

Where is the region of the Marches? The region of the Marches is located in the center of Italy. With which other regions does it border? It borders with five other regions: with Emilia-Romagna to the north, with Tuscany to the west, with Umbria to the southwest, and with Abruzzo and Lazio to the south. It also borders with the Republic of San Marino to the north and with the Adriatic Sea to the east.

What is the capital of the Marches? The capital is Ancona, a city on the sea and a port. What is its climate like? Its climate is similar to that of Basilicata: Close to the sea, the climate is Mediterranean, but in the inland and in the mountains, the climate is continental. What is the topography of this area? The topography of this area is similar to that of Abruzzo. Both have the Apennines to the east. But the mountains of the Marches are not as high as those of Abruzzo. In the Marches, there are lower mountains and hills that descend toward the coast. There are also very fertile plains and many fields of sunflowers. What are some national parks in this area? There are two: the Sibillini National Park and Monte Conero Park. What are the names of the provinces in the Marches? There are five provinces: Ancona, Ascoli Piceno, Fermo, Macerata and Pesaro, and Urbino. In Urbino, there is the Montefeltro Palace, where you can see works of art.

Who is famous for art and for literature from the Marches? There are many historical figures who come from the Marches! The region of the Marches is also the land of the Renaissance, since Rafaello Sanzio, known as Raphael, was born here in 1483. You can see his paintings in the Montefeltro Palace. There are many cities and many towns that still have castles and medieval and Renaissance towers, such as in Ascoli Piceno, Cingoli, Recanati, and Urbino. Giacomo Leopardi, a great Italian poet, was born in Recanati. When? In 1798. Gioacchino Rossini was born in Pesaro. When? In 1792. Here there is a music festival dedicated to him. When? The Rossini Opera Festival takes place each year.

The primary industry is agriculture, but the Marches is also famous for its leather products, such as shoes. There are famous companies that have their headquarters in this region: Todds, for example. But the Marches is famous for the health sciences as well. There are thermal baths, where you can cure many illnesses. Medicine is distinguished in this region.

VOCABOLARIO NUOVO E UTILE / NEW AND USEFUL VOCABULARY

dove	where	**dov'è**	where is
dove sono	where are	**quale**	which, what
qual è	which, what is	**quali sono**	which, what are
come	how	**com'è**	how is
come sono	how are	**che**	what, that
chi	who	**quando**	when
quanto/a	how much	**quanti/e**	how many
entrambi	both	**vicino (a)**	near (to)
il clima	climate	**la zona**	area
la topografia	topography	**l'entroterra**	inland
il campo	field	**il girasole**	sunflower
il parco nazionale	national park	**la provincia**	province
la figura storica	historical figure	**il quadro**	painting, portrait
il cuoio	leather	**la ditta**	company, business
le terme	thermal baths	**la malattia**	sickness, disease
il pregio	virtue, value	**l'istituto**	institute
continentale	continental	**mediterraneo/a**	Mediterranean [adj.]
marchigiano/a	from the Marches	**riflessivo/a**	reflexive

RIPASSO GENERALE / GENERAL REVIEW

A. Notes about le Marche

Le Marche—or the Marches, as they're known in English—is a region of Italy that abuts the Adriatic Sea. It is known for the medieval cities of Urbino, Ancona, Pesaro, and Ascoli Piceno. It is also the birthplace of the famous Renaissance painter Raphael, as well as other famous authors and musicians, such as Giacomo

Leopardi and Gioacchino Rossini. Like many other Italian regions, this one is geographically diverse: It ranges from seaside towns to mountainous inlands, and everything in between.

In this lesson, you'll learn reflexive verbs and their pronouns, as well as the vocabulary necessary to tell time and talk about the body. By the end of the lesson, you'll be able to say how you're feeling as you climb a mountain at 2:00 pm!

B. Reflexive Verbs and Pronouns

Reflexive verbs are verbs whose actions reflect back on themselves. All the verbs you have seen so far are (mostly) nonreflexive verbs; that is, the action of the verb, if there is one, is not the subject of the verb. For instance, you can wash a car, and the car is the direct object of the verb. But what if you are washing yourself?

Reflexive verbs in Italian require an extra part to them: a reflexive pronoun that precedes the conjugated verb. You've seen some reflexive verbs before, such as *chiamarsi* (meaning "to call oneself," which is used in introducing yourself by name). Reflexive verbs end in *-arsi*, *-ersi*, and *-irsi*, which denotes that they are reflexive.

Let's look at the conjugation of *chiamarsi*:

mi chiamo	**ci** chiamiamo
ti chiami	**vi** chiamate
si chiama	**si** chiamano

Notice that each conjugation has a different reflexive pronoun that matches up with it. Reflexive pronouns can only go with the reflexive verb conjugation to which they belong—you can't mix and match. As for the verb itself, it is conjugated exactly the same as a normal *-are*, *-ere*, or *-ire* verb with a pronoun in front.

Let's look at one more verb (*mettersi*):

mi metto	**ci** mettiamo
ti metti	**vi** mettete
si mette	**si** mettono

As you can see, it's just a regularly conjugated *-ere* verb with the correct pronouns in front. Practice this with the verbs *alzarsi* ("to get up"), *radersi* ("to shave oneself"), and *vestirsi* ("to dress oneself").

C. How to Tell Time

In Italian, telling time is slightly different than how it's done in English. For starters, to ask for the time, you'd essentially say, "What hour is it/are they?" and answer "It is the [number]/They are the [number]," where the word *the* stands in for "the hour(s)." So, you would ask "*Che ora è?/Che ore sono?*" and someone would respond "*È l'una*" or "*Sono le quattro e venti.*"

The two questions are interchangeable, but the answer does depend on the time. *È* is only used with noon (*È mezzogiorno*), midnight (*È mezzanotte*), and one o'clock (*È l'una*). *Sono* is used with all other hours. To express minutes after the hour, just add *e* and the number of minutes (*Sono le undici e dieci* = It's 11:10). You can also use *e un quarto* (:15), *e mezzo* (:30), and [an hour] *meno un quarto* (:45).

To denote the time of day, simply add *di mattina* (in the morning), *del pomeriggio* (in the afternoon), *di sera* (in the evening), or *di notte* (in the nighttime). Just keep in mind that the Italians keep time a little differently than Americans do; for instance, *sera* might begin around 2:00 or 3:00 pm in some regions! To avoid this confusion, simply use the 24-hour clock.

To ask at what time something begins, add the preposition *a* to the beginning of the aforementioned questions. For example, you might ask someone at what time your Italian lesson begins: "*A che ora è la lezione d'italiano?*" The speaker would respond, "*È alle 3 e mezzo*" ("It's at 3:30"). He or she might even say, "*È dalle 3 e mezzo alle 4 e un quarto*" ("It's from 3:30 to 4:15"). Review articulated prepositions (lesson 8) to write out your weekly schedule using *da* and *a*.

D. Body Vocabulary

As you have learned previously, some body parts are very irregular from singular to plural. You've seen words like *la mano*, which are also irregular in their singular form in that they seem to be masculine but have a feminine article. The reason for this is that many body parts are derived from Latin, which had three genders instead of just two.

Here are a few body parts that are irregular between their singular and plural forms:

Singular	Plural	Meaning
l'orecchio	le orecchie	ear(s)
il labbro	le labbra	lip(s)
il dito	le dita	finger(s)
la mano	le mani	hand(s)
il braccio	le braccia	arm(s)
il ginocchio	le ginocchia	knee(s)

As always, you'll be able to tell which gender you'll be working with by the article. For instance, you'd say *il mio labbro* (my lip) but *le mie labbra* (my lips). Practice this with other irregular body parts!

ATTIVITÀ / ACTIVITIES

Alberto e Arianna sono amici e stanno organizzando una festa per Stella, una loro amica. Devono parlare dell'orario della festa, chi invitare e chi non invitare, e altre cose importanti. La cosa più importante è che la festa è una sorpresa! (Alberto and Arianna are friends and are organizing a party for their friend Stella. They need to talk about the timing of the party, about whom to invite and whom not to invite, and other important things. The most important thing is that the party is a surprise!)

1. Scrivi la forma corretta del verbo tra parentesi. (Write the correct form of the verb in the parentheses.)

Arianna: Alberto, dobbiamo parlare della festa per Stella! A che ora 1. _____ (noi, alzarsi) sabato per decorare la casa? Chi invitiamo? Chi non invitiamo? Che cosa dobbiamo comprare?

Alberto: Veramente non lo so...il sabato di solito io non 2. _____ (svegliarsi) fino a mezzogiorno e non 3. _____ (alzarsi) fino all'una. Poi 4. _____ (radersi), poi 5. _____ (vestirsi)...

Arianna: Questo sabato sarà un po' diverso. Tu 6. _____ (svegliarsi) alle otto e mi incontri al supermercato, dove compriamo tutte le cose. Dimmi, però – chi invitiamo?

Alberto: Va bene, io 7. _____ (mettersi) a lavorare un po' presto. Invitiamo Alessia e Pietro?

Arianna: Alessia e Pietro sì; il fratello di Pietro, no. Io non 8. _____ (sentirsi) bene con lui dopo che ci siamo lasciati.[1]

Alberto: Allora non invitiamo lui. Come 9. _____ (chiamarsi)?

Arianna: Lui e la sua nuova fidanzata 10. _____ (chiamarsi) Paolo e Angela. Puah!

....
1 *ci siamo lasciati* = we broke up

Alberto: Okay, va bene! Incontriamoci alle sei con tutti gli amici – tranne[1] Paolo – e loro arriveranno[2] alle sei e mezzo. Tutto a posto!

Arianna: Non vedo l'ora![3]

2. Scrivi l'ora in italiano. (Write the time in Italian. Note: Don't forget to add *È* or *Sono* and the definite article where necessary. There may be more than one correct answer if you use military time!)

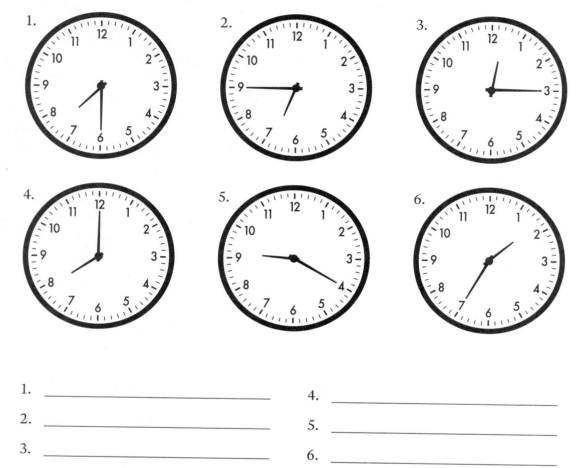

1. _____

2. _____

3. _____

4. _____

5. _____

6. _____

3. Abbina il pronome riflessivo alla sinistra al verbo riflessivo alla destra. (Match the reflexive pronoun on the left to the reflexive verb on the right.)

1. vi   a. chiama

2. si   b. rado

3. ti   c. mettiamo

....

1 except

2 they will arrive

3 *non vedo l'ora* = I can't wait

4. mi   d. alzi

5. ci   e. svegliate

4. Scrivi la parte corretta del corpo nello spazio. (Write the correct body part in the blank space.)

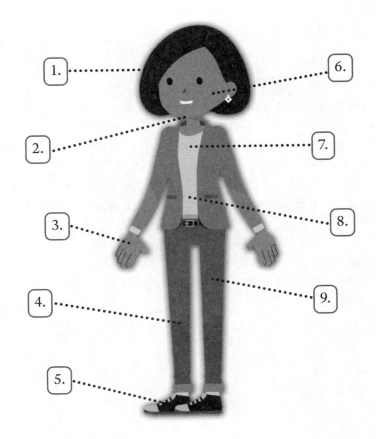

1. _____   6. _____

2. _____   7. _____

3. _____   8. _____

4. _____   9. _____

5. _____

ANSWER KEY

1.

1. ci alziamo
2. mi sveglio
3. mi alzo
4. mi rado
5. mi vesto
6. ti svegli
7. mi metto
8. mi sento
9. si chiama
10. si chiamano

2.

1. Sono le sette e mezzo / Sono le diciannove e mezzo / Sono le sette e trenta / Sono le diciannove e trenta
2. Sono le sette meno un quarto / Sono le diciannove meno un quarto / Sono le sette meno quindici / Sono le diciannove meno quindici / Sono le sei e quarantacinque / Sono le diciotto e quarantacinque
3. Sono le dodici e un quarto / Sono le dodici e quindici / È mezzogiorno e un quarto / È mezzogiorno e quindici / È mezzanotte e un quarto / È mezzanotte e quindici
4. Sono le otto / Sono le venti
5. Sono le nove e venti / Sono le ventuno e venti
6. È l'una e trentacinque / Sono le tredici e trentacinque

3.

1. e.
2. a.
3. d.
4. b.
5. c.

4.

1. la testa
2. il collo
3. la mano
4. il ginocchio
5. il piede
6. l'orecchio
7. il petto
8. lo stomaco
9. la gamba

MAP OF LE MARCHE BY PROVINCES

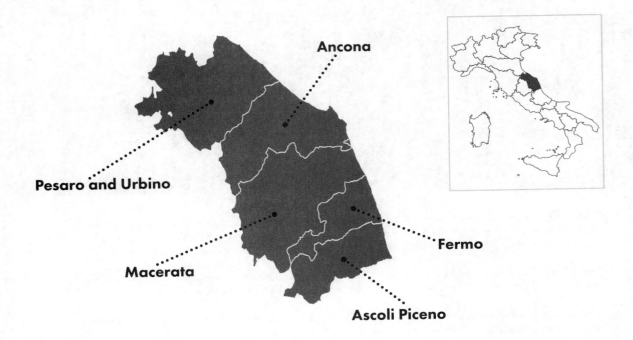

Ancona

Pesaro and Urbino

Macerata

Fermo

Ascoli Piceno

RECIPROCAL VERBS AND NEGATIVES / VENETO

Dov'è la regione del Veneto? La regione del Veneto si trova nel nordest d'Italia. Con quali altre regioni confina? Confina con quattro altre regioni: a nord-ovest con il Trentino—Alto Adige, a sud con l'Emilia-Romagna, a sud-ovest con la Lombardia e ad est con il Friuli—Venezia Giulia. Confina a nord con l'Austria e a sud-est con il mare Adriatico.

Qual è il capoluogo del Veneto? Il capoluogo è Venezia, una città sul mare e un porto. Si chiama anche la Serenissima—"la più serena." Ma Venezia è veramente un arcipelago di 118 piccole isole!

Com'è il clima di questa regione? Il suo clima è simile a quello della Basilicata e delle Marche, ma ancora più incredibile: vicino al mare il clima è mediterraneo, ma nell'entroterra nelle montagne, come le Dolomiti, fa freddissimo! Qual è la topografia di questa zona? La topografia di questa regione è simile a quella dell'Abruzzo. Ma, invece degli Appennini ci sono le Alpi, che in questa regione si chiamano Dolomiti. Nel Veneto ci sono varie regioni climatiche: c'è la regione alpina, con un inverno molto freddo, poi c'è una zona collinare dove non fa troppo caldo né troppo freddo, poi le pianure dove può fare molto caldo d'estate. In questa regione c'è anche il bellissimo Lago di Garda, il lago più grande di tutta Italia!

Quali sono alcuni parchi nazionali di questa zona? Il parco nazionale si chiama il Parco delle Dolomiti Bellunesi. Come si chiamano le province venete? Ci sono sei province: Belluno, Padova, Rovigo, Treviso, Venezia e Vicenza.

Chi è un veneto famoso nell'arte e nella letteratura? Ci sono davvero tanti artisti, poeti e drammaturghi che vengono dal Veneto! Questa è la terra dell'arte: c'è la cappella degli Scrovegni con gli affreschi di Giotto a Padova. Andrea Mantegna, Giovanni Belli, Tiziano, Tintoretto, Tiepolo e Canova, sono tutti veneti e puoi vedere le loro opere d'arte in tanti musei e chiese. Questa regione è anche conosciuta per l'architettura di Andrea Palladio e la sua "Rotonda" o la Villa Capra, un sito UNESCO nella provincia di Vicenza, e d'ispirazione per Monticello. Anche per la letteratura e il teatro il Veneto è una regione molto importante. Per esempio, Ugo Foscolo è nato a Zante nel 1778, un'isola greca del Veneto. Il Settecento è un'epoca molto importante sia per l'arte visiva che per l'arte teatrale per la presenza del drammaturgo Carlo Goldoni nato nel 1708. Il Teatro che si chiama la Fenice si trova a Venezia. Non abbiamo neanche nominato Marco Polo!

Il Veneto è una regione molto ricca. Le industrie più importanti sono la finanza e il turismo, come puoi immaginare. Ma il Veneto è anche famoso per l'industria petrolchimica ed i tessuti come l'azienda Benetton. L'agricoltura è ancora importante con la produzione di mais (granturco) e anche di vino. Quasi tutti conoscono questa regione per le tante città sulla laguna di Venezia, il Carnevale con tutte le bellissime maschere, i canali e le strade piccole, chiamate "calli," le gondole, la Basilica di San Marco, oppure le bellezze di Verona, la città di Romeo e Giulietta dove c'è anche l'Arena, il teatro romano. È una regione che pensiamo di conoscere bene, ma forse non conosciamo bene la sua storia né i suoi ricchi dialetti. Il veneziano è un dialetto molto particolare, con suoni diversi, ma anche con una tradizione letteraria ricca.

▶ Find this translation on the next page

Where is the Veneto region? The Veneto region is located in the northeast of Italy. With which other regions does it border? It borders with four other regions: to the northwest with Trentino–Alto Adige, to the south with Emilia-Romagna, to the southeast with Lombardy, and to the east with Friuli–Venezia Giulia. It borders with Austria to the north and with the Adriatic Sea to the southeast.

What is the capital of Veneto? The capital is Venize, a city on the ocean and a port. It is also called la Serenissima—"The Most Serene." But Venice is truly an archipelago of 118 small islands!

What is the climate of this region? Its climate is similar to that of Basilicate and the Marches but still more drastic: Close to the sea, the climate is Mediterranean, but in the mountains, like the Dolomites, in the inland, it is very cold! What is the topography of this area? The topography of this region is similar to that of Abruzzo. But instead of the Apennines, there are the Alps, which in this region are called the Dolomites. In Veneto, there are various climactic regions: There is the Alpine region, with a very cold winter; then there is a hilly area, where it is neither too hot nor too cold; and then the plains, where it can be very hot in the summer. In this region, there is also the beautiful Garda Lake, the largest lake in all of Italy!

What are some of the national parks in this area? The national park is called the National Park of the Belluno Dolomites. What are the provinces in Veneto called? There are six provinces: Belluno, Padova, Rovigo, Treviso, Venezia, and Vicenza.

Who is famous for art and for literature from Veneto? There are truly many artists, poets, and playwrights who come from Veneto! This is the land of art: There is the Scrovegni Chapel with Giotto's frescoes in Padova. Andrea Mantegna, Giovanni Belli, Tiziano, Tintoretto, Tiepolo, and Canova are all from Veneto, and you can see their works of art in many museums and churches. This region is also known for Andrea Palladio's architecture and his "Rotonda," or Villa Capra, a UNESCO site in the province of Vicenza and an inspiration for Monticello. Veneto is also a very important region for literature and theater. For example, Ugo Foscolo was born in Zante, a Greek island of Veneto, in 1778. The 18th century is a very important period both for the visual arts and for theatrical arts, given the presence of the playwright, Carlo Goldoni, born in 1708. The theater called La Fenice ("The Phoenix"), is located in Venice. We haven't even mentioned Marco Polo!

Veneto is a very wealthy region. The most important industries are finance and tourism, as you can imagine. But Veneto is also famous for the petrochemical industry and textiles, such as the Benetton company. Agriculture is still important for the production of corn and also wine. Almost everyone knows this region because of the many cities in the laguna of Venice; the Carnival, with all its beautiful masks; the canals and the small streets, called *calli*; the gondolas; Saint Mark's Basilica; or the beauties of Verona, the city of Romeo and Juliet where there is also the Arena, the Roman theater. It is a region that we think we know well, but perhaps we don't know its history nor its rich dialects well. Venetian is a very special dialect with different sounds but also with a rich literary tradition.

VOCABOLARIO NUOVO E UTILE / NEW AND USEFUL VOCABULARY

l'arcipelago	archipelago	l'isola	island
la temperatura	temperature	l'artista	artist
il poeta	poet [masc.]	la poetessa	poet [fem.]
l'arte	art	il drammaturgo	playwright
la cappella	chapel	l'affresco	fresco
l'opera d'arte	work of art	il museo	museum
l'architettura	architecture	la letteratura	literature

il teatro	theater	**l'ispirazione**	inspiration
l'arte visiva	visual art	**l'arte teatrale**	theater art
il mais	corn	**la finanza**	finance
il turismo	tourism	**la petrolchimica**	petrochemistry
il tessuto	textile	**l'azienda**	business, store
sereno/a	serene	**alpino/a**	alpine [adj.]
freddo/a	cold	**caldo/a**	hot, warm
veneto/a	Venetian	**greco/a**	Greek
non...neanche	not even	**sia...che**	both...and
ancora	still, yet	**quasi**	almost, kind of
la laguna	lagoon	**la maschera**	mask
la canale	canal	**la strada**	street
la calle	street (Venetian)	**la gondola**	gondola (boat)

RIPASSO GENERALE / GENERAL REVIEW

A. Notes about Veneto

Veneto is one of the most famous regions of Italy due to the fact that it's home to cities like Venice, Padua, Verona, Vicenza, and others. This region is far north enough to have a border with Austria. Home to some of the most famous composers and artists, Veneto houses some of the best cultural sites to visit, including UNESCO sites. Visit one of the many libraries, villas, art museums, or theaters to enjoy it fully!

In this lesson, you'll learn about reciprocal constructions, which are very similar to the reflexive verbs you've learned, as well as negative constructions and adverbs. By the end of the lesson, you and a friend will be able to meet each other in front of a Canaletto painting, hug each other, but not leave each other just yet, and head swiftly over to la Fenice for a theater performance.

B. Reciprocal Construction

Reciprocal constructions are so similar to reflexive verbs that you won't need to learn a new construction at all. In fact, they're essentially just the plural forms of reflexive verbs (the *noi*, *voi*, and *loro* forms). Why are these only in the plural? Because they are verbs that denote actions that two or more people can do to each other, reciprocally. These are verbs like *parlarsi* ("to talk to each other"), *conoscersi* ("to meet each other"/"to know each other"), and *capirsi* ("to understand each other").

Let's look at the conjugations of these verbs:

	parlarsi	conoscersi	capirsi*
noi	ci parliamo	ci conosciamo	ci capiamo
voi	vi parlate	vi conoscete	vi capite
loro	si parlano	si conoscono	si capiscono

They translate to "**we** _____ each other," "**you [pl.]** _____ each other" and "**they** _____ each other," respectively.

Other verbs that take this construction are *abbracciarsi* ("to hug each other"), *aiutarsi* ("to help each other"), *baciarsi* ("to kiss each other"), *farsi regali* ("to give each other gifts"), *fidanzarsi* ("to get engaged"), *frequentarsi* ("to go out together"), *guardarsi* ("to look at each other"), *incontrarsi* ("to encounter each other"), *lasciarsi* ("to leave each other"), *salutarsi* ("to greet each other"), *scriversi* ("to write each other"), and *vedersi* ("to see each other"). Try to conjugate each one of these for practice.

> Mi sveglio tardi, e mi alzo con calma. Faccio colazione a letto o nella sala grande del palazzo. Poi scrivo una lettera d'amore al mio Romeo. Poi mi vesto e mi trucco per tutta la mattina. Non lavoro—sono ricca! Mi annoio spesso. Pranzo all'una e poi faccio un sonnellino. Riprendo a scrivere le poesie e le lettere d'amore nella mia camera da letto. Non esco di casa quasi mai, e mi lamento spesso con i miei genitori. Ceno tardi, se ho fame. Sono innamorata, quindi spesso non mi sento bene! Mi addormento mentre guardo la luna dal balcone.

▶ I wake up late, and I get up gradually. I eat breakfast in bed or in the great hall of the palace. Then I write a love letter to my Romeo. Then I get dressed and put makeup on for the whole morning. I don't work—I'm rich! I often get bored. I eat lunch at 1 and then I take a nap. I go back to writing poetry and love letters in my bedroom. I hardly ever leave my house, and I often complain to my parents. I eat dinner late, if I have dinner. I'm in love, so I often don't feel well! I fall asleep while watching the moon from my balcony.

A. Negative Constructions

Negative expressions in Italian might look a bit strange to a native English speaker because they are almost always paired with, and preceded by, the word *non*, making the sentence appear to have a double negative. However, the word *non* simply denotes that what is to follow in the sentence will be negative.

Here are some affirmative expressions in Italian that are paired with corresponding negative expressions:

Espressioni Affermative	Espressioni Negative
qualcosa (*anything*)	non...niente/nulla (*nothing*)
tutto (*everything*)	non...niente/nulla (*nothing*)
qualcuno (*everyone* [sing.])	non...nessuno (*nobody/no one*)
tutti (*everyone* [pl.])	non...nessuno (*nobody/no one*)
sempre (*always*)	non...mai (*never*)
qualche volta (*sometimes*)	non...mai (*never*)
mai (*ever*)	non...mai (*never*)
già (*already*)	non...ancora (*not yet*)
ancora (*still*)	non...più (*no longer*)
e...e (*both...and*)	né...né (*neither...nor*)

Note that verbs typically occur where the ellipses (...) are in the chart, but not always.

If someone asks you a question using an adverb or phrase in the first column, you can answer negatively with an expression in the second. For example, you might be asked, "*Suoni **ancora** il pianoforte?*" ("Do you **still** play the piano?"). If you don't, you can respond, "***Non** suono **più** il pianoforte*" ("I **no longer** play the piano") or, simply, "***Non più**."

B. Adverbs

An *avverbio* (adverb) is a word that modifies or qualifies verbs, adjectives, or other adverbs, usually in relation to time, manner, and degree. In English, these are words that often end in *-ly* (e.g., *swiftly, slowly, traditionally*, etc.). Some do not end in *-ly*, such as *often, always, sometimes, early*, etc. This is also true for Italian: While many adverbs end in *-mente*, there are many that do not. Here are a few (with their corresponding negative expressions):

sempre (always)	*non...mai* (never)
prima (first)	*dopo* (after)
spesso (often)	*qualche volta / a volte* (sometimes)
presto (early)	*tardi* (late)
già (already)	*non...ancora* (not yet)
molto (very / a lot)	*poco* (not much)
ancora (still)	*non...più* (not anymore)
bene (well)	*male* (badly)

Adverbs that end in *-mente* use specific rules to form them. If the original adjective ends in *-o*, it changes to *-a*, and then *-mente* is added. If an adjective ends in *-e*, it stays the same, and the *-mente* ending is simply tacked on. However, if an adjective ends in *-le* or *-re*, the *e* is dropped before *-mente* is added. Let's see how this works:

*rar**o***	→	*rar**a***	→	*rar**amente***
*felic**e***	→	*felice*	→	*felic**emente***
*genera**le***	→	*general_*	→	*general**mente***
*regola**re***	→	*regolar_*	→	*regolar**mente***

What are some things that you do during the day? In what manner do you do them? Do you get dressed rapidly (*rapido → rapidamente*)? Do you eat breakfast happily (*contento → contentamente*)? Try to think of adjectives that you can turn into adverbs to describe your whole day.

Chi sono Francesca da Rimini e Paolo? Sono due amanti nel secondo cerchio dell'Inferno di Dante Alighieri, il poeta medievale, condannati per il peccato della lussuria. Francesca è la figlia di Guido da Polenta, il signore di Ravenna nell'Emilia-Romagna. Francesca è la moglie di Giovanni Malatesta, ma lei si annoia e lui non le piace. Lei poi incontra Paolo, il fratello di Giovanni e suo cognato. Si conoscono e si innamorano. Si abbracciano e si baciano. Si capiscono perché si amano. Si guardano e parlano della storia di Lancillotto e Ginevra, una storia romantica. Non vogliono mai lasciarsi! Ma poi arriva Gianciotto, il marito di Francesca, e li uccide insieme! Che storia triste.

▶ Who are Francesca da Rimini and Paolo? They are two lovers in the second circle in the Hell of the medieval poet Dante Alighieri who are condemned for the sin of lust. Francesca is the daughter of Guido da Polenta, a lord in Ravenna, in Emilia-Romagna. Francesca is the wife of Giovanni Malatesta, but she gets bored and doesn't find him attractive. She then meets Paolo, Giovanni's brother and her brother-in-law. They meet each other and they fall in love. They hug and they kiss. They understand each other because they love each other. They look at each other and speak about the story of Lancelot and Guinevere, a romantic story. They never want to leave each other! But then Gianciotto, Francesca's husband, arrives, and he kills them together! What a sad story.

ATTIVITÀ / ACTIVITIES

Sabrina e Chiara sono sorelle e sono di Verona. Stanno parlando dei loro genitori, che hanno tutti e due compleanni nel prossimo mese. Devono preparare una festa per la loro famiglia. (Sabrina and Chiara are sisters who are from Verona. They are talking about their parents, who both have birthdays next month. They must prepare a party for their family.)

1. Scrivi la forma corretta del verbo reciproco nello spazio. (Write the correct form of the reciprocal verb in the blank space.)

Sabrina: Chiara! Sono mesi che non 1. _____ (noi, vedersi)!

Chiara: È vero! Sai che ad aprile ci sono i compleanni di mamma e papà? Noi 2. _____ (aiutarsi) ad organizzare la festa e comprare i regali?

Sabrina: Ma certo. 3. _____ (noi, incontrarsi) al centro commerciale per fare shopping, poi invitiamo la famiglia. Posso invitare Giacomo? È il mio nuovo fidanzato.

Chiara: Da quanto tempo 4. _____ (voi, conoscersi)?

Sabrina: Da quattro giorni, ma 5. _____ (noi, sposarsi) a maggio.

Chiara: Wow, che veloce! Forse questo è il regalo più bello per la nostra mamma.

Sabrina: Allora lasciamo a loro che 6. _____ (loro, farsi regali), io porto solo le belle notizie!

2. Trasforma l'aggettivo in un avverbio. (Turn the adjective into an adverb.)

1. chiaro   _____
2. triste   _____
3. contento   _____
4. particolare   _____
5. veloce   _____

3. Scegli l'opzione giusta per completare la frase. (Choose the correct option to complete the sentence.)

1. Valentina, leggi mai il giornale?   a. No, non conosco nessuno.
2. Giorgio, suoni ancora il pianoforte?   b. No, non voglio niente, grazie.
3. Angelica, conosci qualcuno in questa città?   c. No, non lo leggo mai.
4. Fabio, preferisci Pepsi o Coca Cola?   d. Non mi piace né questo né quello.
5. Pino, vuoi qualcosa da bere?   e. No, non lo suono più.

4. Traduci le frasi italiane in inglese. (Translate the Italian sentences into English.)

1. Io e Francesca ci abbracciamo quando ci incontriamo.

   _____

2. Com'è che tu e Luigi vi conoscete?

   _____

3. Mia sorella e io ci facciamo regali per Natale.

   _____

4. Gli amici si salutano quando si vedono per strada.

   _____

5. Quando è che tu e Antonio vi fidanzate?

   _____

ANSWER KEY

1.

1. ci vediamo
2. ci aiutiamo
3. Ci incontriamo
4. vi conoscete
5. ci sposiamo
6. si fanno regali

2.

1. chiaramente
2. tristemente
3. contentamente
4. particolarmente
5. velocemente

3.

1. c.
2. e.
3. a.
4. d.
5. b.

4.

1. Francesca and I hug each other when we meet up with each other.
2. How is it that you and Luigi know each other?
3. My sister and I give each other gifts for Christmas.
4. The friends greet each other when they see each other on the street.
5. When is it that you and Antonio will get engaged to each other? (When will you and Antonio get engaged?)

MAP OF VENETO BY PROVINCES

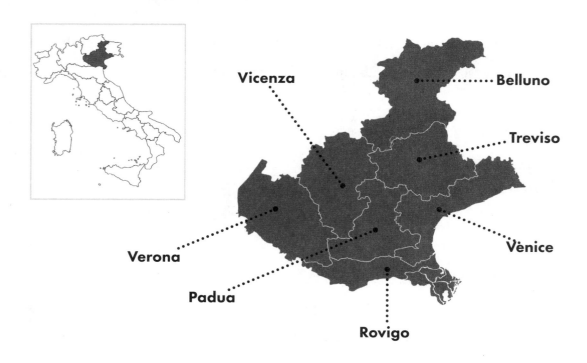

PRESENT PROGRESSIVE AND SUFFIXES / PIEDMONT

Dov'è la regione del Piemonte? La regione del Piemonte si trova nel nordovest d'Italia. Con quali altre regioni confina? Confina con quattro altre regioni: a nord-ovest con la Valle d'Aosta, a sud-est con l'Emilia-Romagna, a sud con la Liguria e ad est con la Lombardia. Confina ad ovest con la Francia e a nord con la Svizzera. È la regione più occidentale di tutta l'Italia!

Qual è il capoluogo del Piemonte? Il capoluogo è Torino, una bellissima città con una ricca cultura e storia. È famosa per la sua architettura, come la Mole Antonelliana, un edificio altissimo e grandissimo che è stato costruito nel 1869. Adesso è la sede del Museo Nazionale del Cinema. Torino era anche l'importantissima sede dei Giochi Olimpici Invernal nel 2006.

Com'è il clima di questa regione? Il suo clima è continentale e simile a quello della Lombardia: sulle montagne delle Alpi, però, fa freddo e anche freddissimo!

Qual è la topografia di questa zona? Questa zona è prevalentemente montagnosa: le montagne circondano la regione. Ci sono le Alpi e ci sono pure gli Appennini. Ci sono anche le colline dove non fa troppo caldo né troppo freddo e anche le pianure dove può fare molto caldo a causa di un vento caldissimo e secchissimo che si chiama *favonio*. In questa regione ci sono anche tanti fiumi, come il fiume Po che origina qui: nasce dal Monviso nelle Alpi. C'è il Lago Maggiore, con tante isole bellissime che si chiamano isole Borromee. Il Lago Maggiore è una destinazione turistica.

Quali sono alcuni parchi nazionali in questa zona? Due parchi nazionali sono il Parco del Gran Paradiso e il Parco Val Grande. Come si chiamano le province piemontesi? Ci sono sette province: Alessandria, Asti, Biella, Cuneo, Novara, Verbano-Cusio-Ossola e Vercelli.

Il Piemonte è una regione molto ricca dove sia l'industria che l'agricoltura vanno forte. Anche il turismo va molto forte per quelli che cercano di godere delle montagne facendo sport oppure rilassandosi. Qui gli sport invernali sono popolarissimi.

Questa è la regione conosciuta per il "Made in Italy": prodotti come il cioccolato, il vino, il caffè e le macchine come la FIAT, che significa Fabbrica Italiana Automobili Torino. A Torino c'è il Lingotto, la sede industriale della FIAT. All'epoca del boom economico durante gli anni Cinquanta, tantissime persone del Sud sono emigrate in Piemonte per trovare lavoro. Ci sono tanti vigneti dove i lavoratori coltivano l'uva per fare questi vini pregiati: il Barolo, il Nebbiolo, il Barbera e l'Asti Spumante. Ci sono anche delle risaie dove cresce il riso. La produzione del riso e del frumento è importantissima in questa regione da tanti anni.

▶ Find this translation on the next page

Where is the Piedmont region? The Piedmont region is located in the northwest of Italy. With which other regions does it border? It borders with four other regions: to the northwest with Valle d'Aosta, to the southeast with Emilia-Romagna, to the south with Liguria, and to the east with Lombardy. It borders to the west with France and to the north with Switzerland. It is the most western region of Italy!

What is the capital of Piedmont? The capital is Turin, a beautiful city with a rich culture and history. It is famous for its architecture, such as the Mole Antonelliana, a very tall and large building that was built in 1869. Now it is the location of the National Museum of Cinema. Turin was also the very important center of the Winter Olympic Games in 2006.

What is the climate of this region? Its climate is continental and similar to that of Lombardy: In the mountains of the Alps, however, it is cold—even extremely cold!

What is the topography of this area? This area is predominantly mountainous: Mountains surround the region. There are the Alps and there are also the Apennines. There are also the hills, where it is neither too hot nor too cold, and also the plains, where it can be very hot because of a very hot and dry wind called *favonio*. In this region there are also many rivers, such as the Po River, which originates here: It begins in Monviso in the Alps. There is Lago Maggiore, with many beautiful islands that are called the Borromean Islands. Lago Maggiore is a tourist destination.

What are some national parks in this area? Two national parks are the Gran Paradiso Park and Val Grande Park. What are the provinces in Piedmont? There are seven provinces: Alessandria, Asti, Biella, Cuneo, Novara, Verbano-Cusio-Ossola, and Vercelli.

Piedmont is a very wealthy region where both industry and agriculture are strong. Even tourism is very strong, with those who try to enjoy the mountains by doing sport or by relaxing. Here winter sports are very popular.

This is the region known for "Mady in Italy": products like chocolate, wine, coffee, and cars, such as FIAT, which stands for Fabbrica Italiana Automobili Torino ("The Italian Automobile Factory of Turin"). The Lingotto, the industrial headquarters, is in Turin. In the period of the economic boom during the 1950s, many people from the South emigrated to Piedmont to find work. There are many vineyards, where the workers cultivate the grapes to make these valued wines: Barolo, Nebbiolo, Barbera, and Asti Spumante. There are also rice paddies, where rice grows. Rice and wheat production has been very important in this region for many years.

VOCABOLARIO NUOVO E UTILE / NEW AND USEFUL VOCABULARY

bellissimo/a	very beautiful	**altissimo/a**	very high/tall
grandissimo/a	very big/great	**importantissimo/a**	very important
freddissimo/a	very cold	**caldissimo/a**	very hot
secchissimo/a	very dry	**popolarissimo/a**	very popular
tantissimo/a	very much	**tantissimi/e**	very many
adesso	now	**montagnoso/a**	mountainous
andare forte	to be popular	**godere**	to enjoy
oppure	or (else)	**invernale**	winter [adj.]
la macchina	car	**la sede**	seat (of industry)
il cinema	film, movie theater	**i Giochi Olimpici**	Olympic Games

il cioccolato	chocolate	**il vino**	wine
il boom economico	economic boom	**il vigneto**	vineyard
il lavoratore	worker	**la risaia**	rice paddy/field
il riso	rice	**il frumento**	wheat

RIPASSO GENERALE / GENERAL REVIEW

A. Notes about Piemonte

Piemonte is a region in the far north of Italy that's home to many different types of food and famous landmarks. Its close proximity to France and Switzerland introduces many influences from those countries, especially the wine and chocolate that make the region famous. Piemonte—or more specifically, its capital, Torino—was the host of the Winter Olympic Games in 2006. It is the home of the car company FIAT (Fabbrica Italiana Automobili Torino).

In this lesson, you'll learn the present progressive and suffixes. What are you doing right now? Is it very interesting? You'll learn how to express both of these actions and sentiments after learning these grammatical structures.

B. Present Progressive

The present progressive is one of the easiest tenses to form in Italian, but its usage is a bit different than that of English. In English, native speakers tend to overuse gerunds and the present progressive. Think of your summer plans, for instance: "I'm **going** to the beach this summer." Italians only use the present progressive right in the moment that it's happening. What are you doing right now? You are reading. You can also simply use the present tense with these actions in Italian.

For now, let's look at how to form the gerund, and then the present progressive.

The gerund (-ing verbs in English) is formed by cutting off the -are, -ere, and -ire endings of infinitive verbs and replacing them with -ando (-are) or -endo (-ere and -ire). That's it! There are a few irregular verbs, such as fare (facendo), dire (dicendo), and bere (bevendo), but almost all other verbs will simply take these new endings. Even essere and avere are regular in this tense!

Now that we know how to form the gerund, let's put it into the present progressive.

First, let's review the verb *stare* (it'll be important):

io **sto**	noi **stiamo**
tu **stai**	voi **state**
lui/lei/Lei **sta**	loro/Loro **stanno**

Now all you need to do is add the gerund after the correct form of *stare* and you have the present progressive. The gerund by itself means "_____ing"; the gerund with *stare* means "I am _____ing," "you are _____ing," etc.

You can practice this tense by looking around the room and describing what other people are doing in the present moment (e.g., *Lui sta studiando*; *Lei sta guardando la TV*; *Io sto imparando!*)

Come noi vediamo nel bellissimo film *Riso amaro* di Giuseppe De Santis, il lavoraccio delle mondine è molto difficile. Il narratore all'inizio del film dice che solo le manine delle donne possono fare questo lavoro. Il tempaccio non le scoraggia. Loro devono chinarsi per mettere le piantine nella terra. Così cresce il riso. I capi sono proprio dei ladroni, perché non le pagano tanto. Ma le donne si sostengono, cantano delle canzoncine e a notte tornano alla casetta dove dormono nei loro lettini.

▶ As we see in the beautiful film *Bitter Rice* by Giuseppe De Santis, the tough job of the rice workers is very difficult. At the beginning of the film, the narrator says that only the small hands of women can do this job. The bad weather doesn't discourage them. They have to bend over to put the small plants in the ground. This is how rice grows. The bosses are truly thieves, because they don't pay them much. But the women support each other, they sing little songs, and at night they return to the little house where they sleep in their small beds.

A. Suffixes

Suffixes are a very fun part of the Italian language. Instead of adding an adjective to modify a word, you can sometimes build it into the word itself. Suffixes can be used to intensify a word, to diminish a word, and sometimes to make a word a term of endearment. Here are some of these categories:

Superlativo assoluto

In Italian, there are two types of superlatives: relative ("It is the most _____ in the world") and absolute, the latter of which takes a suffix. To make a word an absolute superlative, simply remove the final letter and add *-issimo/a/i/e*.

Buono becomes *buonissimo*, *felice* becomes *felicissimo*, and *brava* becomes *bravissima*. Easy! Adding this suffix adds "very" to the meaning in English. So, *buonissimo* means "very good," *felicissimo* means "very happy," etc.

Note: Since these endings begin with -*i*, watch out for words that end in -*co*/-*ca* and -*go*/-*ga*; you'll need to add an *h* to keep those hard sounds (*lungo* → *lunghissimo*).

Diminutivo

Adding the suffixes -*ino*/*a*, -*etto*/*a*, -*ello*/*a*, or -*uccio*/*a* can make a word smaller or simply add affection. If *gatto* is a "cat," then *gattino* is a "little cat," or "kitten." It's a bit rude to call a child "fat" (*grasso*), but *grassotello* means "plump" or "chubby" (in a nice way!). The suffixes -*ino*/*a* and -*uccio*/*a* are used in many Italian nicknames (e.g., Giuseppe → Giuseppino/Pino; Elena → Lenuccia).

Accrescitivo

The opposite of diminutive suffixes is the *accrescitivo*, which makes words bigger. These new words end in -*one* and become masculine even if they refer to something feminine originally. For example, a big door (*una porta*) becomes *un portone*, and a large woman (*una donna*) becomes *un donnone*!

Peggiorativo

Pejorative suffixes, as you can probably guess, make things bad. These new words most commonly end in -*accio*/*a* or -*astro*/*a*. So, *un ragazzo* is a "boy," but a "bad little boy" would be called a *ragazzaccio*.

These examples are not the only suffixes in the Italian language, but they are the most common.

Mimì, il protagonista di questo film, recitato dal bravissimo attore Giancarlo Gianini, è un uomo siciliano. Lui deve nascondersi dalla mafia e quindi lascia la moglie Rosalia e si trasferisce a Torino. Lì, Mimì trova lavoro in un cantiere. Poi trova un buon posto di lavoro come operaio metallurgico in una fabbrica automobilistica. Dopo conosce Fiore, una bella donna settentrionale, indipendente e intelligente. Loro si fraintendono molto perché vengono da due mondi diversi. In una scena molto memorabile, si parlano ad un incrocio usando la lingua dei gesti quando succede una cosa imprevista. Si innamorano l'uno dell'altro e poi c'è confusione!

▶ Mimì, the protagonist of this film, played by the very talented actor Giancarlo Giannini, is a Sicilian man. He has to hide himself from the Mafia and so leaves his wife Rosalia and moves to Turin. There, Mimì finds work on a construction site. Then, he finds a good job as a metal worker in an automobile factory. Afterward he meets Fiore, a beautiful northern woman, who is independent and intelligent. They misunderstand each other a lot because they come from two different worlds. In a very memorable scene, they speak to each other at an intersection using the language of gestures when an unforeseen thing occurs. They fall in love with each other and then there's chaos!

ATTIVITÀ / ACTIVITIES

1. Traduci le frasi dall'italiano in inglese. (Translate the sentences from Italian to English.)

1. Il ragazzino è cattivello.

   _____

2. Questo lavoraccio non mi piace!

   _____

3. Che carino quel gattino! Quanti anni ha?

   _____

4. Imparare bene l'italiano è importantissimo.

   _____

5. Quel portone è bellissimo!

   _____

2. Cambia la parola in un superlativo assoluto. (Change the word into an absolute superlative.)

1. terribile   _____
2. bene   _____
3. interessante   _____
4. sicura   _____
5. lungo   _____
6. vecchi   _____
7. delicata   _____
8. male   _____
9. cattive   _____
10. stanco   _____

3. Formula una frase al presente progressivo con il verbo. (With the verb given, form a sentence using the present progressive.)

1. Lucia e Domenico _____ (preparare) una bella cena per la famiglia.

2. Samuele _____ (fare) una foto della sua ragazza.

3. Ragazzi, che cosa _____ (mangiare)?

4. Teresa ed io _____ (guardare) il nostro programma preferito.

5. Lisa, perché non _____ (suonare) il pianoforte?

4. *Esercizio di scrittura: Cosa stanno facendo?*

Write a paragraph about what your friends are doing at this exact moment to practice the present progressive. Don't forget to use the verb *stare*.

_____

_____

_____

_____

_____

_____

_____

ANSWER KEY

1.
1. The little boy is naughty.
2. I do not like this terrible job!
3. What a cute kitten! How old is it?
4. It is very important to learn Italian well.
5. That large door is very beautiful!

2.
1. terribilissimo/a
2. benissimo
3. interessantissimo/a
4. sicurissima
5. lunghissimo
6. vecchissimi
7. delicatissima
8. malissimo
9. cattivissime
10. stanchissimo

3.
1. stanno preparando
2. sta facendo
3. state mangiando
4. stiamo guardando
5. stai suonando

4. Answers will vary. Example:

Caterina e Francesco stanno giocando a baseball. Io sto leggendo il mio libro preferito. Oscar sta ballando...

MAP OF PIEMONTE BY PROVINCES

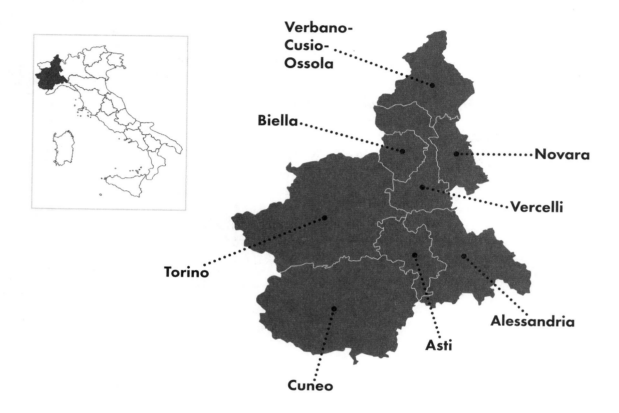

LEZIONE 17

INDEFINITE PRONOUNS, CI, AND NE / SARDINIA

L'isola della Sardegna si trova nel Mar Tirreno, a sud dell'isola della Corsica, l'isola francese. Ci sono tante isole nel Mediterraneo e la Sicilia è l'isola più grande di tutte. Ma la Sardegna è più grande di tutte le altre isole—è la numero due! La Sardegna è più grande di Cipro, un'isola greca—la numero tre! Come la Sicilia, la Sardegna è anche una regione.

Il capoluogo della Sardegna è Cagliari, una bellissima città con una ricca cultura e storia. Altre città importanti sono Sassari, Nuoro e Oristano. Ci sono tanti monumenti che fanno parte della lunga storia dell'isola. In Sardegna ci sono ancora i segni della presenza cartaginese, bizantina, romana e spagnola—e di tante altre culture! Dal 1324 al 1848, c'è stato il Regno della Sardegna e Cagliari era la capitale.

Il clima della Sardegna, come la sua geografia, è molto diversificato. Alcuni scienziati lo chiamano un "micro-continente." Ci sono le montagne, le pianure, le rocce, i boschi e le spiagge con le acque limpidissime, come la Costa Smeralda, una destinazione turistica per i ricchi! Le spiagge settentrionali sono quelle dove vanno tanti turisti. Le industrie principali sono il turismo e l'agricoltura. Ma ce ne sono delle altre, come la pastorizia e l'attività mineraria. Sull'isola ci sono più capre e pecore che in altre regioni italiane. Una stima del numero delle pecore è di 4 millioni! Le pecore producono il formaggio famoso dell'isola, il pecorino sardo. Non ha rivali!

Conosci la storia dei nuraghi? Forse non ne sai niente, o forse ne sai qualcosa. I nuraghi sono case antiche delle famiglie reali di 1600 anni avanti Cristo. Risalgono all'età del Bronzo! Alcune sembrano come delle torri, oppure come degli alveari. Queste case sono fatte con grandissime pietre, ma senza cemento!

Forse non hai intenzione di andare in Sardegna, ma devi pensarci bene. È proprio un'isola bella e ha una storia affascinante e unica.

The island of Sardinia is located in the Tyrrhenian Sea, south of the island of Corsica, the French island. There are many islands in the Mediterranean, and Sicily is the largest of all of them. But Sardinia is the largest of all the other islands—it is number two! Sardinia is larger than Cyprus, a Greek island—number three! Like Sicily, Sardinia is also a region.

The capital of Sardinia is Cagliari, a beautiful city with a rich culture and history. Other important cities are Sassari, Nuoro, and Oristano. There are many monuments that are part of the island's long history. In Sardinia, there are still the signs of the Carthaginian, Byzantine, Roman, and Spanish presence—and many other cultures! From 1324 to 1848, there was the Kingdom of Sardinia, and Cagliari was the capital.

The climate of Sardinia, like its geography, is very diversified. Some scientists call it a "micro-continent." There are mountains, plains, cliffs, forests, and beaches with extremely clear water, such as the Emerald Coast, a tourist destination for the wealthy! The northern beaches are where many tourists go. The main industries are tourism and agriculture. But there are some others, such as livestock rearing and mining. On the island, there are more goats and sheep than in other Italian regions. An estimate of the number of sheep is approximately 4 million! The sheep produce the famous cheese of the island, Sardinian pecorino. It has no rivals!

Do you know the history of the nuraghi? Maybe you don't know anything about them, or perhaps you know something about them. The nuraghi are ancient homes of royal families from 1600 BC. They date back to the Bronze Age! Some look like towers, or even like beehives. These homes are made with very large stones but without cement!

Maybe you don't intend to go to Sardinia, but you have to think about it well. It is truly a beautiful island and has a fascinating and unique history.

VOCABOLARIO NUOVO E UTILE / NEW AND USEFUL VOCABULARY

tanto/a	very, much	**tante/i**	many
tutto/a	all [sing.]	**tutti/e**	all [pl.]
altro/a/i/e	other	**alcuno/a**	some [sing.]
alcuni/e	some [pl.]		
fare parte (di)	to be part (of)	**avere intenzione (di)**	to mean (to)
esserci	there is/there are	**pensarci**	to think about something
il monumento	monument	**la presenza**	presence
il segno	sign	**lo scienziato**	scientist
il bosco	forest	**la pastorizia**	pastoralism
la capra	goat	**la pecora**	sheep
la stima	estimate	**il cemento**	cement
il pecorino	sheep's milk cheese	**il rivale**	rival
la pietra	rock	**l'alveare**	beehive
cartaginese	Carthaginian	**bizantino/a**	Byzantine
romano/a	Roman	**spagnolo/a**	Spanish
diversificato/a	diversified	**limpido/a**	clear, limpid
smeraldo/a	emerald [adj.]	**settentrionale**	northern
minerario/a	mining [adj.]	**sardo/a**	Sardinian

RIPASSO GENERALE / GENERAL REVIEW

A. Notes about Sardegna

Sardegna (spelled *Sardinia* in English) is an island to the west of Italy that's situated south of Corsica in the middle of the Tyrrhenian Sea. It is a beautiful island with a climate as diversified as its history. Its coastlines are famous, but its inland cities and landmarks are also quite fascinating, especially the ancient nuraghi. Often overlooked as a tourist destination among those traveling to Italy, it is not to be missed!

In this lesson, you'll examine indefinite pronouns (*some, all, few, every*, etc.) and the particles *ci* and *ne*, which are harder to translate into English. Have you ever been to Sardinia? If you've been there, you've probably seen some landmarks mentioned previously. There are many of them!

B. Indefinite Adjectives and Pronouns

As mentioned previously, adjectives such as *many, some, all*, and the like are called indefinite because they are not very specific or because they don't represent something that is a whole entity. Although adjectives usually follow nouns in Italian, these adjectives all go before the noun. Some of these adjectives and pronouns have both singular and plural forms; others only have the singular form. Let's take a look at them and their meanings:

Indefinite Adjectives

Adjective	Meaning	Example
ogni [sing. only]	every, each	Ogni persona è speciale.
qualche [sing. only]	some, a few	Qualche persona è speciale.
qualunque* [sing. only]	any	Qualunque persona che incontri* sarà speciale.
alcuni/e	some, a few	Alcune persone sono speciali.
tutto/a/i/e**	all, every	Tutte le persone sono speciali.

* *Qualunque* requires the subjunctive mood, which you won't meet in this course.
** *Tutto* in all forms requires the use of the appropriate definite article with it (e.g., *Tutto il giorno, Tutta la notte*, etc.)

Indefinite Pronouns

Pronoun	Meaning	Example
ognuno [sing. only]	everyone	Ognuno è speciale.
qualcuno [sing. only]	someone, anyone	Qualcuno è speciale.
tutto [sing. only]	all, everything	Tutto è speciale.
qualcosa/qualche cosa [sing. only]	something, anything	Dimmi qualcosa di* speciale.
alcuni/e	some, a few	Alcuni sono speciali.
tutti/e	everyone, everybody	Tutti sono speciali.

* *Qualcosa*, when followed by an adjective, requires the use of the preposition *di* and the masculine singular form of the adjective. When followed by a verb (e.g., "Is there anything to eat?"), it uses the preposition *da* and the infinitive form of the verb.

As you can see, some of the adjectives and pronouns are exactly the same, but the pronouns can stand on their own. Among them, there are also meanings that are exactly the same, while they differ in that they are singular or plural. Singular-only adjectives and pronouns can only go with singular nouns, adjectives, and verbs, while plural ones go with plurals.

C. *Ci* and *ne*

These two small words are called particles, and they stand in for very specific words and phrases in the Italian language. In a sentence, they function the same way that pronouns do.

You've seen *ci* many times before, mostly with *è* and *sono* to mean "there is" and "there are." *C'è* means "there is _____" (singular), and *Ci sono* means "there are _____" (plural). You've also seen *ci* as a direct object pronoun, an indirect object pronoun, and a reflexive and reciprocal pronoun, all replacing the *noi* (first person plural).

In this lesson, *ci* will be used a bit differently. *Ci* can now be used to replace entire prepositional phrases that begin with *in*, *a*, *con*, *da*, and *su*, as well as prepositional phrases relating to places. If someone asks you if you go to a certain place often—e.g., "*Vai spesso in Italia?*"—you can respond, "*Sì, vado spesso in Italia,*" but that's a bit redundant. You can also replace the phrase in bold with *ci* and say, "*Sì, ci vado spesso.*" The pronoun goes before the verb and replaces *in Italia*, a place and a prepositional phrase that begins with *in*.

Ne behaves similarly to *ci* but is used to replace quantities and prepositional phrases beginning with *di* ("of"). Do you need something? If someone asks you if you need water ("*Hai bisogno di acqua?*"), you could respond, "*Sì, ho bisogno di acqua,*" or you could be less repetitive and say, "*Sì, ne ho bisogno.*" If someone asks you if you are afraid of snakes ("*Hai paura di serpenti?*"), you can respond, "*No, non ne ho paura.*"

As for quantities, you can replace phrases beginning with *di*, like the ones you learned as part of lesson 8 on the partitive. However, if you use *ne* with a quantity, you must still list the number with it, even if you replace the thing that is being quantified. For example, look at this exchange:

> "*Compri dei pomodori?*" "*Sì, ne compro 5.*"
> ("Do you buy some tomatoes?" "Yes, I buy 5 **of them**.")

Here, the pronoun *ne* implies "of them" and the quantity is still listed, but the thing being quantified is not being repeated. It's just an easier, simpler way to respond to a question.

Come possiamo vedere la Sardegna sullo schermo? Ci sono tanti film che sono stati girati in Sardegna. Ce ne sono tanti!

Un esempio di un film dove si vede la bellezza naturale della Sardegna si chiama *Deserto rosso* di Michelangelo Antonioni, con l'attrice famosa Monica Vitti. Verso la fine del film, la protagonista, Giuliana, che vive nel nord dell'Italia industriale degli anni Sessanta (1960s), fa un sogno. Nel suo sogno c'è una spiaggia deserta con la sabbia rosa e le acque limpide. Una piccola ragazza nuota nel mare e vede una barca. I colori di questa scena sono molto vivaci! Altre scene del film—per esempio a Ravenna nel nord e nella fabbrica dove lavora il marito di Giuliana—sono meno colorate. Antonioni, in questo film, fa vedere il Nord inquinato e industriale e la natura selvaggia e la bellezza incontaminata della Sardegna. Si vede anche questa bellezza naturale della Sardegna nel film di Lina Wertmüller che si chiama *Travolti da un insolito destino nell'azzurro mare d'agosto*. È un titolo lunghissimo!

La bellezza della Sardegna sembra quasi un'utopia. Devi andarci per crederlo!

▶ How can we see Sardinia on the screen? There are many films that were shot in Sardinia! There are many of them!

One example of a film where one sees the natural beauty of Sardinia is called *Red Dessert* by Michelangelo Antonioni, with the famous actress Monica Vitti. Toward the end of the film, the protagonist, Giulia, who lives in the north of industrial Italy in the 1960s, has a dream. In her dream, there is a deserted beach with red sand and clear waters. A small girl swims in the sea and sees a ship. The colors of this scene are very bright! Other scenes in the film—for example, in Ravenna in the north and in the factory where Giuliana's husband works—are less colorful. In this film, Antonioni shows us the polluted and industrial North and the wild nature and uncontaminated beauty of Sardinia. One also sees the natural beauty of Sardinia in Lina Wertmüller's film called *Swept Away by an Unusual Destiny in the Blue Sea of August*. It is a very long title!

Sardinia's beauty seems almost like a utopia. You have to go there to believe it!

ATTIVITÀ / ACTIVITIES

1. Traduci le seguenti frasi in inglese. Poi sottolinea la parte della frase che va sostituita da *ci* o *ne*. (Translate the following sentences from Italian to English. Then, underline the part of the first sentence that is being replaced by *ci* or *ne*.)

1. Vado al supermercato oggi e compro del latte. Ne compro un gallone.

   _____

2. Non penso molto al mio ragazzo. Non ci penso molto.

   _____

3. Vai mai in Francia? Io non ci vado spesso.

   _____

4. Michele non crede ai fantasmi. Non ci crede.

   _____

5. Hai paura dei ragni? Leonardo ne ha molta paura!

   _____

2. Sostituisci l'aggettivo indefinito con un pronome indefinito e riscrivi la frase. (Replace the indefinite adjective with an indefinite pronoun and rewrite the sentence. Pay attention to singular and plural!)

1. Parlo con ogni persona alla festa.

   _____

2. Non c'è qualche studente che possa parlare giapponese?

   _____

3. Tutte le persone nella mia famiglia mangiano la pizza.

   _____

4. Alcune persone pensano di essere intelligenti.

   _____

5. C'è qualche cosa di buono nelle notizie oggi.

   _____

3. Abbina la frase alla sinistra alla sostituzione appropriata alla destra. (Match the sentence on the left with the appropriate substitution on the right.)

1. tutte le persone   a. qualcosa

2. ogni persona   b. alcuni

3. qualche cosa   c. tutto

4. alcune persone   d. tutti

5. tutte le cose   e. ognuno

4. *Ci* o *ne*? Scegli l'opzione giusta. (Would this phrase be replaced by *ci* or *ne*? Choose the correct option.)

1. Compro 5 banane.   ci   ne

2. Ho bisogno di aiuto.   ci   ne

3. Penso a te sempre.   ci   ne

4. Lavoriamo sui pronomi.   ci   ne

5. Viaggio a Parigi quest'estate.   ci   ne

5. *Esercizio di scrittura: Non ci credo!*

Write some questions to your Italian pen pal about things that you do and do not believe to be true. Ask them if they believe in the same things or not.

_____

_____

_____

_____

_____

_____

_____

ANSWER KEY

1.

1. I'm going to the supermarket today and buying some milk. I will buy one gallon of it.
   del latte
2. I don't think about my boyfriend much. I don't think about him much.
   al mio ragazzo
3. Do you ever go to France? I don't go there often.
   in Francia
4. Michele does not believe in ghosts. He does not believe in them.
   ai fantasmi
5. Are you afraid of spiders? Leonardo is very afraid (has much fear) of them!
   dei ragni

2.

1. Parlo con ognuno alla festa.
2. Non c'è qualcuno che possa parlare giapponese?
3. Tutti nella mia famiglia mangiano la pizza. / Ognuno nella mia famiglia mangia la pizza.
4. Alcuni pensano di essere intelligenti.
5. C'è qualcosa di buono nelle notizie oggi.

3.

1. d.	3. a.	5. c.
2. e.	4. b.	

4.

1. ne	3. ci	5. ci
2. ne	4. ci	

5. Answers will vary. Example:

Credi all'oroscopo? Veramente non ci credo. Credi ai fantasmi? Ci credo io!

MAP OF SARDEGNA BY PROVINCES

PASSATO PROSSIMO WITH AVERE / UMBRIA

La regione dell'Umbria è il cuore verde dell'Italia, proprio nel centro della penisola. Si chiama "il cuore verde" perché ci sono tanti boschi in questa regione e anche tante colline, valli e fiumi. Il fiume Tevere attraversa la regione. L'Umbria è anche molto conosciuta per il Lago Trasimeno, un bellissimo lago. La regione si trova a sud e ad est della Toscana, ad ovest delle Marche, e a nord del Lazio. Sai che l'Umbria è l'unica regione che non confina con un mare o un altro paese straniero? È veramente il "cuore" della nazione! Forse non sai che l'Umbria è grande come lo stato americano del Connecticut!

Ci sono due province umbre che sono anche nomi di città umbre: Perugia e Terni. Il capoluogo dell'Umbria è Perugia, una città collinare con una storia etrusca, medievale e rinascimentale molto ricca. A Perugia c'è la famosa Università per Stranieri, dove tanti studenti internazionali studiano l'italiano. C'è anche il festival della musica jazz, Umbria Jazz, che si svolge ogni estate. Hai mangiato i cioccolatini Baci? Vengono da un'industria che si chiama Perugina che è stata fondata a Perugia nel 1907! Hai letto il nome di San Francesco? In Umbria si trova la sua città d'origine: Assisi, dove puoi andare a vedere la Basilica dedicata al santo. San Francesco è il santo patrono d'Italia. Nella Basilica puoi vedere alcuni dipinti degli artisti più famosi del medioevo e del Rinascimento. Hai visto i quadri di Giotto, Cimabue o Simone Martini?

L'Umbria non è solo famosa per la sua arte figurativa, ma anche per la sua architettura gotica. Un esempio è il Duomo di Orvieto, con i suoi mosaici di oro, marmi di vari colori e sculture. Andrea Orcagna, Beato Angelico e Luca Signorelli hanno lavorato in questo duomo.

Questa regione ha anche prodotto della ceramica artistica. Produce anche altri prodotti alimentari. Hai mangiato la pasta Buitoni? Hai bevuto l'acqua San Benedetto? Hai assaggiato l'olio d'oliva? San Benedetto è tra alcuni dei tanti santi famosi di questa regione, come San Francesco, Santa Chiara e Santa Rita.

Forse non sei mai andato in Umbria. Forse sei andato in Toscana. Ma l'Umbria ha un suo fascino unico ed è ricchissima di arte, cultura e storia religiosa.

The region of Umbria is the green heart of Italy, right in the center of the peninsula. It is called "the green heart" because there are many forests in this region, and also many hills, valleys, and rivers. The Tiber River passes through the region. Umbria is also well known for Lake Trasimene, a beautiful lake. The region is located to the south and to the east of Tuscany, to the west of the Marches, and to the north of Lazio. Do you know that Umbria is the only region that does not border with an ocean or another foreign country? It truly is the "heart" of the nation! Perhaps you don't know that Umbria is as big as the American state of Connecticut!

There are two Umbrian provinces that are also the names of Umbrian cities: Perugia and Terni. Umbria's capital is Perugia, a hilly city with a very rich Etruscan, medieval, and Renaissance history. In Perugia there is the famous Università per Stranieri ("University for Foreigners"), where many international students study Italian. There is also the jazz music festival, Umbria Jazz, which takes place each summer. Have you eaten Baci chocolates? They come from a company that is called Perugina, which was founded in Perugia in 1907! Have you read of the name Saint Francis? In Umbria is his city of origin: Assisi, where you can go to see the Basilica dedicated to the saint. Saint Francis is the patron saint of Italy. In the Basilica you can see some of the paintings by the most famous artists of the Middle Ages and the Renaissance. Have you seen the paintings by Giotto, Cimabue, or Simone Martini?

Umbria is not only famous for its figurative arts but also for its Gothic architecture. One example is the cathedral in Orvieto, with its mosaics of gold, marbles of various colors, and sculptures. Andrea Orcagna, Beato Angelico, and Luca Signorelli worked in this cathedral.

This region has also produced artistic ceramics. It also produces other food items. Have you eaten Buitoni pasta? Have you drunk water by San Benedetto? Have you tried olive oil? San Benedetto is among some of the many famous saints of this region, such as Saint Francis, Saint Chiara, and Saint Rita.

Perhaps you have never gone to Umbria. Maybe you went to Tuscany. But Umbria has its own unique appeal, and it is extremely rich with art, culture, and religious history.

VOCABOLARIO NUOVO E UTILE / NEW AND USEFUL VOCABULARY

attraversare	to cross over	**svolgersi**	to unfold, to occur
mangiato	eaten	**letto**	read
visto	seen	**lavorato**	worked
prodotto	produced	**bevuto**	(had) drunk
assaggiato	tasted	**andato/a**	gone
conosciuto/a	known	**unico/a**	unique
straniero/a	foreign	**verde**	green
umbro/a	Umbrian	**collinare**	hilly
etrusco/a	Etruscan	**internazionale**	international
fondato/a	founded	**d'origine**	of origin
dedicato/a	dedicated	**gotico/a**	Gothic
il santo patrono	patron saint	**il dipinto**	painting
il mosaico	mosaic	**l'oro**	gold
il marmo	marble	**la scultura**	sculpture
la ceramica	ceramics	**l'olio d'oliva**	olive oil

RIPASSO GENERALE / GENERAL REVIEW

A. Notes about Umbria

You might be wondering why Umbria is called "the green heart" of Italy: It's partly due to the ecology of the region and partly due to its position right in the center of the boot. The region is full of lakes, forests, trees, and valleys that contribute to its "greenness." You've probably heard of the city of Assisi, especially if you know Saint Francis of Assisi. Umbria is also home to the famous cities of Terni and Perugia. It's a splendid mix of new and old, north and south.

In this lesson, you'll learn how to express things in the past tense for the first time. The *passato prossimo* (recent past) can be a bit difficult until you learn to notice certain patterns and shortcuts. Imagine you traveled to Umbria last month and talk about your trip!

B. The *passato prossimo* with *avere*

The recent past—the *passato prossimo* in Italian—has two distinct categories: verbs that use *avere* as an auxiliary verb and those that use *essere*. You will learn about verbs that use *essere* in lesson 19. Verbs that use *avere* are known as transitive verbs, and those that use *essere* are intransitive verbs. If you already know what that means, great! If not, here's how you can tell the difference:

Transitive verbs are verbs that can possibly take a direct object. They are verbs whose action can be done upon something else. For example, you can *hit* a table (the action verb is *to hit* and the direct object is *a table*), but you can't *go* a table or *be* a table. Those would be intransitive verbs—verbs of movement or states of being.

The *passato prossimo* is made up of two words. First is an auxiliary (or helping) verb, and then a past participle. This is a past tense that describes recent actions: actions that occurred today, yesterday, in the past month or year. These actions are completed and did not occur over and over again; they are one-and-done actions.

To begin, let's review the verb *avere*, which is the auxiliary verb you'll work with in this lesson:

io **ho**	noi **abbiamo**
tu **hai**	voi **avete**
lui/lei/Lei **ha**	loro/Loro **hanno**

You will then add a past participle. These are words like *done, made, painted, seen,* etc. (English speakers sometimes use these on their own to mean the same thing as verbs in the *passato prossimo*; try not to compare this to English so as not to get confused.)

To form the past participle, cut off the *-are, -ere,* and *-ire* endings from infinitive verbs and replace them with *-ato, -uto,* and *-ito,* respectively. This doesn't work for every single verb (as you will see in the next section), but this is the pattern that you should remember. So, *parlare* becomes *parlato, avere* becomes *avuto,* and *dormire* becomes *dormito.*

Added to the auxiliary verb, you now have the complete verbal phrase: *ho parlato* (I spoke), *hai avuto* (you had), *avete dormito* (you all slept).

Easy, right? Unfortunately, there are many irregular past participles! Let's meet a few and try to recognize some patterns.

C. Irregular Past Participles

Irregular past participles are not easy to spot and must be memorized. Once you have memorized these verbs, it will be much easier to decide which verbs are regular and which will be irregular.

Here's a chart that shows the various patterns that irregular past participles can take (you don't need to know the meaning of every one):

-tto	fare	**fatto**		prendere	pre**so**
	dire	de**tto**		rendere	re**so**
	leggere	le**tto**		accendere	acce**so**
	correggere	corre**tto**		spendere	spe**so**
	scrivere	scri**tto**		scendere	sce**so**
	friggere	fri**tto**		offendere	offe**so**
	rompere	ro**tto**	**-so**	decidere	deci**so**
	cuocere	co**tto**		uccidere	ucci**so**
	tradurre	trado**tto**		ridere	ri**so**
-rto	aprire	ape**rto**		dividere	divi**so**
	offrire	offe**rto**		chiudere	chiu**so**
	soffrire	soffe**rto**		concludere	conclu**so**
	coprire	cope**rto**		diffondere	diffu**so**
	scoprire	scope**rto**		rimanere	rima**sto**
	morire	mo**rto**		chiedere	chie**sto**
	accorgersi	acco**rto**		rispondere	rispo**sto**
-rso	perdere	pe**rso**	**-sto**	comporre	compo**sto**
	correre	co**rso**		proporre	propo**sto**
-lto	scegliere	sce**lto**		disporre	dispo**sto**
	togliere	to**lto**		vedere	vi**sto**
	raccogliere	racco**lto**		mettere	me**sso**
	sciogliere	scio**lto**		succedere	succe**sso**
	risolvere	riso**lto**	**-sso**	permettere	perme**sso**
	rivolgersi	rivo**lto**		esprimere	espre**sso**
-nto	piangere	pia**nto**		muovere	mo**sso**
	spegnere	spe**nto**		discutere	discu**sso**
	spingere	spi**nto**			
	vincere	vi**nto**			
	aggiungere	aggiu**nto**			
	dipingere	dipi**nto**			
	assumere	assu**nto**			

D. Agreement of Direct Object Pronouns in the Past Tense

By definition, transitive verbs take a direct object with their actions. You can *kick* a ball, *give* a gift, and *take* a nap. If you decide to replace these direct objects with their appropriate direct object pronoun, you'll have to change the past participle to agree with the pronoun in number and gender.

Let's review direct object pronouns:

mi	ci
ti	vi
lo/la/La	li/le/Li/Le

If you say you did something, such as "I took a picture" ("*Ho fatto una foto*"), you could simply write it like it is in the parentheses. If you replace *una foto* with *la*, then you put the pronoun before the verbal phrase (*lo* and *la* can be shortened to *l'*) and change the *fatto* to *fatta* to reflect the fact that the direct object is singular and feminine. If it is plural, it would also change to reflect that plural object:

Ho fatto una foto → ***L'ho fatta.***

Ho fatto le foto → ***Le ho fatte.***

What else can you replace with direct object pronouns? You can practice this in the Activities for this lesson.

ATTIVITÀ / ACTIVITIES

1. Traduci le seguenti frasi in inglese. Sottolinea il verbo al passato prossimo. (Translate the following phrases from Italian to English. Underline the verb in the *passato prossimo*.)

1. Ieri ho parlato con la mia amica.

   _____

2. Stamattina abbiamo mangiato gli spaghetti per colazione.

   _____

3. Hai dormito bene, Angelina?

   _____

4. Loro hanno aperto la porta del negozio.

   _____

5. Avete mai ballato il tango?

   _____

2. Scrivi il participio passato corretto del verbo. (Write the correct past participle of the verb.)

   1. scrivere   _____

   2. fare   _____

   3. vedere   _____

   4. prendere   _____

   5. rispondere   _____

   6. morire   _____

   7. conoscere   _____

   8. correre   _____

   9. succedere   _____

   10. nascere   _____

3. Riscrivi la frase al passato prossimo con un pronome di oggetto diretto. (Rewrite the sentence in the *passato prossimo* with a direct object pronoun. Note: Pay attention to the agreement!)

   1. Ho cucinato una torta.   _____

   2. Abbiamo mangiato i tortellini.   _____

   3. Hanno fatto i loro compiti.   _____

   4. Hai chiuso tutte le porte?   _____

   5. Luca ha comprato un telefono.   _____

4. *Esercizio di scrittura: Ho avuto una bella giornata!*

Tell your Italian pen pal about the day you had yesterday. What did you do? What did you eat? What did you see? Use the *passato prossimo*. For extra practice, rewrite each sentence with a direct object pronoun where necessary.

_____

_____

_____

_____

_____

_____

_____

ANSWER KEY

1.

1. Yesterday I spoke with my friend.
   ho parlato
2. This morning we ate spaghetti for breakfast.
   abbiamo mangiato
3. Did you sleep well, Angelina?
   Hai dormito
4. They opened the door of the store.
   hanno aperto
5. Have you [pl.] ever danced the tango?
   Avete...ballato

2.

1. scritto
2. fatto
3. visto/veduto
4. preso
5. risposto
6. morto
7. conosciuto
8. corso
9. successo
10. nato

3.

1. L'ho cucinata.
2. Li abbiamo mangiati.
3. Li hanno fatti.
4. Le hai chiuse?
5. Luca l'ha comprato.

4. Answers will vary. Example:

Ieri ho mangiato una bella torta al cioccolato. Ho dormito per tre ore. Ho ballato con mio figlio.

MAP OF UMBRIA BY PROVINCES

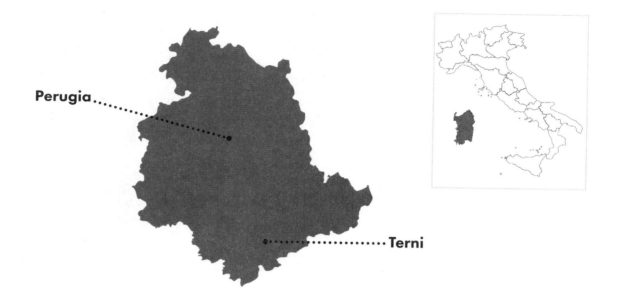

WHERE ARE YOU NOW?

Congratulations! You've made it through the first three-quarters of the workbook. By now, you should be familiar with the following topics in vocabulary:

1. question words
2. body parts
3. the arts
4. telling time

You have also covered quite a bit of grammar:

1. irregular plurals
2. interrogatives
3. reflexive verbs
4. reciprocal verbs
5. negative and affirmative phrases
6. adverbs
7. the present progressive
8. suffixes
9. indefinite adjectives and pronouns
10. *ci* and *ne*
11. the *passato prossimo* with avere
12. irregular past participles
13. agreement with direct objects in the past tense

Next to each topic, rate your comfort level from 1 to 5, with 1 being the least comfortable and 5 being the most. What can you work on more?

Some helpful tools and methods are listed in the first Where Are You Now? section in this workbook.

PASSATO PROSSIMO WITH *ESSERE* / TUSCANY

La famosissima regione della Toscana si trova nel centro della penisola. La regione si trova a sudest della Liguria, a sud dell'Emilia-Romagna, a nordovest dell'Umbria, ad ovest delle Marche, e a nord del Lazio. Confina con il mare Tirreno sulla costa occidentale. Ci sono due piccole isole vicino alla costa: l'Elba e l'Isola del Giglio. Confina anche con il mare Ligure a nord. Ci sono tanti boschi, colline, montagne e fiumi in questa regione. Il fiume Arno attraversa le città di Firenze, Siena ed Empoli.

La Toscana è la culla del Rinascimento. *Rinascere* significa nascere una seconda volta. È la riscoperta del mondo classico. In Toscana c'è l'origine di tanta storia artistica e politica della nazione. Tante città come Firenze (il suo capoluogo), Siena, San Gimignano, Lucca, Pisa, Arezzo e l'area di Chianti sono destinazioni turistiche molto popolari. Infatti, la regione della Toscana è così policentrica che alcuni la chiamano "una nazione dentro una nazione." Ci sono nove province: Arezzo, Firenze, Grosseto, Livorno, Lucca, Massa e Carrara, Pisa, Pistoia, Prato e Siena. Ti ricordi quante province ha l'Umbria? Ne ha solo due! La Toscana invece ne ha nove.

La Toscana produce tanti vini famosi e pregiati. Hai mai bevuto il vino Montepulciano, il Chianti o il Brunello? Altri prodotti toscani molto importanti sono i prodotti di cuoio come le borse e le scarpe. Hai mai comprato una borsa a Firenze? La regione è molto nota per i salumi e la bistecca. Ci sono delle mucche che vivono nella valle di Chiana che si usano per la bistecca fiorentina. Hai mai mangiato una bistecca fiorentina? Poi ci sono anche tanti posti e spettacoli per tutta la regione. Hai mai visto la torre che pende a Pisa? Oppure sei mai andato a Piazza del Campo di Siena per vedere la corsa di cavalli che si chiama Palio?

Firenze è la prima destinazione turistica della regione. Sei mai andato a Firenze? Tanti autori medievali e rinascimentali di Firenze sono diventati importanti, come le "tre corone" della letteratura italiana: Dante Alighieri, Francesco Petrarca e Giovanni Boccaccio. Dante ha scritto il poema epico *La Divina commedia*. Dante è nato a Firenze, ma non è morto lì: è morto a Ravenna in esilio. Anche Niccolò Machiavelli è nato a Firenze, ma è morto nella sua città natale. Machiavelli ha scritto tanti libri importanti come *Il principe*. Lui ha lavorato per la potente famiglia fiorentina dei Medici. La corte dei Medici è stata la culla dell'Umanesimo. Hai mai letto le opere di questi autori fiorentini?

Firenze è anche importante per la sua arte medievale e rinascimentale. Hai mai visto le opere di Michelangelo o di Botticelli? Michelangelo Buonarotti era un artista fondamentale del Rinascimento. Ha fatto tanto nella sua carriera. Ha dipinto, ha disegnato, ha scritto poesie e ha fatto delle sculture importanti come la *Pietà*. Anche Sandro Botticelli era un artista molto importante. Ha dipinto tanti quadri importanti come la *Primavera* e *La nascita di Venere*.

Probabilmente sei già andato in Toscana. Ma vale sempre la pena tornarci!

▶ Find this translation on the next page

The extremely famous region of Tuscany is located in the center of the peninsula. The region is located to the southeast of Liguria, to the south of Emilia-Romagna, to the northwest of Umbria, to the west of the Marches, and to the north of Lazio. It borders with the Tyrrhenian Sea on the western coast. There are two small islands close to the coast: Elba and the Island of Giglio. It also borders with the Ligurian Sea to the north. There are many forests, hills, mountains, and rivers in this region. The Arno River crosses the cities of Florence, Siena, and Empoli.

Tuscany is the cradle of the Renaissance. *Rinascere* means "to be born a second time." It is the rediscovery of the classical world. In Tuscany there is the origin of much artistic and political history of the nation. Many cities, such as Florence (its capital), Siena, San Gimignano, Lucca, Pisa, Arezzo, and the Chianti region, are very popular tourist destinations. Indeed, the region of Tuscany is so polycentric that some call it "a nation inside a nation." There are nine provinces: Arezzo, Firenze, Grosseto, Livorno, Lucca, Massa-Carrara, Pisa, Pistoia, Prato, and Siena. Do you remember how many provinces Umbria has? It only has two of them. Tuscany, instead, has nine of them.

Tuscany produces many famous and valued wines. Have you ever drunk Montepulciano, Chianti, or Brunello wines? Other very important Tuscan products are the leather products, such as bags and shoes. Have you ever purchased a bag in Florence? The region is very famous for its cured meats and steak. There are cows that live in the Chiana valley which are used for Florentine steaks. Have you ever eaten a Florentine steak? Then there are also many places and sights throughout the region. Have you ever seen the leaning tower in Pisa? Or have you ever gone to the Piazza del Campo in Siena to see the horse race called the Palio?

Florence is the first tourist destination of the region. Have you ever gone to Florence? Many medieval and Renaissance authors in Florence became important, such as the "three crowns" of Italian literature: Dante Alighieri, Francesco Petrarca, and Giovanni Boccaccio. Dante wrote the epic poem *The Divine Comedy*. Dante was born in Florence, but he did not die there: He died in Ravenna in exile. Niccolò Machiavelli was also born in Florence, but he died in his native city. Machiavelli wrote many important books, such as *The Prince*. He worked for the powerful Florentine family of the Medici. The Medici court was the cradle of Humanism. Have you ever read the works of these Florentine authors?

Florence is also important for its medieval and Renaissance art. Have you ever seen the works by Michelangelo or by Botticelli? Michelangelo Buonarotti was a fundamental artist of the Renaissance. He did much during his career. He painted, he drew, he wrote poetry, and he made important sculptures, such as the *Pietà*. Sandro Botticelli was also an important artist. He painted many important paintings, such as the *Spring* and *The Birth of Venus*.

You have probably already gone to Tuscany. But it is always worthwhile to return there!

VOCABOLARIO NUOVO E UTILE / NEW AND USEFUL VOCABULARY

famosissimo/a	very famous	**policentrico/a**	having many centers
natale	native	**potente**	powerful
fiorentino/a	Florentine	**toscano/a**	Tuscan
fondamentale	fundamental	**probabilmente**	probably
la culla	cradle	**il Rinascimento**	the Renaissance
la borsa	purse, bag	**la pelle**	skin, pelt

la bistecca	steak	**la mucca**	cow
il cavallo	horse	**la corte**	court
il poema	poem	**il libro**	book
l'Umanesimo	Humanism	**l'opera**	work (of art)
pendere	to lean	**rinascere**	to be reborn
comprato	bought	**diventato/a**	(had) become
nato/a	born	**morto/a**	died
scritto	written	**lavorato**	worked
stato/a	was	**fatto**	did, made
dipinto	painted	**disegnato**	drawn
già	already	**mai**	ever, never
non...mai	never	**non...ancora**	not yet
sempre	always	**spesso**	often
qualche volta	sometimes	**scorso/a**	last
fa	ago	**presto**	early

RIPASSO GENERALE / GENERAL REVIEW

A. Notes about Toscana

Toscana (or Tuscany, as it is called by English speakers) is one of the most famous Italian regions because it has as its capital Firenze (Florence), the cradle of the Renaissance and hometown to authors such as Dante Alighieri. In fact, you can visit the Casa di Dante in Florence! With cities like Chianti and Montepulciano, Tuscany boasts superb wines and olive oil as well as the mouthwatering *bistecca fiorentina*. Don't miss Siena, Pisa, Lucca, and other treasures as well.

In this lesson, you'll continue learning about the *passato prossimo*, this time with intransitive verbs, which take *essere* as their auxiliary. You'll also discover expressions of time. Have you ever been to Tuscany? Now's your chance to talk about that experience.

B. The *passato prossimo* with *essere*

The *passato prossimo* with *essere* is formed almost exactly the same way as with *avere*. You'll start with the conjugated form of *essere* that is appropriate to the subject and then add a past participle. However, there's a twist here: The past participle, when used with *essere*, must agree with the subject in number and gender (like an adjective).

First, let's review the conjugations of *essere*:

io **sono**	noi **siamo**
tu **sei**	voi **siete**
lui/lei/Lei **è**	loro/Loro **sono**

Now let's look at the verb *andare* in the past tense. *Andare* goes with *essere* in the past perfect because it is an intransitive verb, which is a verb of movement or state of being. You'll be introduced to some mnemonic devices later in this lesson to help you differentiate between transitive and intransitive verbs.

sono andato/a	siamo andati/e
sei andato/a	siete andati/e
è andato/a	sono andati/e

As you can see, the past participle must agree in gender and number for each person of the verb.

One particularity of the verb *essere* is that it takes *essere* as its auxiliary. If you've studied French before, you know that *to be* does not behave similarly! The past participle for *essere* is actually *stato/a/i/e*, which is also the past participle for *stare*. Here are the forms of *essere* in the *passato prossimo*:

sono stato/a	siamo stati/e
sei stato/a	siete stati/e
è stato/a	sono stati/e

Don't worry about the fact that the *io* and *loro* forms look similar; you'll be able to tell the difference by looking at the past participles, which are different.

C. Expressions of Time

When using expressions of time in the *passato prossimo*, you should know that certain words can go between the auxiliary verb and the past participle. Expressions like *non...mai* and *non...ancora* can sandwich these verbs. Here are a few examples:

> "*Hai **già** mangiato?*" (Have you already eaten?)
> "*No, **non** ho **ancora** mangiato.*" (No, I have not yet eaten.)

> "*Sei **mai** stata in Italia?*" (Have you ever been to Italy?)
> "*No, **non** sono **mai** stata in Italia.*" (No, I have never been to Italy.)

Words that can act this way are *mai, ancora, già,* and *sempre.*

D. The Difference between Transitive and Intransitive Verbs

Lesson 18 offered a brief introduction to transitive and intransitive verbs and the differences between them. In that lesson, and as mentioned previously in this one, intransitive verbs are verbs of movement and states of being (verbs like *to go, to be, to become, to live, to die,* etc.). Think of them as verbs you can do around a house; for this reason, a visual of a house is very important.

La casa di essere

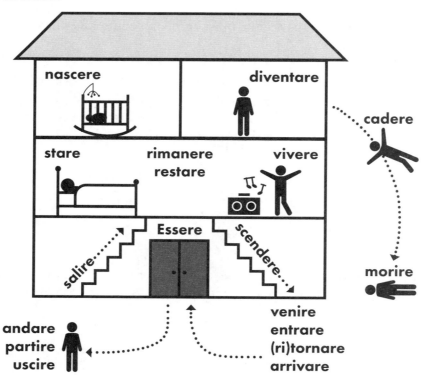

Here you can see all the different verbs that take *essere* as their auxiliary—they're all intransitive verbs.

If you're less of a visual learner and more into acronyms, here's a handy one that fits almost all of these verbs: SUPERMAN DAVE.

STARE

USCIRE

PARTIRE

ENTRARE

RIMANERE

MORIRE

ANDARE

NASCERE

DIVENTARE

ARRIVARE

VENIRE

ESSERE

If you've got these verbs down, then you can (almost, but not always) assume that any other verb is transitive (and thus takes *avere* as its auxiliary).

Michelangelo Buonarotti era un artista fondamentale del Rinascimento. È nato il 6 marzo 1475 a Firenze. Ma non ci è rimasto. Ha fatto tanto nella sua carriera. Ha dipinto, ha disegnato, ha scritto poesie e ha fatto delle sculture importanti come la *Pietà*. In pochi anni, è diventato l'artista più importante del Rinascimento. È restato per molti anni nella corte dei Medici. Ha fatto alcune delle sue opere più notevoli, per esempio la Capella Sistina, per i papi sotto i Medici, per esempio Leone X e Clemente V. È morto a Roma nel 1564.

Michelangelo Buonarotti was a fundamental artist of the Renaissance. He was born on March 6, 1475, in Florence. But he did not remain there. He did much in his career. He painted, he drew, he wrote poetry, and he made important sculptures, such as the *Pietà*. In a few years, he became the most important artist of the Renaissance. He remained for many years in the Medici court. He made some of his most noteworthy works, for example, the Sistine Chapel, for the popes under the Medici, for example, Leo X and Clement V. He died in Rome in 1564.

Mi sono svegliato presto. Mi sono alzato subito, con la luce del sole toscano! Non posso fare la doccia, perché ancora non esiste. E non mi sono cambiato i vestiti: porto sempre le stesse cose da una settimana intera! Ho fatto colazione e ho bevuto del vino caldo. Poi sono andato nello studio a dipingere. Ho pranzato con i miei assistenti a mezzogiorno. Ho ripreso a lavorare subito dopo e sono rimasto nello studio a lavorare fino a tardi. Non ho cenato, perché avevo troppa voglia di dipingere! Mi sono addormentato tardi sui miei pennarelli. Questo quadro sarà fantastico!

▶ I woke up early. I got up immediately, with the light of the Tuscan sun! I can't take a shower, because they don't exist yet. And I didn't change my clothes: I've been wearing the same items for a whole week! I ate breakfast and drank warm wine. Then I went into the study to paint. I ate lunch with my assistants at noon. I went back to work right away and stayed in the studio to work until late. I didn't eat dinner, because I had too large a desire to paint! I fell asleep late on my brushes. This painting will be fantastic!

ATTIVITÀ / ACTIVITIES

1. Traduci le seguenti frasi in inglese. Sottolinea i verbi che sono al passato prossimo. (Translate the following sentences from Italian into English. Underline the verbs that are in the *passato prossimo*.)

   1. Stamattina sono andato al supermercato e ho comprato delle banane.

      _____

   2. Siete mai stati a Londra? Avete visto Big Ben?

      _____

   3. Ieri Alessia ha corso una maratona. Non è stata facile!

      _____

   4. Perché Riccardo non è venuto alla nostra festa? Cosa ha fatto invece?

      _____

   5. Oggi è arrivata una lettera per te. Asuka ti ha scritto da Giappone.

      _____

2. Riscrivi la frase, cambiando il soggetto ogni volta. (Rewrite the sentence, changing the subject each time.)

1. Piero è nato 34 anni fa. (i miei genitori / io / tu e Gianni / io e Chiara)

2. Daniele e Tommaso sono arrivati in ritardo. (Elena ed Emma / tu / noi studenti / Bella)

3. Io non sono mai andata in crociera (*cruise*). (Edoardo / Emidio ed io / voi / i bambini)

4. Quando siete ritornate tu ed Erica? (tu / Giuseppe e Filippo / Franca / noi)

3. Regolare o irregolare? Scegli l'opzione giusta per ogni participio passato. (Regular or irregular? Choose the correct option for each past participle.)

1. morire → morto   I   R

2. arrivare → arrivato   I   R

3. nascere → nato   I   R

4. essere → stato   I   R

5. rimanere → rimasto   I   R

6. andare → andato   I   R

7. venire → venuto   I   R

8. stare → stato   I   R

4. Transitivo o intransitivo? Scegli l'opzione giusta. (Transitive or intransitive? Choose the correct option. Note: Remember the *casa di essere* and SUPERMAN DAVE!)

1. cadere   I   T

2. fare   I   T

3. diventare   I   T

4. morire   I   T

5. giocare   I   T

6. rientrare   I   T

7. avere   I   T

8. trovare   I   T

5. *Esercizio di scrittura: Sono andato/a a/in…*

List all of the places you have been to (or gone to) using the verb *andare* or *stare*. For extra practice, talk about the things that you did there.

_____

_____

_____

_____

_____

_____

_____

ANSWER KEY

1.

1. This morning I went to the supermarket and I bought some bananas.
   sono andato, ho comprato
2. Have you [pl.] ever been to London? Did you [pl.] see Big Ben?
   Siete stati, Avete visto
3. Yesterday Alessia ran a marathon. It was not easy!
   ha corso, è stata
4. Why didn't Riccardo come to our party? What did he do instead?
   è venuto, ha fatto
5. Today a letter arrived for you. Asuka wrote to you from Japan.
   è arrivata, ha scritto

2.

1. I miei genitori sono nati 34 anni fa.
   Io sono nata 34 anni fa.
   Tu e Gianni siete nati 34 anni fa.
   Io e Chiara siamo nati 34 anni fa.
2. Elena ed Emma sono arrivate in ritardo.
   Tu sei arrivato/a in ritardo.
   Noi studenti siamo arrivati in ritardo.
   Bella è arrivata in ritardo.
3. Edoardo non è mai andato in crociera.
   Emidio ed io non siamo mai andati in crociera.
   Voi non siete mai andati/e in crociera.
   I bambini non sono mai andati in crociera.

4. Quando sei ritornato/a tu?
   Quando sono ritornati Giuseppe e Filippo?
   Quando è ritornata Franca?
   Quando siamo ritornati/e noi?

3.

1. I	4. I	7. I
2. R	5. I	8. R
3. I	6. R	

4.

1. I	4. I	7. T
2. T	5. T	8. T
3. I	6. I	

5. Answers will vary. Example:

Sono andata in Italia due anni fa. Ho visto il Colosseo, ho mangiato gli spaghetti, ho visitato i musei...

MAP OF TOSCANA BY PROVINCES

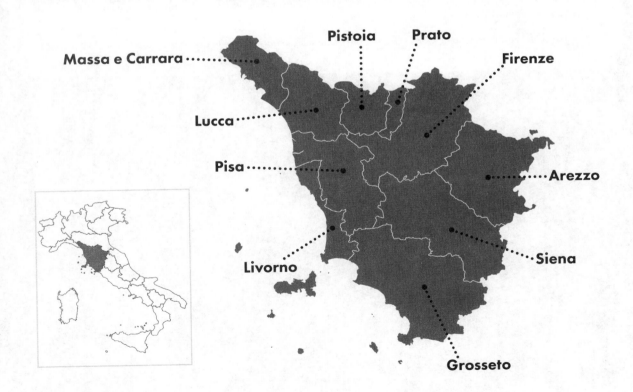

THE IMPERFECT TENSE / CALABRIA

La regione della Calabria si trova nel sud della penisola. È il punto dello stivale che dà un calcio alla Sicilia! La regione si trova a sud della Basilicata. È bagnata dal mare Tirreno sulla costa occidentale e dal mare Ionico sulla costa orientale. È separata dalla Sicilia dallo Stretto di Messina. Il capoluogo è Catanzaro.

La Calabria è una regione molto montagnosa. Ci sono tre catene montuose: l'Aspromonte, il Pollino e la Sila. Le montagne del Pollino si trovano nel nord della regione. Separano la Calabria dalla Basilicata. Lì c'è il parco nazionale più grande dell'Italia. La Sila, invece, si trova nel centro della regione. L'Aspromonte è il punto più a sud della penisola. Sull'Aspromonte c'è stata una battaglia molto importante durante il Risorgimento italiano nel 1860. Garibaldi comandava le truppe durante il Risorgimento!

La storia in Calabria è molto importante. I segni del primo essere umano si trovano in Calabria! Si chiamava *Homo erectus* e viveva sulla costa settecentomila anni prima di Cristo. Nell'epoca paleolitica gli uomini preistorici erano anche artisti! Hanno disegnato il primo toro, il *Bos primigenius*, nella grotta del Romito. Sapevano già disegnare anche in quell'epoca! Circa 800 e 700 anni avanti Cristo, la regione della Calabria faceva parte della Magna Grecia. C'erano tante colonie greche sulla costa come Gioia Tauro. Ci sono parti della Calabria dove i dialetti sono molto simili alla lingua greca.

Le statue dei Bronzi di Riace si trovano nel Museo della Magna Grecia a Reggio Calabria. Sono due uomini, forse guerrieri o dei. Reggio era un centro di attività molto importante. La Calabria ha anche monumenti bizantini molto importanti, come la chiesa che si chiama la Cattolica a Stilo. Il filosofo importante Tommaso Campanella è nato a Stilo. Lui ha scritto *La città del sole*.

Se ti interessa la storia antica, o hai voglia di prendere il sole sulle spiagge più belle del mondo, devi visitare la Calabria!

The region of Calabria is located in the south of the peninsula. It is the tip of the boot that gives a kick to Sicily! The region is located to the south of Basilicata. It is washed by the Tyrrhenian Sea on the western coast and by the Ionian Sea on the eastern coast. It is separated from Sicily by the Strait of Messina. Its capital is Catanzaro.

Calabria is a very mountainous region. There are three mountain ranges: Aspromonte, Pollino, and Sila. The Pollino mountains are located in the north of the region. They separate Calabria from Basilicata. In that place is the largest national park of Italy. On the other hand, Sila is located in the center of the region. Aspromonte is the southernmost point of the peninsula. At Aspromonte was a very important battle during the Italian Unification of 1860. Garibaldi led the troops during the Unification!

History is very important in Calabria. The signs of the first human being can be found in Calabria! It was called *Homo erectus* and it used to live on the coast 700,000 years before Christ. In the Paleolithic Period, the prehistoric humans were even artists! They drew the first bull, *Bos primigenius*, in the cave at Romito. They already knew how to draw in that period! Around 800 or 700 BC, the region of Calabria was a part of Magna Grecia. There were many Greek colonies on the coast, like Gioia Tauro. There are parts of Calabria where dialects are very similar to the Greek language.

The statues of the Bronzes of Riace are located in the Museum of Magna Grecia in Reggio Calabria. They are two men, perhaps soldiers or gods. Reggio was a very important center of activity. Calabria also has very important Byzantine monuments, such as the church called the Catholic at Stilo. The important philosopher Tommaso Campanella was born in Stilo. He wrote *The City of the Sun*.

If you are interested in ancient history, or if you wish to sunbathe on the most beautiful beaches of the world, you should visit Calabria!

il calcio	soccer	lo stretto	strait
il punto	point	la catena	chain
l'albero	tree	l'abete	fir, spruce
il pino	pine	la battaglia	battle
la truppa	troop	la vite	vine
l'agrume	citrus tree	il bergamotto	bergamot tree
il fungo porcino	porcini mushroom	l'oliva	olive
la castagna	chestnut	l'essere umano	human being
il toro	bull	la colonia	colony
il bronzo	bronze	la scoperta	discovery
il guerriero	warrior	il dio	god
il filosofo	philosopher	le cuffie	headphones
sviluppato/a	developed	selvaggio/a	wild
preistorico/a	prehistoric	fresco/a	fresh
comandare	to command	vivere	to live
sapere	to know	fare chiasso	to make noise
di solito	usually	anzi	even so, rather

RIPASSO GENERALE / GENERAL REVIEW

A. Notes about Calabria

Calabria is the toe of the Italian boot, the southernmost point of Italy before reaching Sicily. It has a range of different influential cultures, from ancient Greek and Byzantine to modern eastern European; in fact, many Calabrians speak a dialect of Albanian called Arbërisht. Calabria was a point of exodus for many Italians in the wave of immigration to the United States (1880–1920). This peninsula of the Italian peninsula has much to offer to tourists!

In this lesson, you'll learn another past tense, the imperfect (*imperfetto*). It is similar to the *passato prossimo* in that it can narrate recent past events, but dissimilar in the type of actions it describes. Why did so many Italians want to emigrate in the last century? What did you always do as a child? You'll be able to describe these actions now.

B. The *imperfetto*

The *imperfetto* is one of the easiest tenses to conjugate in Italian, mostly because the forms are all uniform and there are very few irregular verbs. To form the imperfect, simply cut off the -*re* ending of (almost) any verb and add the following endings:

-vo	-vamo
-vi	-vate
-va	-vano

So, your typical -*are*, -*ere*, and -*ire* verbs will look like this:

parlare	mettere	dormire	finire
parlavo	mettevo	dormivo	finivo
parlavi	mettevi	dormivi	finivi
parlava	metteva	dormiva	finiva
parlavamo	mettevamo	dormivamo	finivamo
parlavate	mettevate	dormivate	finivate
parlavano	mettevano	dormivano	finivano

It's important to know where the stress falls in pronunciation of these verbs. For the first three persons (singular) and the third person plural, the stress falls on the syllable that precedes the *VA* (*par-LA-vo, par-LA-vi, par-LA-va, par-LA-va-no*). For the *noi* and *voi* forms, the stress falls on the *VA* syllable (*par-la-VA-mo, par-la-VA-te*).

In the *imperfetto*, *essere* is irregular, but *avere* is not.

essere	avere
ero	avevo
eri	avevi
era	aveva
eravamo	avevamo
eravate	avevate
erano	avevano

Here are three more commonly used verbs that are irregular in the *imperfetto*: *bere*, *dire*, and *fare*:

bere	dire	fare
bevevo	dicevo	facevo
bevevi	dicevi	facevi
beveva	diceva	faceva
bevevamo	dicevamo	facevamo
bevevate	dicevate	facevate
bevevano	dicevano	facevano

As you'll see in the next section, the imperfect is used for very specific actions that occurred in the past.

Da bambino ero molto attivo e curioso. Avevo i capelli molto lunghi e portavo la pelle di un tigre. Non avevo tanti amici, ma giocavo a nascondino con gli altri bambini. Mi piaceva fare scarabocchi sui muri delle grotte. Mi piaceva anche pescare e nuotare. Nuotavo spesso nel mare. Mangiavo il pesce, gli animali piccoli, le castagne, le olive e bevevo l'acqua fresca dei torrenti. Vivevo in una grotta nelle montagne.

When I was a child, I was very active and curious. I had very long hair and I wore a tiger skin. I didn't have many friends, but I played hide-and-seek with other children. I liked to doodle on cave walls. I also liked to fish and swim. I often used to swim in the sea. I would eat fish, small animals, chestnuts, olives, and I would drink the fresh water from the streams. I used to live in a cave in the mountains.

A. Differences between the *imperfetto* and the *passato prossimo*

The difference between the imperfect and present perfect in English is very subtle, and sometimes English speakers don't use them in the same way as they are used in Italian, so be patient with yourself as you are learning these two tenses.

You know that the *passato prossimo* is used for actions that are complete in the past or that only happened once in a defined period of time. In contrast, the imperfect is used when you are describing actions that are incomplete, ongoing, or occurring during a vaguely defined period of time. The imperfect can also be used to talk about habitual actions, to set up the background of a story, and to talk about weather and time in the past.

Think about some things you did yesterday and some things you always used to do as a child. If yesterday you ate breakfast at 9, you'd express that in the *passato prossimo* (it's a complete, one-time action occurring at a set time): *Ieri **ho mangiato** colazione alle 9.* If you're telling someone that you always used to eat breakfast at 9 as a child, that's habitual, so it would be in the imperfect: *Da bambino/a **mangiavo** sempre la colazione alle 9.*

You can have two actions occurring in the same sentence, one of each verb type. This is for times when an ongoing action (in the imperfect) is interrupted by a one-time action (in the *passato prossimo*): for example, "While I was taking a shower, someone knocked at the door" ("*Mentre **facevo** una doccia, qualcuno **ha bussato** alla porta*"). You can also express that two imperfect actions are occurring at the same time (e.g., "*Mentre **studiavo**, mio fratello **ascoltava** la musica*") and two *passato prossimo* actions that occur simultaneously ("*Quando Marco **ha bussato** alla porta, io **sono caduta***"). In all of these sentences, you can see the difference between the actions. Try a few for yourself!

Faceva bello: c'era tanto sole. Sono andata alla spiaggia con i miei amici. Eravamo lì sdraiati sulla sabbia. Io avevo tanta energia e volevo nuotare, quindi mi sono alzata. Ho camminato fino all'acqua. L'acqua non era troppo fredda. Mi sono tuffata. L'acqua era limpida. Ho potuto vedere i pesci e il fondo. Mentre guardavo il fondo del mare, ho visto qualcosa. Sembrava il dito di un piede, ma sembrava anche vero. Non potevo crederci! Mi sono tuffata una seconda volta. Il piede sembrava duro, come di metallo. Sono uscita dall'acqua gridando dalla gioia. Ho scoperto qualcosa importante!

It was beautiful outside: There was a lot of sun. I went to the beach with my friends. We were lying outstretched there on the sand. I had a lot of energy and wanted to swim, so I got up. I walked up to the water. The water wasn't too cold. I dove in. The water was clear. I could see the fish and the bottom. While I was looking at the bottom of the sea, I saw something. It seemed like the toe of a foot, but it also seemed real. I couldn't believe it! I dove in a second time. The foot seemed hard, like metal. I got out of the water shouting with joy. I discovered something important!

1. Traduci le seguenti frasi in inglese. Sottolinea tutti i verbi. (Translate the following sentences from Italian to English. Underline all of the verbs.)

   1. Mentre Ivano era a scuola, io dipingevo.

      _____

   2. Mentre Lauretta faceva i suoi compiti, Dino è entrato nella camera.

      _____

   3. Quando Pinocchio ha detto una bugia (*lie*), il suo naso è cresciuto.

      _____

   4. Quando tu hai gridato (*screamed*), io mi sono svegliata.

      _____

   5. Mentre Aldo e Carlo sciavano, voi eravate a casa e bevevate il cioccolato caldo.

      _____

2. Decidi se il verbo tra parentesi è all'imperfetto o al passato prossimo. Poi scrivi la forma corretta del verbo. (Decide whether the verb in parentheses is in the imperfect or *passato prossimo*. Then write the correct form of the verb. Note: Pay attention to verbs that might need to take *essere* or *avere* as their auxiliary!)

   Cenerentola 1. _____ (essere) una povera ragazza. Un giorno, 2. _____ (ricevere) un invito a un ballo. Cenerentola 3. _____ (volere) tanto andare al ballo ma le sue sorellastre (*stepsisters*) le 4. _____ (dire) di no. Gli animali 5. _____ (fare) un abito per lei. La zucca 6. _____ (diventare) una carrozza e i topi 7. _____ (diventare) cavalli. 8. _____ (essere) quasi mezzanotte quando lei 9. _____ (arrivare) al ballo. Il principe 10. _____ (essere) molto bello!

3. Scrivi la forma corretta del verbo all'imperfetto. (Write the correct form of the verb given in the *imperfetto*.)

   1. dire, lui   _____

   2. mangiare, io   _____

   3. scrivere, lei   _____

4. essere, noi _____

5. avere, voi _____

6. fare, loro _____

7. finire, tu _____

8. andare, noi _____

9. rilassare, loro _____

10. giocare, tu _____

4. Completa la tabella con le forme corrette dei verbi. (Complete the chart with the correct forms of the verbs.)

abitare	perdere	salire	capire
1.	perdevo	7.	capivo
abitavi	4.	salivi	10.
2.	5.	saliva	capiva
3.	perdevamo	salivamo	11.
abitavate	6.	8.	capivate
abitavano	perdevano	9.	12.

5. *Esercizio di scrittura: Mentre io...tu...*

Write to your Italian pen pal talking about things that you might have been doing at the same time yesterday. They might be quite different due to the time difference. You can mix and match the *imperfetto* and *passato prossimo*, but make sure that they make sense!

_____

_____

_____

_____

_____

_____

_____

_____

_____

_____

1.

1. While Ivano was at school, I was painting.
    era, dipingevo
2. While Lauretta was doing her homework, Dino entered the room.
    faceva, è entrato
3. When Pinocchio told a lie, his nose grew.
    ha detto, è cresciuto
4. When you screamed, I woke up.
    hai gridato, mi sono svegliata
5. While Aldo and Carlo were skiing, you [pl.] were staying at home and drinking hot chocolate.
    sciavano, stavate, bevevate

2.

1. era
2. ha ricevuto
3. voleva
4. hanno detto
5. hanno fatto
6. è diventata
7. sono diventati
8. Era
9. è arrivata
10. era

3.

1. diceva
2. mangiavo
3. scriveva
4. eravamo
5. avevate
6. facevano
7. finivi
8. andavamo
9. rilassavano
10. giocavi

4.

1. abitavo
2. abitava
3. abitavamo
4. perdevi
5. perdeva
6. perdevate
7. salivo
8. salivate
9. salivano
10. capivi
11. capivamo
12. capivano

5. Answers will vary. Example:

Mentre tu facevi colazione, io dormivo. Quando io mi sono svegliata, tu eri al lavoro.

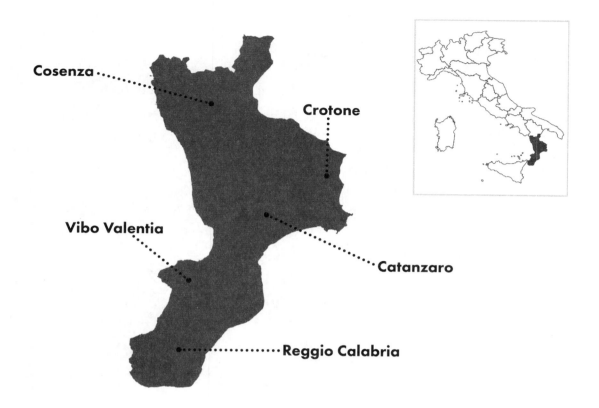

Cosenza

Crotone

Vibo Valentia

Catanzaro

Reggio Calabria

THE IMPERSONAL VOICE / LIGURIA II

Conosci già la Liguria? Forse! La Liguria è una regione molto bella nella parte nordovest dell'Italia, conosciuta da tanti turisti. Sembra una striscia lunga sulla costa. Confina con il paese della Francia (ad ovest), e con le regioni del Piemonte (a nord) e quelle dell'Emilia-Romagna e la Toscana (ad est). Il capoluogo della Liguria è Genova, una città situata tra il mare e le colline. È una città molto importante per la sua storia, per le figure storiche e per la sua funzione di un porto sul mare Mediterraneo. Sai chi è Cristoforo Colombo, per esempio? Certo! Lui è nato a Genova nel 1451. Sai che la parola *jeans* viene dal nome della città di Genova? Forse sì o forse no!

La parte del mare Mediterraneo che è vicina alla costa si chiama Mar Ligure. Altre città importanti sono Savona, Rapallo, Sestri Levante e La Spezia. La Liguria è una regione multicolore per l'abbondanza di fiori e piante che possono crescere in questo clima. Devi assolutamente andare a vedere il Parco Nazionale delle Cinque Terre, che sono cinque paesi pittoreschi—Riomaggiore, Manarola, Corniglia, Vernazza e Monterosso—dove il paesaggio naturale è davvero bellissimo da vedere, con tanti terrazzi e viti sui muri. Nella Liguria, crescono l'olivo, gli agrumi e le nocciole. Voglio spesso mangiare il pesto alla Genovese, una specialità ligure!

La Liguria è anche nota per i suoi spettacoli teatrali e musicali. Conosci San Remo? Il festival della canzone italiana si svolge ogni anno a San Remo, dove tanti musicisti, quelli famosi e soprattutto quelli nuovi, esibiscono i loro talenti. Sai che ci sono tantissimi teatri a Genova, più che in ogni altra città italiana? È un fatto interessante!

••••▶ Are you already familiar with Liguria? Perhaps! Liguria is a very beautiful region in the northwestern part of Italy, known by many tourists. It looks like a long stripe on the shore. It borders with France (to the west) and with the regions of Piedmont (to the north) and those of Emilia-Romagna and Tuscany (to the east). The capital of Liguria is Genoa, a city that is situated between the ocean and the hills. It is very important for its history and its historical figures, and for its function as a port on the Mediterranean. Do you know who Christopher Columbus is, for example? Of course! He was born in Genoa in 1451. Do you know that the word *jeans* comes from the city name of Genova? Perhaps, or maybe not!

The part of the Mediterranean Sea that is close to the coast is called the Ligurian Sea. Other important cities are Savona, Rapallo, Sestri Levante, and La Spezia. Liguria is a multicolored region with its abundance of flowers and plants that can grow in this climate. You absolutely have to go and see the National Park of the Cinque Terre, which is five picturesque towns—Riomaggiore, Manarola, Corniglia, Vernazza and Monterosso—where the natural landscape is truly very beautiful to see, with many terraces and vines on the walls. In Liguria, olives, citrus, and nuts grow. I often want to eat Genoese pesto, a Ligurian specialty!

Liguria is also known for its theatrical and musical performances. Do you know San Remo? The festival of Italian music takes place every year at San Remo, where many musicians, those who are famous and most of all those who are new, exhibit their talent. Do you know that there are so many theaters in Genoa, more than in any other Italian city? It's an interesting fact!

la striscia	stripe	**la collina**	hill
la funzione	use, function	**la figura storica**	historical figure
l'abbondanza	abundance	**la pianta**	plant
il paesaggio	landscape	**la terrazza**	terrace
il muro*	wall	**l'olivo**	olive tree
l'agrume	citrus tree	**la nocciola**	hazelnut
il festival	festival	**il talento**	talent
il musicista	musician	**il movimento**	movement
l'acciuga	anchovy	**l'epoca**	era, age
situato/a	situated	**multicolore**	multicolored
pittoresco/a	picturesque	**noto/a**	noted
teatrale	theatrical	**musicale**	musical
verace	true, genuine	**genovese**	from Genoa
distante	distant	**entrambi**	both
soprattutto	above all	**giusto**	right
d'accordo	agreed	**lungo**	along
altrimenti	otherwise	**presto**	soon
dovere	to need to, must	**potere**	to be able to, can
volere	to want to	**crescere**	to grow
esibire	to exhibit	**svolgersi**	to take place
camminare	to walk	**addormentarsi**	to fall asleep

* *Muro* is a tricky word because it can take two different plurals and mean two different things: *Il muro/I muri* refers to the walls within a house or building, while *il muro/le mura* refers to the walls of a city.

RIPASSO GENERALE / GENERAL REVIEW

A. **Review: Modal Verbs** (*dovere, potere, volere*)

You may remember these three verbs—often called modal verbs—from lesson 9, which is also the last time you studied the region of Liguria. Let's review their present tense conjugations:

dovere	potere	volere
devo	posso	voglio
devi	puoi	vuoi
deve	può	vuole
dobbiamo	possiamo	vogliamo
dovete	potete	volete
devono	possono	vogliono

You'll also remember that these verbs typically, but not always, precede another verb in the infinitive. It's right there in their definitions in English: *to want **to**, to need **to**, to be able **to**.* However, *volere* and *dovere* can also be followed by nouns when they mean *to want* _____ and *to owe* _____, respectively.

Modal Verbs in Past Tenses

Since you've learned two past tenses (the *passato prossimo* and the *imperfetto*), you can now learn how to use modal verbs in these tenses. It's a little tricky at first, since there are subtle differences in meaning between them, but with a little practice, it will become easier.

When modal verbs are used in the *passato prossimo*, they refer to completed, fulfilled actions in the past. In the imperfect, there is an implication that these actions were not fulfilled. They are things that you should have done, wanted to do, or could have done, but you didn't do these things. Maybe you should have cleaned your room, but you didn't because you had to study instead. Maybe you could have gone skiing, but you had to work, so you didn't end up going. The first parts of these sentences—and remember, they'll have a negative outcome—are going to be in the *imperfetto* and the second part in the *passato prossimo*:

> ***Dovevo*** *pulire la mia camera, ma non l'ho fatto perché **ho dovuto** studiare invece.*
>
> ***Potevo*** *andare a sciare, ma **ho dovuto lavorare**, allora non ci sono andata.*

You can see in these sentences which actions were completed and which were not. What were you supposed to do this past week? What did you do instead? Practice using both past tenses with the three modal verbs to master them!

Il capoluogo della Liguria è Genova, una città situata tra il mare e le colline. È una città molto importante per la sua storia, per le figure storiche e per la sua funzione di un porto sul mare Mediterraneo. Sai chi è Cristoforo Colombo, per esempio? Certo! Lui è nato a Genova nel 1451. All'epoca di Cristoforo Colombo non si andava in aereo, ma si andava in barca e in nave come lui. Si andava a piedi e a cavallo, ma non si andava in macchina, in bici o in motocicletta!

▶ Liguria's capital is Genoa, a city located between the sea and the hills. It is a very important city for its history, for its historical figures, and for its role as a port on the Mediterranean Sea. Do you know who Christopher Columbus is, for example? Of course! He was born in Genoa in 1451. In the days of Christopher Columbus, people didn't travel by airplane, but they went by boat or ship like he did. People walked and rode horses, but they didn't go in cars, on bikes, or on motorcycles!

A. Review: *Conoscere* and *sapere*

You also met the verbs *conoscere* and *sapere* in lesson 9. To refresh your memory, these two verbs both mean "to know" but have slightly different connotations: *Conoscere* means "to be familiar with," and *sapere* means "to know (as a fact)." *Conoscere* is generally used with people, places, and things with which you can be familiar (such as a language or a famous person), while *sapere* goes with skills and action verbs. Let's review their conjugations:

conoscere	sapere
conosco	so
conosci	sai
conosce	sa
conosciamo	sappiamo
conoscete	sapete
conoscono	sanno

Note the irregularities in these verbs, especially in their pronunciation.

When put into a sentence, *conoscere* is followed by direct objects and *sapere* is followed by direct objects, verbs, and interrogative pronouns, such as *chi* and *che*. Do you know how to snowboard (*sapere*)? Are you familiar with Lady Gaga (*conoscere*)? Do you know who is the president of Italy (*sapere*)? The differences between these two verbs are important!

Conoscere and *sapere* in Past Tenses

Using these two verbs in the past tenses isn't as difficult as using the modal verbs, but it's still something to practice and memorize. In the *passato prossimo, conoscere* means "to have met" and *sapere* means "to have found out"/"to have heard." In the *imperfetto*, both verbs mean "to have (always) known." So, if you just met Lady Gaga yesterday, which one would you use? You'd use *conoscere* ("*Ho conosciuto Lady Gaga ieri*"). If you just found out that her real name is Stefani Germanotta, which one would you use? You'd use *sapere* ("*Ho saputo che il suo vero nome non è Lady Gaga!*").

B. **The Impersonal Voice (*si impersonale*)**

The *si impersonale* is a very useful construction in Italian. It is commonly used in the same way that in English we say "one" or "we" or "you"—even if we don't mean "you" personally. It's used to give a rough idea of what people generally do in a certain situation: for example, "If you go to Rome, you should see the Colosseum" (or "If one goes to Rome, one should see the Colosseum"). When asking how to say something in Italian, you would say, "*Come **si dice** _____?*" ("How does **one**/ How do **you** say _____?"), and someone would respond, "***Si dice** _____,*" telling you the Italian word.

In Italian, this is formed by using the pronoun *si* and the present tense, third person singular or plural form of the verb. You'd use the singular form with singular objects (or if there is no object at all) and the plural form with plural objects. So, you would say, "*Se **si va** a Roma, **si deve** vedere il Colosseo*" or "***Si devono** mangiare gli spaghetti.*" It all depends on what comes after the verb that is in the *si impersonale*.

There are a few special rules for using this construction. First, when using it with a reflexive verb (which already has the pronoun *si* with it), you don't say "*si si alza*" ("one gets up") but rather "***ci si alza.***" This is to avoid repetition.

When using the construction with modal verbs (the ones listed previously in this lesson), the modal verb is the one that changes in regard to singular or plural objects. So, you would say, "***Si può** vedere il Colosseo*" but "***Si possono** vedere tanti musei.*"

Renzo Piano è un architetto genovese famoso. È nato a Genova nel settembre 1947. Ha disegnato tantissimi edifici famosi in tutto il mondo. Si sa che sono le sue creazioni. A Genova ha dovuto ridisegnare il porto principale, che si chiama il Porto Antico, perché era stato distrutto dalla guerra. Ha voluto creare una struttura che si chiama Bigo che assomiglia una gru che si usa al porto con delle braccia lunghe. Si può salire il Bigo per vedere il panorama del porto! Lui ha potuto creare anche uno spazio dove si possono tenere concerti e spettacoli teatrali e un nuovo acquario che si chiama La Bolla. Lui voleva anche ricostruire il viadotto Morandi sul Polcevera che è crollato nel 2018. Non doveva farlo, ma voleva ricostruirlo gratis.

▶ Renzo Piano is a famous Genoese architect. He was born in Genoa in September 1947. He designed many famous buildings all over the world. It is known that they are his creations. He redesigned the main port at Genova, which is called the Porto Antico, because it had been destroyed by the war. He wanted to create a structure that is called Bigo, which resembles a crane with long arms used at a port. You can go up the Bigo to see the panorama of the port! He was able to create a space where concerts and theatrical shows can be held, and a new aquarium that is called La Bolla ("The Bubble"). He also wanted to rebuild the Morandi viaduct on the Polcevera, which collapsed in 2018. He didn't have to do it, but he wanted to rebuild it for free.

ATTIVITÀ / ACTIVITIES

1. Traduci le seguenti frasi in inglese. Sottolinea tutti i verbi modali. (Translate the following sentences from Italian into English. Underline all of the modal verbs.)

1. Dovevo andare a Genova questo fine settimana ma non ho potuto perché non avevo i soldi.

   _____

2. Volevo vedere il nuovo film di *Star Wars* ma ho dovuto lavorare.

   _____

3. Volevo visitare il museo archeologico ma ho dovuto stare a casa invece.

   _____

4. Potevo andare in montagna con i miei amici ma non ho voluto.

   _____

5. Dovevo studiare per l'esame d'italiano ma ho dovuto anche dormire.

_____

2. Traduci le seguenti frasi in italiano. (Translate the following sentences from English into Italian.)

1. I wanted to go to a concert this weekend, but I couldn't because I had to work.

_____

2. I found out yesterday that you have a cat.

_____

3. Do you [pl.] know how to swim?

_____

4. I should have ordered a coffee, but I wanted tea.

_____

5. Did he meet your [male] cousin?

_____

3. Sapere o conoscere? Scegli l'opzione giusta e coniuga il verbo. (*Sapere* or *conoscere*? Choose the correct option and conjugate the verb.)

1. We know who the secretary is. _____ chi è il segretario.

2. We know the secretary. _____ il segretario.

3. They found out the truth. _____ la verità.

4. You [sing.] met me a year ago. Tu mi _____ un anno fa.

5. Are you familiar with Italian? _____ l'italiano?

4. Riempi gli spazi vuoti nella tabella per tutti i tre verbi modali. (Fill in the blank spots in the table for all three modal verbs.)

volere	dovere	potere
voglio	4.	7.
1.	devi	puoi
vuole	deve	8.
2.	5.	possiamo
volete	6.	9.
3.	devono	possono

5. Scrivi la forma corretta del si impersonale. (Write the correct form of the *si impersonale*.)

1. In Italia _____ (vivere) bene!

2. Quando _____ (sentirsi) male, _____ (andare) dal dottore.

3. A scuola _____ (imparare) molto.

4. A Genova _____ (mangiare) gli spaghetti al pesto.

5. In Liguria _____ (potere visitare) le Cinque Terre.

6. *Esercizio di scrittura: Cosa si fa? Cosa non si fa?*

Tell your Italian pen pal about things that one typically does in your hometown and things that you absolutely do not do. Use the *si impersonale* to express these things.

_____

_____

_____

_____

_____

ANSWER KEY

1.

1. I should have gone to Genoa this weekend, but I couldn't because I had no money.
   Dovevo, ho potuto
2. I wanted to see the new Star Wars film, but I had to work.
   Volevo, ho dovuto
3. I wanted to visit the archaeological museum, but I had to stay at home instead.
   Volevo, ho dovuto
4. I could have gone to the mountains with my friends, but I didn't want to.
   Potevo, ho voluto
5. I should have studied for my Italian test, but I also had to sleep.
   Dovevo, ho dovuto

2.

1. Volevo andare a un concerto questo fine settimana ma non ho potuto perché ho dovuto lavorare.
2. Ho saputo ieri che tu hai un gatto.

3. Sapete nuotare?
4. Dovevo ordinare un caffè, ma ho voluto un tè.
5. Ha conosciuto tuo cugino?

3.

1. Sappiamo
2. Conosciamo
3. Hanno saputo
4. hai conosciuto
5. Conosci

4.

1. vuoi
2. vogliamo
3. vogliono
4. devo
5. dobbiamo
6. dovete
7. posso
8. può
9. potete

5.

1. si vive
2. ci si sente, si va
3. si impara
4. si mangiano
5. si possono visitare

6. Answers will vary. Example:

A Filadelfia si mangiano i cheesesteak. Non si tifa per (*root for*) le squadre di Pittsburgh!

THE IMPERATIVE WITH PRONOUNS / CAMPANIA II

"Vedi Napoli e poi muori!" Forse conosci questa frase? Napoli è una bella città sulla baia e la sua bellezza è famosa e conosciuta al mondo. È il capoluogo della regione della Campania, una regione meridionale dell'Italia. La Campania è la regione più popolata del Sud. Confina con le regioni del Lazio (a nordovest), del Molise (a nord) e la Puglia e la Basilicata (ad est). Ad ovest c'è il mar Tirreno. La Campania ha quattro golfi sulle sue coste.

La Campania è una regione nota per la sua storia che risale ai tempi prima dei greci e dei romani. Ci sono sei siti che fanno parte del Patrimonio dell'Umanità dell'UNESCO in questa regione. Includono il centro storico di Napoli, gli Scavi di Pompei ed Ercolano e la Costiera Amalfitana. La Campania è tra le tre regioni più visitate d'Italia, e tra quelle zone più visitate d'Europa. È una regione con tante montagne e colline ed anche con quattro vulcani come Vesuvio! Ci sono anche delle isole molto belle, come Capri, Ischia e Procida.

Napoli è famosa per il panorama della baia, per le sue chiese barocche, per la pizza margherita, per i suoi attori e i suoi cantanti. Conosci Totò, il grande attore comico? O Enrico Caruso, il tenore napoletano? Ci sono anche grandi filosofi che sono nati o vissuti a Napoli: Giambattista Vico e Benedetto Croce ne sono degli ottimi esempi.

C'è tanto da dire su Napoli e sulla regione della Campania. Forse hai parenti che vengono da questa zona!

▶ "See Naples and then die!" Perhaps you know this phrase? Naples is a beautiful city on the bay and its beauty is famous and known throughout the world. It is the capital of the Campania region, a southern region in Italy. Campania is the most populated region of the South. It borders with the regions of Lazio (to the northwest), Molise (to the north), and Puglia and Basilicata (to the east). To the west is also the Tyrrhenian Sea. Campania has four gulfs on its coasts.

Campania is a region known for its history that hearkens back to the times before the Greeks and the Romans. There are six sites that are part of UNESCO's Patrimony of Humanity in this region. They include the historic center of Naples, the sites of Pompei and Ercolano, and the Amalfi Coast. Campania is among the most visited regions in Italy, and one of the most visited in all of Europe! It's a region with many mountains and hills, and even four volcanos, such as Vesuvius! There are also many beautiful islands, such as Capri, Ischia, and Procida.

Naples is also famous for the panorama of the bay, for its baroque churches, for *pizza margherita*, for its actors and its singers. Are you familiar with Totò, the great comic actor? Or with Enrico Caruso, the Neapolitan tenor? There are also many great philosophers who were born or who lived in Naples: Giambattista Vico and Benedetto Croce are some excellent examples of them.

There is much to say about Naples and the Campania region. Perhaps you have relatives who come from this area!

VOCABOLARIO NUOVO E UTILE / NEW AND USEFUL VOCABULARY

il meridione	the south	il settentrione	the north
la foto(grafia)	photo(graph)	il tempio	temple
il golfo	gulf	il centro storico	historical center
la chiesa	church	la montagna	mountain
la collina	hill	il vulcano	volcano
il panorama	panorama	i parenti	relatives
vietato/a	prohibited	volentieri	willingly
ripieno/a	filled	diverso/a	different
realizzare	to actualize	visitare	to visit
nuotare	to swim	raggiungere	to reach
salire	to climb	sembrare	to seem
Dimmelo!	Tell it to me!	Smettila!	Stop it!
Vattene!	Get out of here!	Vacci!	Go there!

RIPASSO GENERALE / GENERAL REVIEW

A. Review: The *imperativo*

The imperative, as you learned in lesson 10, is a tense that commands someone to do something. In this lesson, you'll review the tenses and then learn how to use imperatives with pronouns, which you learned in lesson 11.

As you may remember, the imperative has both informal and formal conjugations. Let's review the informal first:

AFFERMATIVO	parlare	mettere	aprire	capire
tu	parla	metti	apri	capisci
noi	parliamo	mettiamo	apriamo	capiamo
voi	parlate	mettete	aprite	capite

NEGATIVO	parlare	mettere	aprire	capire
tu	non parlare	non mettere	non aprire	non capire
noi	non parliamo	non mettiamo	non apriamo	non capiamo
voi	non parlate	non mettete	non aprite	non capite

The informal imperative, with the exception of the *tu* form of -*are* verbs, looks exactly the same as regular conjugations. In the negative, it is the same, also with the exception of the *tu* form of -*are* verbs. If you remember that those two forms are irregular, you're pretty much set.

There are also quite a few irregular verbs in the informal imperative:

	avere	essere	andare	dare	fare	stare	dire
tu	abbi	sii	va'/vai	da'/dai	fa'/fai	sta'/stai	di'
noi	abbiamo	siamo	andiamo	diamo	facciamo	stiamo	diamo
voi	abbiate	siate	andate	date	fate	state	dite

And now let's look at the formal imperative:

AFFERMATIVO	parlare	mettere	aprire	capire
Lei	parli	metta	apra	capisca
Loro	parlino	mettano	aprano	capiscano

NEGATIVO	parlare	mettere	aprire	capire
Lei	non parli	non metta	non apra	non capsica
Loro	non parlino	non mettano	non aprano	non capiscano

The formal imperative has the opposite forms of the *tu* forms in the informal imperative: Instead of -*a*, -*i*, -*i*, -*isci*, they're -*i*, -*a*, -*a*, -*isca*. If you put a *non* in front of these forms, you have the negative.

Here are some irregular verbs in the formal imperative:

	avere	essere	bere	venire	uscire
Lei	abbia	sia	beva	venga	esca
Loro	abbiano	siano	bevano	vengano	escano

	andare	dare	fare	stare	dire
Lei	vada	dia	faccia	stia	dica
Loro	vadano	diano	facciano	stiano	dicano

B. Double Pronouns

Double pronouns are a bit difficult in Italian, but as always, they become easier with practice. These pronouns are the result of combining direct and indirect object pronouns (listed in the chart below). The indirect object pronoun comes first, followed by the direct object pronoun. See if you can notice any patterns and changes that you'll have to make and observe:

+	lo	la	li	le	ne
mi	me lo	me la	me li	me le	me ne
ti	te lo	te la	te li	te le	te ne
gli/le/Le	glielo	gliela	glieli	gliele	gliene
ci	ce lo	ce la	ce li	ce le	ce ne
vi	ve lo	ve la	ve li	ve le	ve ne
gli/...loro	glielo/ lo...loro	gliela/ la...loro	glieli/ li...loro	gliele/ le...loro	gliene/ ne...loro

As you can see, there are a lot of changes to the indirect object pronouns. *Mi, ti, ci,* and *vi* change to *me, te, ce,* and *ve,* and there is an extra *e* added between double pronouns that start with *gli* (all third person pronouns). In the third person plural, you can choose to sandwich the verb with the indirect pronoun and *loro,* or you can use the same pronoun as the third person singular.

C. Imperative with Single and Double Pronouns

Now let's review just single direct and indirect object pronouns, since you'll be working with them together with the imperative:

Direct	Indirect
mi	mi
ti	ti
lo/la/La	gli/le/Le
ci	ci
vi	vi
li/le/Loro	gli/...loro/...Loro

For the informal imperative, you can tack these pronouns right on the end of the word (you have to remove the final *e* in the negative *tu* form). So if you want to tell someone to eat (*mangia*) an apple (*una mela*), you would say, "*Mangiala!*" If you want to instruct multiple people to tell (*dire*) the truth (*la verità*), you would say, "*Ditela!*" Some of the irregular commands (the ones that end in apostrophes in the chart on the previous page) necessitate a doubling of the first letter of the pronoun, so you'll see commands like *Dimmi!* (Tell me!) or *Fallo!* (Do it!).

For the formal imperative, pronouns do not attach to the end of the word; rather, they're put in front of it. So instead of *Dimmi!*, you'd see *Mi dica!*

With double pronouns, the same rules follow for attaching them (or not attaching them). You can stick a double pronoun onto the end of an informal imperative, making it all one word, and you can put a double pronoun in front of a formal imperative. Which type of imperative is *Dammelo!* and which is *Me lo dia!*? If you guessed informal and formal, respectively, you're correct!

You'll practice these more in the Activities.

ATTIVITÀ / ACTIVITIES

1. Traduci le seguenti frasi in inglese. (Translate the following sentences from Italian into English.)

    1. Da' una pizza a Daniele, per favore.

       _____

    2. Di' la verità a me.

       _____

    3. Regalate un osso al cane.

       _____

    4. Cantate le canzoni alle ragazze.

       _____

    5. Leggi i libri a noi.

       _____

2. Scrivi l'imperativo con un pronome doppio. (Write the imperative with a double pronoun.)

    1. Da' una pizza a Daniele, per favore.

       _____

    2. Di' la verità a me.

       _____

3. Regalate un osso al cane.

   _____

4. Cantate le canzoni alle ragazze.

   _____

5. Leggi i libri a noi.

   _____

3. Il tuo amico è molto pigro. Digli cosa fare! (Your friend is very lazy. Tell him what to do!)

   1. Wake up! (alzarsi)

      _____

   2. Eat breakfast! (fare colazione)

      _____

   3. Go to the doctor! (andare dal dottore)

      _____

   4. Call your mother! (telefonare alla mamma)

      _____

   5. Put your phone on the table! (mettere il cellulare sul tavolo)

      _____

4. Scrivi il pronome doppio giusto nello spazio. (Write the correct double pronoun in the blank space.)

   1. Devo dare un regalo a mia madre, ma non voglio dar_____.

   2. Posso regalare una sciarpa a lei, ma non ho i soldi per regalar_____.

   3. Voglio fare una domanda al professore, ma non posso far_____.

   4. Voglio comprare i biglietti ai miei amici, ma non posso comprar_____.

   5. Devo leggere un libro a voi, ma non voglio legger_____.

5. *Esercizio di scrittura: Dammelo!*

You are still talking to your lazy friend from Activity 3. Give him (or her) more commands that are based on healthy decisions. Try to use the double pronouns after each sentence, when possible.

_____

_____

_____

_____

_____

ANSWER KEY

1.

1. Give a pizza to Daniele, please.
2. Tell the truth to me.
3. Give (Gift) a bone to the dog.
4. [You pl.] Sing the songs to the girls.
5. Read the books to us.

2.

1. Dagliela!
2. Dimmela!
3. Regalaglielo!
4. Cantategliele!
5. Leggiceli!

3.

1. Alzati!
2. Fai (Fa') colazione!
3. Vai (Va') dal dottore!
4. Telefona alla mamma!
5. Metti il cellulare sul tavolo!

4.

1. darglielo
2. regalargliela
3. fargliela
4. comprarglieli
5. leggervelo

5. Answers will vary. Example:

Mi devi pagare l'affitto (*rent*). Pagamelo! È molto importante mangiare le verdure (*vegetables*). Mangiale ogni giorno!

THE FUTURE TENSE / LAZIO II

Oggi parleremo del Lazio. Il Lazio è una regione nella parte centro-ovest dell'Italia. Si trova al confine con la Toscana e l'Umbria (al nord), l'Abruzzo e il Molise (all'est), e la Campania (al sud). Il Mar Tirreno bagna la costa occidentale della regione. Il Lazio contiene la capitale della nazione: Roma! Ci sono quattro province: Frosinone, Latina, Rieti e Viterbo. Segue direttamente la Lombardia in due cose: ha una popolazione grande e un'economia molto forte. C'è tanta storia antica, particolarmente romana, in questa regione. Ci sono tante cose da fare e da vedere per i turisti. La Città del Vaticano si trova in questa regione, anche se non fa parte della nazione italiana.

Noi chiamiamo la regione Lazio ma gli antichi lo chiamavano Latium. Alcuni credono che questo nome venga dal *latus* in latino, che significa "largo." Questa regione è molto piana. Il Latium era la regione del re Latinus, il capo dei latini, i popoli antichi che precedevano i romani.

Quando noi pensiamo a Lazio e a Roma forse pensiamo ai film di Federico Fellini, come *La dolce vita*. Questo film parla della vita mondana a Roma e ci porta al mare di Ostia. O forse, quando pensiamo a Roma pensiamo ai film di Nanni Moretti, come *Caro diario*, quando lui va in motorino per alcuni quartieri di Roma. Oppure pensiamo al film di Paolo Sorrentino, *La grande bellezza*, che fa vedere la Roma di Fellini sotto una luce contemporanea.

A Roma non mancano le cose da vedere e da visitare. A Roma si trovano il Campidoglio, il Colosseo, la Basilica di San Pietro alla Città del Vaticano, il Castel Sant'Angelo, il Pantheon e la Fontana Trevi. Il fiume del Tevere percorre Roma. È la città eterna e la capitale del mondo.

Today we will speak about Lazio. Lazio is a region in the central-western part of Italy. It borders with Tuscany and Umbria (to the north), Abruzzo and Molise (to the east), and Campania (to the south). The Tyrrhenian Sea washes its western shore. Lazio contains the nation's capital: Rome! There are four provinces: Frosinone, Latina, Rieti, and Viterbo. It directly follows Lombardy in two things: It has a large population and a very strong economy. There is a lot of ancient history, particularly Roman history, in this region. There are many things for tourists to do and to see. Vatican City is located in this region, even if it is not part of the Italian nation.

We call the region Lazio, but the ancients called it Latium. Some believe that this name comes from *latus* in Latin, which means "wide." This region is very flat. Latium was the region of King Latinus, the leader of the Latins, the ancient peoples who preceded the Romans.

When we think about Lazio and Rome, maybe we think about Federico Fellini's films, such as *La dolce vita* (*The Sweet Life*). This film talks about the social life of Rome, and it brings us to the sea at Ostia. Or perhaps when we think about Rome, we think about Nanni Moretti's films, such as *Dear Diary*, when he goes on his moped through some neighborhoods in Rome. Or we think about the film by Paolo Sorrentino, *The Great Beauty*, which shows us Fellini's Rome in a contemporary light.

Things to do and to see are not missing in Rome. The Campidoglio, the Colosseum, St. Peter's Basilica in Vatican City, the Castel Sant'Angelo, the Pantheon, and the Trevi Fountain are located in Rome. The Tiber River runs through Rome. It is the eternal city and the capital of the world.

VOCABOLARIO NUOVO E UTILE / NEW AND USEFUL VOCABULARY

l'antico	ancient (person)	il popolo	populace
il motorino	scooter	il quartiere	neighborhood
la luce	light	lo schermo	screen
la guerra	war	l'aldilà	the afterlife
il pugno	fist	il fango	mud
il primogenitore	first father	il discendente	descendant
largo/a	wide	piano/a	flat
mondano/a	mundane	recente	recent
contemporaneo/a	contemporary	eterno/a	eternal
appena	as soon as	quando	when
percorrere	to go around	mancare	to be missing, to be lacking
servire	to need, to serve	convenire	to be fitting
bastare	to be sufficient	partire	to depart, to leave
vincere	to win	sposarsi	to get married

RIPASSO GENERALE (GENERAL REVIEW)

A. *Il futuro*

The future tense, like the imperfect tense, is quite easy to conjugate due to its conformity. Sure, there are more irregular stems you'll have to memorize, but for the most part, the future is easy! Let's look at the conjugations:

parlare	mettere	dormire	finire
parlerò	metterò	dormirò	finirò
parlerai	metterai	dormirai	finirai
parlerà	metterà	dormirà	finirà
parleremo	metteremo	dormiremo	finiremo
parlerete	metterete	dormirete	finirete
parleranno	metteranno	dormiranno	finiranno

Notice that the only thing you have to change is the stem of -*are* verbs (changing the *a* to an *e* and then adding the appropriate endings). Since the endings begin with *e* and *i*, you have to watch out for -*are* verbs that end in -*care* and -*gare* (such as *giocare* and *pagare*); they need to add an *h* before the ending in order to keep the hard *C* and *G* sounds. On the other hand, verbs that end in -*ciare* and -*giare* (such as *cominciare* and *mangiare*) need to drop the *i* before taking the future tense endings. Let's see how that looks:

giocare	pagare	cominciare	mangiare
giocherò	pagherò	comincerò	mangerò
giocherai	pagherai	comincerai	mangerai
giocherà	pagherà	comincerà	mangerà
giocheremo	pagheremo	cominceremo	mangeremo
giocherete	pagherete	comincerete	mangerete
giocheranno	pagheranno	cominceranno	mangeranno

And finally, here are some of the most common irregular stems for the future tense:

Verb	Future Stem
andare	andr-
avere	avr-
bere	berr-
dare	dar-
dovere	dovr-
essere	sar-
fare	far-
potere	potr-
rimanere	rimarr-
sapere	sapr-
stare	star-
tenere	terr-
vedere	vedr-
venire	verr-
vivere	vivr-
volere	vorr-

The future tense is used exactly as the future tense is used in English: to talk about actions that will occur in the future. However, there are other usages that aren't typically used in English; you'll see these in the following sections.

B. Future of Possibility

In Italian, you can also use the future tense to make a guess or conjecture about something. If someone asks you what time it is and you don't know, you could respond with the verb in the future tense (*"Non lo so, saranno le nove"*) to indicate that you are guessing. If someone is knocking at the door, you could say, *"Chi sarà a quest'ora?"* ("Whoever **will** that **be** at this hour?"). It sounds quaint in English but perfectly normal in Italian.

Do you remember the idiomatic expressions with *avere* that you met in lesson 5? It was a long time ago! Let's review them here:

Italian Phrase	English Translation
avere fame	to be hungry
avere sete	to be thirsty
avere caldo	to feel hot
avere freddo	to feel cold
avere ragione	to be correct
avere torto	to be incorrect
avere...anni	to be...years old
avere paura (di)	to be afraid (of)
avere bisogno (di)	to have need (of)
avere voglia (di)	to have want (of)
avere fretta	to be in a rush
avere sonno	to be sleepy

These expressions are called idiomatic because they don't match up perfectly to English translations of them. How can you use them? Maybe you could talk about your friend who hasn't yet had lunch today: *Sicuramente **avrà** fame! **Avrà** bisogno di mangiare!*

C. *Futuro anteriore*

The *futuro anteriore*—or the future perfect—is a compound tense much like the *passato prossimo*: It has an auxiliary verb (either *essere* or *avere*) and then a past participle (typically ending in -*ato*, -*uto*, or -*ito*). (You can review irregular past participles in lesson 18.)

This tense is used to talk about an action that will have already taken place in the future by a certain time. For example, by the time you're finished reading this lesson, you *will have learned* (*avrai imparato*) the *futuro anteriore*. And you will be tired after you *will have read* (*avrai letto*) all of these rules!

The *futuro anteriore* can also be used to make speculations. Let's look at a few phrases that make use of both the *futuro anteriore* and the idiomatic expressions with *avere*:

1. *Avranno freddo Sylvia e Marcello?* → Ma **avranno portato** *le giacche, no?*

2. *Avranno sonno?* → Ma **avranno bevuto** *dieci caffè, vero?*

3. *Avranno fame?* → Ma **avranno mangiato** *alla festa, no?*

4. *Avranno bisogno di dormire?* **Avranno** *bisogno di mangiare?* → Ma **avranno fatto** *un sonnellino, vero?*

These translate to the following:

1. **Will** Sylvia and Marcello **be** cold? → But they **will have brought** jackets, no?

2. **Will** they **be** sleepy? → But they **will have drunk** ten coffees, right?

3. **Will** they **be** hungry? → But they **will have eaten** at the party, no?

4. **Will** they **need** to sleep? **Will** they **need** to eat? → Well, they **will have taken** a nap, right?

The "will have" translation seems a bit clunky in English, mostly because English speakers tend to use the past conditional ("would have") instead, but it works for now. For practice, keep thinking of ways to express a speculation or conjecture in English.

ATTIVITÀ / ACTIVITIES

1. Traduci le seguenti frasi in inglese. (Translate the following sentences from Italian into English.)

1. Oggi andrò al supermercato con mia madre.

   _____

2. Quest'estate viaggeremo in Sicilia.

   _____

3. Se hai problemi, dovrai parlare con Caterina.

   _____

4. Dove sono i pesci? Forse il gatto li avrà mangiati!

   _____

5. Marcello e Sylvia nuoteranno nella Fontana di Trevi stasera.

   _____

2. Traduci le seguenti frasi in italiano. (Translate the following sentences from English into Italian.)

1. Tomorrow I will call my aunt.

   _____

2. You [pl.] will eat this sandwich.

   _____

3. Next year we will visit Machu Picchu.

   _____

4. Will you drink this coffee?

   _____

5. He will read the book for class.

   _____

3. Abbina la frase alla sinistra a una frase alla destra. (Match the phrase on the left with a phrase on the right.)

1. Lucia ha sonno.	a. Avrà bisogno di mangiare.
2. Gianni ha fame.	b. Avrà bisogno di partire.
3. Lisa ha sete.	c. Avrà bisogno di dormire.
4. Rita ha fretta.	d. Avrà bisogno di portare una giacca.
5. Giuseppe ha freddo.	e. Avrà bisogno di bere acqua.

4. Scrivi la forma giusta del verbo al futuro anteriore. (Write the correct form of the verb in the *futuro anteriore*.)

1. Danilo verrà alla festa quando _____ (finire) tutti i suoi compiti.

2. Dov'è il mio quaderno? Forse il cane l'_____ (mangiare)!

3. Com'è che hai sonno? _____ (dormire) per dieci ore, no?

4. Jessica e Alessandra sono stanche; _____ (ballare) tutta la notte!

5. Noi _____ (visitare) tutti i paesi del mondo quando avremo compiuto 40 anni.

5. *Esercizio di scrittura: Sarà un bellissimo mondo!*

Tell your Italian pen pal about the world you dream about for the future. What will it look like? What will the people do? What type of person will you be? Make some guesses and speculations using the simple future and the *futuro anteriore*.

_____

_____

_____

_____

_____

_____

_____

_____

ANSWER KEY

1.

1. Today I will go to the supermarket with my mother.
2. This summer we will travel to Sicily.
3. If you have problems, you will need to speak with Caterina.
4. Where are the fish? Maybe the cat will have eaten them!
5. Marcello and Sylvia will swim in the Trevi Fountain this evening.

2.

1. Domani chiamerò/telefonerò a mia zia.
2. Voi mangerete questo panino.
3. L'anno prossimo visiteremo Machu Picchu.
4. Berrai questo caffè?
5. Lui leggerà questo libro per classe.

3.

1. c.
2. a.
3. e.
4. b.

5. d.

4.

1. avrà finito
2. avrà mangiato
3. Avrai dormito
4. avranno ballato
5. avremo visitato

5. Answers will vary. Example:

Tra 50 anni il mondo sarà bellissimo. Non ci saranno guerre. Le persone saranno felici. Io avrò dieci gatti...

COMPARATIVES, SUPERLATIVES, AND ARRIVEDERCI! / TUSCANY II

La famosissima regione della Toscana si trova nel centro della penisola. Qual è la regione centrale più famosa: la Toscana o l'Umbria? Ci sono due piccole isole vicino alla costa: l'Elba e l'isola del Giglio. Qual è l'isola più bella, secondo te: l'Elba o il Giglio? Il fiume Arno attraversa le città di Firenze, Siena ed Empoli. Qual è il fiume italiano più famoso: l'Arno o il Tevere?

Tante città come Firenze (il suo capoluogo), Siena, San Gimignano, Lucca, Pisa, Arezzo e l'area del Chianti sono destinazioni turistiche molto popolari. Qual è la citta toscana più visitata dai turisti: Firenze, Siena o Pisa, secondo te? Ti ricordi quante province ha l'Umbria? Ne ha solo due! La Toscana invece ne ha nove. La Toscana ha più province dell'Umbria.

La Toscana produce tanti vini famosi e pregiati. Hai mai bevuto il vino Montepulciano, il Chianti o il Brunello? Ti è piaciuto? Qual è il vino toscano migliore? La regione è molto nota per i salumi e la bistecca. Ci sono delle mucche che vivono nella valle di Chiana che si usano per la bistecca fiorentina. Hai mai mangiato la bistecca fiorentina? Ti è piaciuta? È migliore della bistecca americana? Poi ci sono anche tanti posti e spettacoli per tutta la regione. Hai mai visto la torre che pende a Pisa? Oppure sei mai andato a Piazza del Campo di Siena per vedere la corsa di cavalli che si chiama Palio? Ti è piaciuta?

Firenze è la prima destinazione turistica della regione. Sei mai andato a Firenze? Ti è piaciuta? Tanti autori medievali e rinascimentali di Firenze sono diventati importanti, come le "tre corone" della letteratura italiana: Dante Alighieri, Francesco Petrarca e Giovanni Boccaccio. Chi è il poeta italiano migliore di tutti i tempi? Anche Niccolò Machiavelli è nato a Firenze, ma è morto nella sua città natale. Hai mai letto delle opere di questi autori fiorentini? Ti sono piaciute? Chi è l'autore più importante del Rinascimento?

Firenze è anche importante per la sua arte medievale e rinascimentale. Hai mai visto le opere di Michelangelo o di Botticelli? Ti sono piaciute? Michelangelo Buonarotti era un artista fondamentale del Rinascimento. Hai mai visto i suoi quadri? Ti sono piaciuti? Anche Sandro Botticelli era un artista molto importante. Chi dipingeva meglio: Michelangelo o Botticelli? Ti piace di più Michelangelo o Botticelli?

▶ Find this translation on the next page

The extremely famous region of Tuscany is located in the center of the peninsula. Which is the more famous central region: Tuscany or Umbria? There are two small islands close to the coast: Elba and the Island of Giglio. Which island is more beautiful: Elba or Giglio? The Arno River crosses the cities of Florence, Siena, and Empoli. Which is the more famous Italian river: the Arno or the Tiber?

Many cities, such as Florence (its capital), Siena, San Gimignano, Lucca, Pisa, Arezzo, and the Chianti region, are very popular tourist destinations. Which is the Tuscan city most visited by tourists: Florene, Siena, or Pisa, do you think? Do you remember how many provinces Umbria has? It only has two of them. Tuscany, instead, has nine of them. Tuscany has more provinces than Umbria.

Tuscany produces many famous and valued wines. Have you ever drunk Montepulciano, Chianti, or Brunello wines? Did you like it? Which is the best Tuscan wine? The region is very famous for its cured meats and steak. There are cows that live in the Chiana valley which are used for Florentine steaks. Have you ever eaten a Florentine steak? Did you like it? Is it better than American steak? Then there are also many places and sights throughout the region. Have you ever seen the leaning tower in Pisa? Or have you ever gone to the Piazza del Campo in Siena to see the horse race called the Palio? Did you like it?

Florence is the first tourist destination of the region. Have you ever gone to Florence? Did you like it? Many medieval and Renaissance authors in Florence became important, such as the "three crowns" of Italian literature: Dante Alighieri, Francesco Petrarca, and Giovanni Boccaccio. Who is the best Italian poet of all time? Niccolò Machiavelli was also born in Florence, but he died in his native city. Have you ever read the works of these Florentine authors? Did you like them? Who is the most important Renaissance author?

Florence is also important for its medieval and Renaissance art. Have you ever seen the works by Michelangelo or by Botticelli? Did you like them? Michelangelo Buonarotti was a fundamental artist of the Renaissance. Have you ever seen his paintings? Did you like them? Sandro Botticelli was also an important artist. Who painted better: Michelangelo or Botticelli? Do you like Michelangelo or Botticelli more?

VOCABOLARIO NUOVO / NEW VOCABULARY

il fiume	river	**l'isola**	island
il quadro	painting	**la corsa**	race
l'autore	author	**la crema solare**	sunblock
la porzione	portion, amount	**la corona**	crown
scotto/a	sunburnt	**centrale**	central
visitato/a	visited	**migliore**	better, best [adj.]
peggiore	worse, worst [adj.]	**l'amato/a**	beloved
piacere	to please	**dispiacere**	to displease
mancare	to be missing, to be lacking	**bastare**	to suffice
servire	to serve	**convenire**	to be convenient
secondo	according to	**purtroppo**	unfortunately
così...come	as...as	**tanto...quanto**	as...as
meglio	better [adv.]	**peggio**	worse [adv.]
più	more	**meno**	less

A. **Past Tense of Verbs like** *piacere*

As you learned in lesson 12, *piacere* is a particular verb that acts a bit differently from other verbs in that it lends itself to a backward sentence structure. That is because, unlike in English, where speakers say, "I like something," in Italian it is "Something is pleasing to me." *Something* thus transforms from a direct object to a subject. Other verbs that follow this structure are *mancare* ("to be missing"/"to be lacking"), *servire* ("to serve"), *bastare* ("to be enough"/"to suffice"), *dispiacere* ("to displease"), and *convenire* ("to be convenient").

In the past tense, all of these verbs must go with *essere*, not *avere*. It *was* pleasing to you, it *was* useful to you, it *was* missing to you, etc. The hard part is that the past participle has to agree with whatever is pleasing/missing/convenient to you; the easy part is that there are only two forms of *essere* that you'll be using (*è* for singular things and *sono* for plural). Let's look at how these sentences change from present to past tense:

Mi **piace** *il gatto.* → *Mi* **è piaciuto** *il gatto.*
(*è* because *gatto* is singular; *piaciuto* because *gatto* is singular masculine.)

Ti **piacciono** *gli spaghetti?* → *Ti* **sono piaciuti** *gli spaghetti?*
(*sono* because *spaghetti* is plural; *piaciuti* because *spaghetti* is plural masculine.)

Gli **manca** *la sua ragazza.* → *Gli* **è mancata** *la sua ragazza.*
(*è* because *ragazza* is singular; *mancata* because *ragazza* is singular feminine.)

Vi **servono** *queste carte.* → *Vi* **sono servite** *queste carte.*
(*sono* because *carte* is plural; *servite* because *carte* is plural feminine.)

Keep going with other verbs in the list and a mix of singular, plural, masculine, and feminine nouns! Remember that they also go with indirect object pronouns (*mi, ti, gli/le/Le, ci, vi, gli*).

B. **Comparisons of Equality**

Comparisons of equality—when two things are equal to each other in quality or quantity—can use two different sets of words: *così...come* or *tanto...quanto*. These sets of words must match up within their own set: They can't be switched around with each other. The word sets will sandwich adjectives: for example, "*Petrarca è* **così** *bravo* **come** *Dante*" or "*Boccaccio è* **tanto** *bravo* **quanto** *Dante*." In both of these sentences, the adjective is the meat of the sandwich. However, many Italians will omit the first word in the set in common parlance: It's just as fine to say, "*Petrarca è bravo* **come** *Dante*" or "*Boccaccio è bravo* **quanto** *Dante*."

While both sets can be used with adjectives, only *tanto...quanto* can be used with nouns, adverbs, and verbs. If it goes with nouns in terms of quantity (i.e., comparing how many apples and oranges you have), then *tanto* and *quanto* must change to agree with those nouns. So, if you say, "I have as many apples as [I have] oranges," you'd say, "*Ho* **tante** *mele* **quante** *arance*." These words are both plural feminine.

C. Comparisons of Minority and Majority

What if you want to compare something to another thing that is more, less, better, or worse than it? You have to use different words again—namely *più...di/che* or *meno...di/che*. When do you use *di*, and when do you use *che*?

Di is used when you are comparing one trait between two entities. If you are comparing your intelligence to your friend's intelligence, the intelligence is the trait, and your friend and you are the entities. So you'd choose *di* ("*Io sono* **più** *intelligente* **di** *lei*"). If you play soccer more than your brother, you'd also choose *di* because you're still comparing one thing between two entities: "*Io gioco a calcio* **più di** *mio fratello*."

Che is used when you are comparing more than one trait among one singular entity. It is also used when there are prepositions in the sentence, and also when there are infinitive verbs. Let's look at a few examples:

- *Io sono* **più** *intelligente* **che** *motivata*. / I am more intelligent than motivated. (This is one entity and two adjectives.)

- *Io ho* **più** *amici* **che** *nemici*. / I have more friends than enemies. (This is one entity and two nouns.)

- *È* **più** *difficile parlare una lingua* **che** *impararla*. / It is more difficult to speak a language than to learn it. (This is comparing two infinitive verbs.)

- *Ci sono* **più** *montagne in Italia* **che** *in Francia*. / There are more mountains in Italy than in France. (This is comparing two prepositional phrases.)

You'll learn some irregular comparison words (*better/best* and *worse/worst*) in the last section of this lesson.

D. *Superlativo relativo*

The *superlativo relativo*, or the relative superlative, is something that is the *most or least* [adjective] out of a certain group. For instance, Italian is the *most beautiful* of all the languages, or Rome is the *most important* city in Italy. Italian is included among all the other languages, and Rome among all the other cities in Italy.

To form the *superlativo relativo*, there are two formulas you can use:

- [Subject] [verb] [definite article] [noun] [*più/meno*] [adjective] [di...]
- [Subject] [verb] [definite article] [*più*] [adjective] [noun] [di...]

Note that you can only use *più* with the second one. Both formulas say the same thing but have slightly different structures. Let's look at a real sentence for both of the formulas:

- *L'italiano è la lingua più bella di tutte le lingue.*
- *Roma è la più importante città di tutta la nazione.*

What is the most important thing in your life? What is the most beautiful country in the world? These are sentences you can use with the *superlativo relativo*.

E. *Superlativo assoluto*

Now let's look at another form of the superlative, the absolute superlative (*superlativo assoluto*). This superlative, unlike the relative superlative, is not counted among a group of other things as the *most/least* [adjective]. It is just *very* [adjective]. If you remember the *-issimo*, *-issima*, *-issimi*, and *-issime* endings from lesson 16, then you're set! All you have to do is remove the final letter of the word and add the appropriate ending. *Buono* becomes *buonissimo*, *cattivo* becomes *cattivissimo*, etc.

F. **Irregular Comparatives and Superlatives**

There are a few irregular comparative words you should know, especially because they are very common: *good → better* and *bad → worse*. They are as follows:

buono (*good*)	**migliore** (*better*)	**(il/la) migliore** (*best*)
cattivo (*bad*)	**peggiore** (*worse*)	**(il/la) peggiore** (*worst*)
bene (*well*)	**meglio** (*better*)	**n/a**
male (*poorly*)	**peggio** (*worse*)	**n/a**

These do not take *più* or *meno* with them: They simply stand alone with *di* or *che*. As you can see, they look very similar among each other; don't get them confused!

1. Traduci le seguenti frasi in inglese. (Translate the following sentences from Italian into English.)

   1. Dante è l'autore italiano più conosciuto di tutti.

   _____

   2. L'Inferno è la storia più affascinante dell'aldilà.

   _____

   3. La Città del Vaticano è il paese più piccolo del mondo.

   _____

   4. L'Italia è il migliore paese dell'Europa.

   _____

   5. Chianti è uno dei vini più popolari di tutti.

   _____

2. Traduci le seguenti frasi in italiano. (Translate the following sentences from English into Italian.)

   1. Palermo is as important as Washington DC.

   _____

   2. Asia is bigger than Africa.

   _____

   3. Italian gelato is better than American ice cream.

   _____

   4. Soccer is very interesting.

   _____

   5. A Lamborghini is faster (*veloce*) than a VW Beetle.

   _____

3. Trasforma le seguenti frasi dal presente al passato. (Change the following sentences from present to past tense.)

1. Le piace la tua giacca.

   _____

2. Non mi servono queste matite.

   _____

3. Questi gnocchi non ci bastano.

   _____

4. Non mi conviene questa lezione.

   _____

5. Ti piacciono le lasagne?

   _____

4. Scegli l'opzione giusta per ogni frase. (Choose the correct option for each sentence.)

1. Vi _____ un piatto per gli spaghetti.

   a. è serviti   b. sono servito   c. sono serviti   d. è servito

2. Mi _____ un computer per questo corso.

   a. è convenuta   b. è convenuto   c. è convenuti   d. è
   convenute

3. Gli _____ i biscotti che hai cucinato.

   a. sono piaciuti   b. sono piaciuto   c. è piaciuto   d. è piaciute

4. Quanto mi _____ questo programma televisivo!

   a. è mancato   b. sono mancata   c. è mancata   d. sono
   mancato

5. Mi dispiace, ma i soldi che mi hai dato non mi _____.

   a. sono bastato   b. è bastato   c. sono bastati   d. sono bastate

5. *Esercizio di scrittura: La più bella di tutte.*

Talk to your friend about your experience taking this course and learning about the Italian language. Exaggerate a lot so that you can use the relative superlative!

_____
_____
_____
_____
_____
_____
_____
_____
_____
_____

ANSWER KEY

1.

1. Dante is the most well-known Italian author of all.
2. *Inferno* is the most fascinating story of the afterlife.
3. Vatican City is the smallest country in the world.
4. Italy is the best country in Europe.
5. Chianti is one of the most popular wines of all.

2.

1. Palermo è (così/tanto) importante come/quanto Washington DC.
2. L'Asia è più grande dell'Africa.
3. Il gelato italiano è migliore del gelato americano.
4. Il calcio è interessantissimo.
5. Una Lamborghini è più veloce di una VW Beetle.

3.

1. She likes your jacket. / Your jacket is pleasing to her.
2. These pencils do not serve me. / These pencils are not useful to me.
3. These gnocchi are not enough for us. / These gnocchi do not suffice to us.
4. This lesson is not useful to me.
5. Do you like the lasagne? / Are the lasagne pleasing to you?

4.

1. d.   3. a.   5. c.
2. b.   4. a.

5. Answers will vary. Example:

Questo corso è stato il più difficile di tutti! Però mi è piaciuto moltissimo. Il superlativo relativo è la cosa più facile...

WHERE ARE YOU NOW?

Congratulations! You've made it through the whole workbook. By now, you should be familiar with the following topics in vocabulary:

1. adverbs of time

You have also covered quite a bit of grammar:

1. the *passato prossimo* with *essere*

2. the difference between transitive and intransitive verbs

3. the imperfect tense

4. the difference between the imperfect and the *passato prossimo*

5. modal verbs in past tenses

6. *conoscere* and *sapere* in past tenses

7. the impersonal *si*

8. double pronouns

9. the imperative with single and double pronouns

10. the future tense

11. the future of possibility

12. the *futuro anteriore*

13. the past tense of verbs like *piacere*

14. comparisons of equality, minority, and majority

15. superlatives (relative and absolute)

16. irregular comparatives and superlatives

Next to each topic, rate your comfort level from 1 to 5, with 1 being the least comfortable and 5 being the most. What can you work on more?

Some helpful tools and methods are listed in the first Where Are You Now? section in this workbook.

APPENDIX A: VERB CHARTS

• • • • • •
Amare

Presente

amo	amiamo
ami	amate
ama	amano

Presente Progressivo

sto amando	stiamo amando
stai amando	state amando
sta amando	stanno amando

Passato Prossimo

ho amato	abbiamo amato
hai amato	avete amato
ha amato	hanno amato

Imperfetto

amavo	amavamo
amavi	amavate
amava	amavano

Imperativo

[tu] ama!	[tu] non amare!
[noi] amiamo!	[noi] non amiamo!
[voi] amate!	[voi] non amate!
[Lei] ami!	[Lei] non ami!
[Loro] amino!	[Loro] non amino!

Futuro

amerò	ameremo
amerai	amerete
amerà	ameranno

Futuro Anteriore

avrò amato	avremo amato
avrai amato	avrete amato
avrà amato	avranno amato

•••••••
Mettere

Presente

metto	mettiamo
metti	mettete
mette	mettono

Presente Progressivo

sto mettendo	stiamo mettendo
stai mettendo	state mettendo
sta mettendo	stanno mettendo

Passato Prossimo

ho messo	abbiamo messo
hai messo	avete messo
ha messo	hanno messo

Imperfetto

mettevo	mettevamo
mettevi	mettevate
metteva	mettevano

Imperativo

[tu] metti!	[tu] non mettere!
[noi] mettiamo!	[noi] non mettiamo!
[voi] mettete!	[voi] non mettete!
[Lei] metta!	[Lei] non metta!
[Loro] mettano!	[Loro] non mettano!

Futuro

metterò	metteremo
metterai	metterete
metterà	metteranno

Futuro Anteriore

avrò messo	avremo messo
avrai messo	avrete messo
avrà messo	avranno messo

Dormire

Presente

dormo	dormiamo
dormi	dormite
dorme	dormono

Presente Progressivo

sto dormendo	stiamo dormendo
stai dormendo	state dormendo
sta dormendo	stanno dormendo

Passato Prossimo

ho dormito	abbiamo dormito
hai dormito	avete dormito
ha dormito	hanno dormito

Imperfetto

dormivo	dormivamo
dormivi	dormivate
dormiva	dormivano

Imperativo

[tu] dormi!	[tu] non dormire!
[noi] dormiamo!	[noi] non dormiamo!
[voi] dormite!	[voi] non dormite!
[Lei] dorma!	[Lei] non dorma!
[Loro] dormano!	[Loro] non dormano!

Futuro

dormirò	dormiremo
dormirai	dormirete
dormirà	dormiranno

Futuro Anteriore

avrò dormito	avremo dormito
avrai dormito	avrete dormito
avrà dormito	avranno dormito

Presente

finisco	finiamo
finisci	finite
finisce	finiscono

Presente Progressivo

sto finendo	stiamo finendo
stai finendo	state finendo
sta finendo	stanno finendo

Passato Prossimo

ho finito	abbiamo finito
hai finito	avete finito
ha finito	hanno finito

Imperfetto

finivo	finivamo
finivi	finivate
finiva	finivano

Imperativo

[tu] finisci!	[tu] non finire!
[noi] finiamo!	[noi] non finiamo!
[voi] finite!	[voi] non finite!
[Lei] finisca!	[Lei] non finisca!
[Loro] finiscano!	[Loro] non finiscano!

Futuro

finirò	finiremo
finirai	finirete
finirà	finiranno

Futuro Anteriore

avrò finito	avremo finito
avrai finito	avrete finito
avrà finito	avranno finito

APPENDIX B: ESSENTIAL GRAMMAR CHARTS

1. **Italian Pronunciation** (Lesson 1)

A	ah (as in *papa*)	**N**	ennay
B	bee	**O**	oh (as in *snow*)
C	chee	**P**	pee
D	dee	**Q**	koo
E	ay (as in *hay*) or eh (as in *end*)	**R**	erray (typically rolled)
F	effay	**S**	essay
G	jee	**T**	tee
H	acca (AH-kah)	**U**	oo (as in *boot*)
I	ee (as in *jeep*)	**V**	voo
L	ellay	**Z**	zeta
M	emmay		

2. **Subject Pronouns** (Lesson 1)

	singular	plural
first person	**io** (I)	**noi** (we)
second person	**tu** (you [informal])	**voi** (you [plural, informal])
third person	**lui/lei/Lei** (she/he/you [formal])	**loro/Loro** (they/you [plural, formal])

3. Indefinite Articles (Lesson 2)

Gender	Article	When Used	Example
Feminine	un'	before a vowel	un'amica
Feminine	una	before a consonant	una stazione
Masculine	un	before most masculine nouns	un mare
Masculine	uno	before masculine nouns beginning with s + consonant, x, y, z, ps, pn, gn	uno studente

4. Definite Articles (Lessons 2 & 3)

Gender	Article	When Used	Example
feminine	l'	before a vowel	l'amica
feminine	la	before a consonant	la stazione
masculine	l'	before a vowel	l'amico
masculine	il	before most masculine nouns beginning with a consonant	il mare
masculine	lo	before masculine nouns beginning with s + consonant, x, y, z, ps, pn, gn	lo studente

5. Plurals (Lesson 3)

gender	singular	plural
feminine	-a	-e
masculine	-o	-i
feminine or masculine	-e	-i

6. Numbers 0–20 (Lesson 3)

Number	Italian	Pronunciation
0	zero	ZEH-ro
1	uno	OO-noh
2	due	DOO-ay
3	tre	TRAY
4	quattro	QUA-tro
5	cinque	CHEEN-quay
6	sei	SAY
7	sette	SEH-tay
8	otto	OH-toh
9	nove	NO-vay
10	dieci	dee-AY-chee
11	undici	OON-dee-chee
12	dodici	DOH-dee-chee
13	tredici	TRAY-dee-chee
14	quattordici	qua-TOR-dee-chee
15	quindici	QUIN-dee-chee
16	sedici	SAY-dee-chee
17	diciassette	dee-cha-SET-tay
18	diciotto	dee-CHO-toh
19	diciannove	dee-cha-NO-vay
20	venti	VEN-tee

7. Numbers 20–100 (Lesson 3)

Number	Italian	Pronunciation
20	venti	VEN-tee
30	trenta	TREYN-tah
40	quaranta	qua-RAHN-tah
50	cinquanta	cheen-QUAN-tah
60	sessanta	seh-SAHN-tah
70	settanta	seh-TAHN-tah

80	ottanta	oh-TAHN-tah
90	novanta	noh-VAHN-tah
100	cento	CHEN-toh

8. **Conjugation of -*are* Verbs** (Lesson 4)

-o	-iamo
-i	-ate
-a	-ano

9. **Conjugation of -*ere* Verbs** (Lesson 5)

[io] -o	[noi] -iamo
[tu] -i	[voi] -ete
[lei, lui, Lei] -e	[loro] -ono

10. **Conjugation of -*ire* Verbs** (Lesson 5)

[io] -o	[noi] -iamo
[tu] -i	[voi] -ite
[lei, lui, Lei] -e	[loro] -ono

11. **Idiomatic Expressions with *avere*** (Lesson 5)

Italian Expression	English Translation	Sample Sentence
avere caldo	to feel warm/hot	Oggi ho caldo e non posso dormire. (Today I feel hot and cannot sleep.)
avere freddo	to feel cold	Se hai freddo, porti una sciarpa. (If you feel cold, you wear a scarf.)
avere fame	to be hungry	Luigi ha fame e mangia un panino. (Luigi is hungry and eats a sandwich.)
avere sete	to be thirsty	I cammelli non hanno mai sete! (Camels are never thirsty!)

avere ragione	to be correct	Ah, avete ragione, i dragoni non sono veri. (Ah, you're right; dragons aren't real.)
avere torto	to be incorrect	Mario dice che 2 + 2 = 5, ma ha torto. (Mario says that 2 + 2 = 5, but he is incorrect.)
avere sonno	to be sleepy	Se hai sonno, vai a letto! (If you're tired, go to bed!)
avere...anni	to be...years old	Oggi è il compleanno di mia madre. Ha 60 anni. (Today is my mother's birthday. She is 60 years old.)
avere bisogno (di)	to need	Ho bisogno di studiare per quest'esame. (I need to study for this exam.)
avere voglia (di)	to want	Hanno voglia di uscire stasera. (They want to go out tonight.)
avere paura (di)	to be afraid (of)	Hai paura dei ragni? (Are you afraid of spiders?)
avere fretta	to be in a rush	Non posso fermarmi, ho fretta! (I can't stop; I'm in a rush!)

12. Irregular -ire Verbs (Lesson 6)

[io] -isco	[noi] -iamo
[tu] -isci	[voi] -ite
[lei, lui, Lei] -isce	[loro] -iscono

Verb	Definition	Conjugation
capire	to understand	capisco, capisci, capisce, capiamo, capite, capiscono
colpire	to hit	colpisco, colpisci, colpisce, colpiamo, colpite, colpiscono
costruire	to construct/build	costruisco, costruisci, costruisce, costruiamo, costruite, costruiscono
distribuire	to distribute	distribuisco, distribuisci, distribuisce, distribuiamo, distribuite, distribuiscono

finire	to finish	finisco, finisci, finisce, finiamo, finite, finiscono
riunire	to reunite	riunisco, riunisci, riunisce, riuniamo, riunite, riuniscono
preferire	to prefer	preferisco, preferisci, preferisce, preferiamo, preferite, preferiscono
pulire	to clean	pulisco, pulisci, pulisce, puliamo, pulite, puliscono
punire	to punish	punisco, punisci, punisce, puniamo, punite, puniscono
scolpire	to sculpt	scolpisco, scolpisci, scolpisce, scolpiamo, scolpite, scolpiscono
spedire	to send	spedisco, spedisci, spedisce, spediamo, spedite, spediscono

13. Possessives (Lesson 7)

	Singular Subjects Singular Objects	Singular Subjects Plural Objects	Plural Subjects Singular Objects	Plural Subjects Plural Objects
first person	il mio la mia	i miei le mie	il nostro la nostra	i nostri le nostre
second person	il tuo la tua	i tuoi le tue	il vostro la vostra	i vostri le vostre
third person	il suo la sua	i suoi le sue	il **loro** la **loro**	i **loro** le **loro**

14. Demonstrative Adjectives (Lesson 7)

	singolare	plurale	singolare	plurale
maschile	**questo** fratello (**quest'**uomo)	**questi** fratelli (**questi** uomini)	**quel** fratello **quell'**uomo **quello** zio	**quei** fratelli **quegli** uomini **quegli** zii
femminile	**questa** sorella (**quest'**amica)	**queste** sorelle (**queste** amiche)	**quella** sorella **quell'**amica	**quelle** sorelle **quelle** amiche

15. Articulated Prepositions (Lesson 8)

+	il	lo	l'	la	i	gli	le
a	al	allo	all'	alla	ai	agli	alle
da	dal	dallo	dall'	dalla	dai	dagli	dalle
di → de	del	dello	dell'	della	dei	degli	delle
in → ne	nel	nello	nell'	nella	nei	negli	nelle
su	sul	sullo	sull'	sulla	sui	sugli	sulle

16. Informal Imperatives (Lesson 10)

	-are	-ere	-ire	-ire (-isc)
tu	-a	-i	-i	-isci
noi	-iamo	-iamo	-iamo	-iamo
voi	-ate	-ete	-ite	-ite

	-are	-ere	-ire	-ire (-isc)
tu = non +	-are	-ere	-ire	-ire
noi = non +	-iamo	-iamo	-iamo	-iamo
voi = non +	-ate	-ete	-ite	-ite

17. Formal Imperatives (Lesson 10)

	-are	-ere	-ire	-ire (-isc)
Lei	-i	-a	-a	-isca
noi	-iamo	-iamo	-iamo	-iamo
Loro	-ino	-ano	-ano	-iscano

18. Direct Objects (Lesson 11)

mi	ci
ti	vi
lo, la, La	li/le, Li/Le

19. Indirect Objects (Lesson 12)

mi	ci
ti	vi
gli/le/Le	gli/...loro/...Loro

20. Tonic Pronouns (Lesson 12)

me	noi
te	voi
lui/lei/Lei	loro/Loro

21. Affirmative and Negative Expressions (Lesson 15)

Espressioni Affermative	Espressioni Negative
qualcosa (*anything*)	non...niente/nulla (*nothing*)
tutto (*everything*)	non...niente/nulla (*nothing*)
qualcuno (*everyone* [sing.])	non...nessuno (*nobody/no one*)
tutti (*everyone* [pl.])	non...nessuno (*nobody/no one*)
sempre (*always*)	non...mai (*never*)
qualche volta (*sometimes*)	non...mai (*never*)
mai (*ever*)	non...mai (*never*)
già (*already*)	non...ancora (*not yet*)
ancora (*still*)	non...più (*no longer*)
e...e (*both...and*)	né...né (*neither...nor*)

22. Indefinite Adjectives (Lesson 17)

Adjective	Meaning	Example
ogni [sing. only]	every, each	Ogni persona è speciale.
qualche [sing. only]	some, a few	Qualche persona è speciale.
qualunque* [sing. only]	any	Qualunque persona che incontri* sarà speciale.
alcuni/e	some, a few	Alcune persone sono speciali.
tutto/a/i/e**	all, every	Tutte le persone sono speciali.

* *Qualunque* requires the subjunctive mood, which you won't meet in this course.
** *Tutto* in all forms requires the use of the appropriate definite article with it (e.g., *Tutto il giorno*, *Tutta la notte*, etc.)

23. Indefinite Pronouns (Lesson 17)

Pronoun	Meaning	Example
ognuno [sing. only]	everyone	Ognuno è speciale.
qualcuno [sing. only]	someone, anyone	Qualcuno è speciale.
tutto [sing. only]	all, everything	Tutto è speciale.
qualcosa/qualche cosa [sing. only]	something, anything	Dimmi qualcosa di* speciale.
alcuni/e	some, a few	Alcuni sono speciali.
tutti/e	everyone, everybody	Tutti sono speciali.

* *Qualcosa*, when followed by an adjective, requires the use of the preposition *di* and the masculine singular form of the adjective. When followed by a verb (e.g., "Is there anything to eat?"), it uses the preposition *da* and the infinitive form of the verb.

24. Irregular Past Participles (Lesson 18)

-tto				-so		
	fare	fatto			prendere	preso
	dire	detto			rendere	reso
	leggere	letto			accendere	acceso
	correggere	corretto			spendere	speso
	scrivere	scritto			scendere	sceso
	friggere	fritto			offendere	offeso
	rompere	rotto			decidere	deciso
	cuocere	cotto			uccidere	ucciso
	tradurre	tradotto			ridere	riso
-rto	aprire	aperto			dividere	diviso
	offrire	offerto			chiudere	chiuso
	soffrire	sofferto			concludere	concluso
	coprire	coperto			diffondere	diffuso
	scoprire	scoperto		-sto	rimanere	rimasto
	morire	morto			chiedere	chiesto
	accorgersi	accorto			rispondere	risposto
-rso	perdere	perso			comporre	composto
	correre	corso			proporre	proposto
-lto	scegliere	scelto			disporre	disposto
	togliere	tolto			vedere	visto
	raccogliere	raccolto		-sso	mettere	messo
	sciogliere	sciolto			succedere	successo
	risolvere	risolto			permettere	permesso
	rivolgersi	rivolto			esprimere	espresso
-nto	piangere	pianto			muovere	mosso
	spegnere	spento			discutere	discusso
	spingere	spinto				
	vincere	vinto				
	aggiungere	aggiunto				
	dipingere	dipinto				
	assumere	assunto				

25. *La casa di essere* ("The House of *essere*") (<u>Lesson 19</u>)

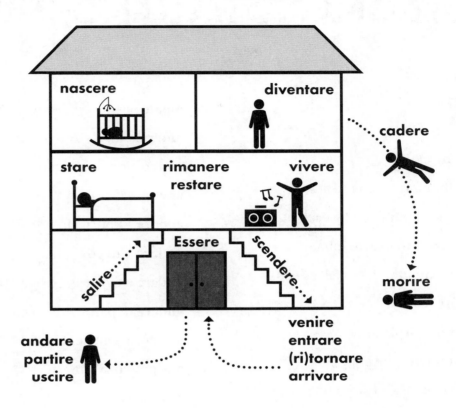

26. **Double Pronouns** (<u>Lesson 22</u>)

+	lo	la	li	le	ne
mi	me lo	me la	me li	me le	me ne
ti	te lo	te la	te li	te le	te ne
gli/le/Le	glielo	gliela	glieli	gliele	gliene
ci	ce lo	ce la	ce li	ce le	ce ne
vi	ve lo	ve la	ve li	ve le	ve ne
gli/...loro	glielo/ lo...loro	gliela/ la...loro	glieli/ li...loro	gliele/ le...loro	gliene/ ne...loro

DIZIONARIO ITALIANO-INGLESE

A

a – to, at, in

abbondanza – abundance

abbracciarsi – to hug each other

abitare – to live, to inhabit

addormentarsi – to fall asleep

adesso – now

aereo – airplane

aeroporto – airport

affascinante – fascinating

agricoltura – agriculture

agrume – citrus tree

aiutare – to help

albergo – hotel

albero – tree

alcuno/a – some [sing.]

alcuni/e – some [pl.]

allora – now

alpinismo – mountain climbing

alto/a – tall

altrimenti – otherwise

altro/a – other

alzarsi – to get up

amare – to love

amato/a – loved, beloved

americano/a – American

amico/amica – friend

anche – also

ancora – yet, again

andare – to go

andare a trovare – to visit (a person)

andare in palestra – to go to the gym

antico/a – ancient

antipatico/a – mean

anzi – even

appena – as soon as

aprire – to open

archeologico/a – archaeological

architettura – architecture

arcipelago – archipelago

arrivare – to arrive

arrivederci – goodbye

arte – art

artista [m./f.] – artist

ascoltare – to listen to

aspettare – to wait for

assaggiare – to taste

assomigliare – to resemble

attento/a – attentive

attenzione – attention

attivo/a – active

attore/attrice – actor/actress

attraversare – to cross over

austriaco/a – Austrian

autobus – bus

automobile [f.] – car

autore/autrice – author

autunno – autumn

avere – to have

avere...anni – to be...years old

avere bisogno (di) – to have need (of)

avere caldo – to feel hot

avere fame – to be hungry

avere freddo – to feel cold

avere fretta – to be in a rush

avere intenzione (di) – to mean to

avere paura (di) – to have fear (of)

avere ragione – to be right

avere sete – to be thirsty

avere sonno – to be sleepy

avere torto – to be incorrect

avere voglia (di) – to have want (of)

avvocato/avvocatessa – lawyer

azienda – business

azzurro/a – light blue

B

baciarsi – to kiss each other

baia – bay

ballare – to dance

banca – bank

bandiera – flag

bar – bar, coffee shop

barista [m./f.] – barista (coffee maker)

barocco – baroque

basso/a – short

bastare – to be enough

bellezza – beauty

bello/a – beautiful

bene – well

bere – to drink

bianco/a – white

bicchiere – glass

bicicletta – bicycle

bisnonno/bisnonna – great-grandparent

bistecca – steak

borsa – purse, bag

bosco – forest

bottiglia – bottle

braccio – arm

bravo/a – good, talented

brutto/a – ugly

buon giorno – good day

buona notte – good night

buona sera – good evening

buono/a – good

C

cadere – to fall

calcio – soccer (*literally*: kick)

caldo/a – hot

calvo/a – bald

cambiare – to change

camera – room

camicia – shirt

camminare – to walk

campo – field

canadese – Canadian

canale – canal, channel

cantante/cantatrice – singer

cantare – to sing

capelli – hair

capire – to understand

capitale – capital

capoluogo – capital (of a region)

caro/a – dear, expensive

casa – house

castano/a – chestnut, brown (hair, eye color)

cattivo/a – bad

cavallo – horse

celeste – sky blue

cena – dinner

centrale – central

centro – center, downtown

cercare – to search for

certo/a – certain

che – what, that

che ora è/che ore sono – what time is it

chi – who

chiamarsi – to call oneself

chiaro/a – clear

chiedere – to ask

chiesa – church

chiudere – to close

ci – we [indirect and direct object, reflexive pronoun], there [particle]

cibo – food

cinema – movie theater

cinese – Chinese

cioccolato – chocolate

città – city

clima – climate

cognato/cognata – brother-in-law/ sister-in-law

colazione – breakfast

collina – hill

collo – neck

come – how

comico/a – funny, comical

cominciare – to begin

compleanno – birthday

composto/a (di) – made (of)

comprare – to buy

con – with

concerto – concert

confine – border

conoscenza – knowledge

conoscere – to know, to be familiar with

consigliare – to advise

consiglio – advice

continuare – to continue

coprire – to cover

corona – crown

correre – to run

corsa – race

corte – court

cosa – thing

così...come – as...as

costa – coast

costoso/a – costly

crescere – to grow

cucinare – to cook

cugino/cugina – cousin

D

d'accordo – agreed

d'origine – originally

da – by, from

dappertutto – everywhere, all over

dare – to give

davvero – really, truly

decidere – to decide

dedicato/a – dedicated

delicato/a – delicate

desiderare – to desire

di – of

di solito – usually

dimenticare – to forget

dio – god

dipingere – to paint

dire – to say

discutere – to discuss

disegnare – to draw

distante – distant

dito – finger

ditta – company

diventare – to become

diversità – diversity

diverso/a – different

divertente – amusing

domanda – question

domani – tomorrow

doppio/a – double

dormire – to sleep

dove – where

dovere – to need to, to owe

dramma [m.] – drama

drammatico/a – dramatic

drammaturgo – playwright

duomo – main church [*literally*: house of god]

E

e...e – both...and

ecco – behold, here (it is)

economia – economy

edificio – building

entrambi – both

entroterra – inland

epoca – era, epoch

equitazione – horseback riding

esame – exam, test

esempio – example

esercizio – exercise

esibire – to exhibit

essere – to be

essere umano – human being

est – east

estate – summer

estivo – summer [adj.]

eterno/a – eternal

F

fa – ago

famiglia – family

famoso/a – famous

fare – to do, to make

fare aerobica – to do exercise

fare bel tempo – to be nice weather

fare brutto tempo – to be bad weather

fare caldo – to be hot (weather)

fare freddo – to be cold (weather)

fare fresco – to be brisk (weather)

fare parte (di) – to be a part (of)

fare sollevamento pesi – to lift weights

farsi regali – to give each other gifts

felice – happy

festival – festival

fidanzarsi – to get engaged to each other

fidanzato/fidanzata – fiancé(e)

figliastro/figliastra – stepson/ stepdaughter

figlio/figlia – son/daughter

figura storica – historical figure

filosofo – philosopher

finanza – finance

fine settimana – weekend

finire – to finish

fiore – flower

fiorentino/a – Florentine

fiume – river

fondamentale – fundamental

fondato/a – founded

fontana – fountain

formaggio – cheese

forse – maybe

foto(grafia) – photo(graph)

francese – French

frase – sentence

fratellastro – stepbrother

fratello – brother

freddo/a – cold

frequentarsi – to go out with each other

fresco/a – brisk

funzione – function, use

G

gelato – ice cream

genero – son-in-law

genitori – parents

genovese – Genoese

gesticolare – to gesticulate

ghiaccio – ice

già – already

giapponese – Japanese

giardino – garden

gigante – giant

ginnastica – exercise

ginocchio – knee

giocare – to play

Giochi Olimpici – Olympic Games

giovane – young

giusto/a – right, correct

gli – the [masc. pl.]

godere – to enjoy

golfo – gulf

gondola – Venetian boat

gotico/a – Gothic

grande – big, great

grasso/a – fat

grazie – thank you

greco/a – Greek

grigio/a – gray

grotta – grotto

guardare – to look at

guerra – war

guerriero – warrior

I

i – the [masc. pl.]

ieri – yesterday

il – the [masc. sing.]

imparare – to learn

in – in, at, to

incontrare – to meet

indicare – to indicate

industria – industry

infatti – in fact

inglese – English

insalata – salad

insegnare – to teach

insieme – together

internazionale – international

invece – instead

invernale – winter [adj.]

inverno – winter

io – I

irlandese – Irish

isola – island

ispirazione – inspiration

istituto – institute

italiano/a – Italian

L

l' – the [masc. or fem. sing.]

la – the [fem. sing.], her [direct object]

labbro – lip

lago – lake

largo/a – wide

lasciarsi – to leave each other

lavare – to wash

lavorare – to work

lavoratore – worker

lavoro – work

le – the [fem. pl.], they [fem. direct object], her/it [indirect object]

leggere – to read

lei/Lei – she/you [formal]

leone – lion

letteratura – literature

letto – bed, read [past part. of *leggere*]

libro – book

ligure – Ligurian

limpido/a – clear

liscio/a – straight (hair)

lo – the [masc. sing.], him/it [masc. direct object]

lontano/a – far

loro/Loro – they/you [formal, pl.]

luce – light

lui – he

lungo/a – long

lupo – wolf

M

macchina – car

madre – mother

magari – hopefully

magro/a – thin

mai – ever, never

mais – corn

malattia – sickness, disease

male – badly

mancare – to be missing/to be lacking

mangiare – to eat

mano [f.] – hand

marchigiano/a – from the Marches

mare – sea

marito – husband

marrone – brown

maschera – mask

matrigna – stepmother

mattina – morning

medico – doctor

medievale – medieval

mediterraneo/a – Mediterranean

meglio – better [adv.]

mela – apple

meno – less

mentre – while

meridionale – southern

meridione – south

messicano/a – Mexican

mettere – to put

mettersi – to put on (clothing)

mezzanotte – midnight

mezzogiorno – midday, the South of Italy

mi – me [direct and indirect object], myself [reflexive pronoun]

migliore – better [adj.], best

minerario/a – mineral

moglie – wife

molto/a – much

molti/e – many

momento – moment

mondano/a – mundane

montagna – mountain

montagnoso/a – mountainous

monumento – monument

morire – to die

mostrare – to show

motocicletta – motorcycle

motorino – scooter

movimento – movement

mucca – cow

multicolore – multicolor

muro – wall

museo – museum

musicale – musical

musicista – musician

N

nascere – to be born

natale – native

ne – of it [particle]

né...né – neither...nor

neanche – not even

negozio – store

nero/a – black

nervoso/a – nervous

nessuno – no one

nevicare – to snow

niente/nulla – nothing

nipote [m./f.] – nephew/niece, grandchild

nocciola – hazelnut

noi – we

nonno/nonna – grandfather/grandmother

nord – north

noto/a – noted, notable

notte – night

numeroso/a – numerous

nuora – daughter-in-law

nuotare – to swim

nuoto – swimming

nuovo/a – new

O

occhiali – glasses

occhio – eye

occidentale – western

offrire – to offer

oggi – today

ogni – every, each

ognuno – everyone, each

olio d'oliva – olive oil

oliva – olive

olivo – olive tree

opera d'arte – work of art

ordinare – to order

orecchio – ear

orientale – eastern

oro – gold

orologio – clock, watch

orso – bear

ovest – west

P

padre – father

paesaggio – landscape

palazzo – palace

pallacanestro – basketball

pallanuoto – water polo

pallavolo – volleyball

pane – bread

panorama [m.] – panorama

pantaloni – pants

parco nazionale – national park

parenti – relatives

parlare – to speak, to talk

parola – word

parte – part

particolare – particular

partire – to leave

passaggio – passage, ride

passare – to pass

passeggiare – to walk

passeggiata – walk

pastorizia – pastoralism, livestock rearing

patrigno – stepfather

patrimonio – patrimony

pattinaggio – skating

pecora – sheep

pecorino – sheep's milk cheese

peggio – worse [adv.]

peggiore – worse [adj.], worst

pelle – skin

penisola – peninsula

pensarci – to think about

pensare – to think

per – for, through

per esempio – for example

perché – because, why

percorrere – to traverse

perdere – to lose

pericolo – danger

però – however

pesce – fish

pesto – pasta sauce with pine nuts and basil

piacere – to please

piano/a – slow, quiet

pianta – plant

pianura – plain (flat land)

piatto – plate

piazza – plaza, square

piccolo/a – little, small

piede – foot

pietra – stone

piovere – to rain

piscina – swimming pool

pista – track (esp. for skiing)

pittore/pittrice – painter

pittoresco/a – picturesque

più – more

poco – few, little

poema – poem

poeta/poetessa – poet

poi – then

pomeriggio – afternoon

popolare – popular

popolato/a – populous

portare – to bring

porto – port

porzione – portion

possedere – to possess

posto – place

potente – potent, powerful

potere – to be able to

povertà – poverty

pranzo – lunch

preferire – to prefer

prego – you're welcome

preistorico/a – prehistoric

prendere – to take

prenotare – to reserve

preoccupato/a – worried

preparare – to prepare

presentare – to present

presenza – presence

presto – soon, early

prima (di) – before

primavera – spring

primo/a – first

principale – principal

probabilmente – probably

problema – problem

processione – procession

prodotto – product

prodotto alimentare – food product

programma – plan, show (television)

provincia – province

psicologo – psychologist

pulire – to clean

punto – point

purtroppo – unfortunately

Q

quadro – painting

qualche volta – sometimes

qualcosa – something

qualcuno – someone

quale – what, which

qualunque – any

quando – when

quanto/a – how much

quanti/e – how many

quartiere – neighborhood, area

quasi – somewhat

quello/a – that

questo/a – this

R

radersi – to shave oneself

radio [f.] – radio

ragazzo/ragazza – boy/girl

raggiungere – to reach

realizzare – to actualize

recente – recent

regalare – to gift

regalo – gift

regione – region

restare – to rest, to stay

riccio/a – curly

ricco/a – rich

ricerca – research

ricevere – to receive

ricordare – to remember

ricuperare – to recuperate

riflessivo/a – reflexive

riflettere – to reflect

rilassare – to relax

rimanere – to remain

rinascimentale – Renaissance [adj.]

Rinascimento – Renaissance

ripetere – to repeat

risalire (a) – to harken back to, to revisit

riso – rice

rispondere – to respond

ristorante – restaurant

roccia – rock

romano/a – Roman

rosa – pink

russo/a – Russian

S

salire – to climb, to go up

salutarsi – to greet each other

salvare – to save

sapere – to know

sapienza – knowledge

sardo/a – Sardinian

sasso – rock

scavo – excavation

scegliere – to choose

scendere – to go down

scherma – fencing

schermo – screen

sci – skiing

sciare – to ski

scienziato – scientist

scoperta – discovery

scorso/a – last

scrittore/scrittrice – writer

scrittura – writing

scrivere – to write

scultura – sculpture

scuola – school

secco – dry

secondo – second, according to

sede – seat

sedere – to sit

segno – sign

seguire – to follow

selvaggio/a – wild

sembrare – to seem

sempre – always

sensibile – sensitive

sentiero – path

sentire – to hear, to smell

sentirsi – to feel

senza – without

sereno/a – serene

servire – to serve

settentrionale – northern

settentrione – north

si – himself/herself/itself [reflexive pronoun], one [*si impersonale*]

sia...che – both...and

siccome – since

siciliano/a – Sicilian

sicuramente – surely

sicuro/a – sure, safe

simpatico/a – nice

sito – place

situato/a – situated

soldi – money

sole – sun

soprattutto – overall, above all

sorella – sister

sorellastra – stepsister

sotterraneo/a – subterranean

sottoterra – underground

spagnolo/a – Spanish

spazio – space

spegnere – to turn off

spendere – to spend

spesso – often

spettacolo – play, show

spiaggia – beach

spingere – to push

sposarsi – to get married

stadio – stadium

stanco/a – tired

stare – to stay, to be

stasera – tonight, this evening

stinco – shin

stivale – boot

storia – history, story

strada – street

straniero/a – stranger, foreign

stressato/a – stressed

stretto – strait

striscia – stripe

struttura – structure

studente/studentessa – student

studiare – to study

stupendo/a – stupendous

su – on

subito – immediately

succedere – to happen

sud – south

suggerire – to suggest

suocero/suocera – father-in-law/
mother-in-law

svegliarsi – to wake up

sviluppare – to develop

svolgersi – to occur, to happen

T

tacco – heel

talento – talent

tanto...quanto – as...as

tanto/a – much

tanti/e – many

tardi – late

tavolo – table

tazza – cup

teatrale – theatrical

teatro – theater

tedesco/a – German

telefono – telephone

televisione – television

tema [m.] – theme, short essay

temperatura – temperature

tempesta – storm

tempio – temple

tempo – time, weather

tenere – to hold

terme – thermal baths

terrazza – terrace

terremoto – earthquake

terribile – terrible

tessuto – fabric

tetto – roof

ti – you [direct and indirect pronoun],
yourself [reflexive pronoun]

tira il vento – the wind is blowing

topografia – topography

tornado – tornado

tornare – to return, to turn

toro – bull

torre – tower

toscano/a – Tuscan

tra/fra – between, among, within

treno – train

triste – sad

trovare – to find

trovarsi – to find oneself

tu – you

turismo – tourism

turista [m./f.] – tourist

tutti/e – every, everyone

tutto/a – all

U

Umanesimo – Humanism

umbro/a – Umbrian

un – a, one [masc.]

un' – a, one [fem.]

una – a, one [fem.]

unico/a – unique, only

università – university

uragano – hurricane

uscire – to go out

V

vacanza – vacation

valigia – suitcase

vecchio/a – old

vedere – to see

vela – sailing

vendere – to sell

veneto/a – Venetian

venire – to come

verace – true

verde – green

vestirsi – to dress oneself

vestiti – clothing [pl.]

vi – you [pl.] [direct and indirect object], yourselves [reflexive pronoun]

viaggiare – to travel

viaggio – trip

vicino (a) – near

vietato/a – prohibited

vigneto – vineyard

vincere – to win

vino – wine

visitare – to visit (a place)

visitato/a – visited

vite – vine

vivere – to live

voi – you [pl.]

volare – to fly

volere – to want to

volontà – desire, willingness

volontieri – willingly

volta – time

vulcano – volcano

vuoto/a – empty

xilofono – xylophone

yoghurt – yogurt

Z

zaino – backpack

zio/zia – uncle/aunt

zitto/a – silent

zona – area, zone

zoo – zoo

DIZIONARIO INGLESE-ITALIANO

A

a – un, un', una, uno

above all – soprattutto

abundance – abbondanza

according to – secondo

active – attivo/a

actor – attore

actress – attrice

actualize – realizzare

advice – consiglio

advise – consigliare

afternoon – pomeriggio

again – ancora

ago – fa

agreed – d'accordo

agriculture – agricoltura

airplane – aereo

airport – aeroporto

all – tutto/a

already – già

also – anche

always – sempre

American – americano/a

among – tra/fra

amusing – divertente

ancient – antico/a

any – qualunque

apple – mela

archaeological – archeologico/a

archipelago – arcipelago

architecture – architettura

arm – braccio

arrive – arrivare

art – arte

artist – artista

as...as – così...come, tanto...quanto

as soon as – appena

ask – chiedere

at – a, in

attention – attenzione

attentive – attento/a

aunt – zia

Austrian – austriaco/a

author – autore/autrice

autumn – autunno

B

backpack – zaino

bad – cattivo/a

badly – male

bag – borsa

bald – calvo/a

bank – banca

bar – bar

barista – barista

baroque – barocco

basketball – pallacanestro

bay – baia

be – essere, stare

be...years old – avere...anni

be a part (of) – fare parte (di)

be able to – potere

be bad weather – fare brutto tempo

be born – nascere

be brisk (weather) – fare fresco

be cold (weather) – fare freddo

be enough – bastare

be familiar with – conoscere

be hot (weather) – fare caldo

be hungry – avere fame

be in a rush – avere fretta

be incorrect – avere torto

be nice weather – fare bel tempo

be right – avere ragione

be sleepy – avere sonno

be thirsty – avere sete

beach – spiaggia

bear – orso

beautiful – bello/a

beauty – bellezza

because – perché

become – diventare

bed – letto

before – prima (di)

begin – cominciare

behold – ecco

best – migliore

better [adj.] – migliore

better [adv.] – meglio

between – tra/fra

bicycle – bicicletta

big – grande

birthday – compleanno

black – nero/a

book – libro

boot – stivale

border – confine

both – entrambi

both...and – e...e, sia...che

bottle – bottiglia

boy – ragazzo

bread – pane

breakfast – colazione

bring – portare

brisk – fresco/a

brother – fratello

brother-in-law – cognato

brown – marrone

brown (hair, eye color) – castano/a

building – edificio

bull – toro

bus – autobus

business – azienda

buy – comprare

by – da

C

call oneself – chiamarsi

Canadian – canadese

canal – canale

capital – capitale

capital (of a region) – capoluogo

car – automobile

car – macchina

center – centro

central – centrale

certain – certo/a

change – cambiare

channel – canale

cheese – formaggio

chestnut – castano/a

Chinese – cinese

chocolate – cioccolato

choose – scegliere

church – chiesa

citrus tree – agrume

city – città

clean – pulire

clear – chiaro/a, limpido/a

climate – clima

climb – salire

clock – orologio

close – chiudere

clothing – vestiti

coast – costa

coffee shop – bar

cold – freddo/a

come – venire

company – ditta

concert – concerto

continue – continuare

cook – cucinare

corn – mais

correct – giusto/a

costly – costoso/a

court – corte

cousin – cugino/cugina

cover – coprire

cow – mucca

cross over – attraversare

crown – corona

cup – tazza

curly – riccio/a

D

dance – ballare

danger – pericolo

daughter – figlia

daughter-in-law – nuora

dear – caro/a

decide – decidere

dedicated – dedicato/a

delicate – delicato/a

desire – desiderare, volontà

develop – sviluppare

die – morire

different – diverso/a

dinner – cena

discovery – scoperta

discuss – discutere

disease – malattia

distant – distante

diversity – diversità

do – fare

do exercise – fare aerobica

doctor – medico

double – doppio/a

downtown – centro

drama – dramma

dramatic – drammatico/a

draw – disegnare

dress oneself – vestirsi

drink – bere

dry – secco

E

each – ogni, ognuno

ear – orecchio

early – presto

earthquake – terremoto

east – est

eastern – orientale

eat – mangiare

economy – economia

empty – vuoto/a

English – inglese

enjoy – godere

era – epoca

eternal – eterno/a

even – anzi

ever – mai

every – ogni, tutti/e

everyone – ognuno, tutti/e

everywhere – dappertutto

example – esempio

excavation – scavo

exercise – esercizio, ginnastica

exhibit – esibire

expensive – caro/a

eye – occhio

F

fabric – tessuto

fall – cadere

fall asleep – addormentarsi

family – famiglia

famous – famoso/a

far – lontano/a

fascinating – affascinante

fat – grasso/a

father – padre

father-in-law – suocero

feel – sentirsi

feel cold – avere freddo

feel hot – avere caldo

fencing – scherma

festival – festival

few – poco

fiancé(e) – fidanzato/fidanzata

field – campo

finance – finanza

find – trovare

find oneself – trovarsi

finger – dito

finish – finire

first – primo/a

fish – pesce

flag – bandiera

Florentine – fiorentino/a

flower – fiore

fly – volare

follow – seguire

food – cibo

food product – prodotto alimentare

foot – piede

for – per

for example – per esempio

foreign – straniero/a

forest – bosco

forget – dimenticare

founded – fondato/a

fountain – fontana

French – francese

friend – amico/amica

from – da

function – funzione

fundamental – fondamentale

funny – comico/a

G

garden – giardino

Genoese – genovese

German – tedesco/a

gesticulate – gesticolare

get engaged to each other – fidanzarsi

get married – sposarsi

get up – alzarsi

giant – gigante

gift – regalare, regalo

girl – ragazza

give – dare

give each other gifts – farsi regali

glass – bicchiere

glasses – occhiali

go – andare

go down – scendere

go out – uscire

go out with each other – frequentarsi

go to the gym – andare in palestra

go up – salire

god – dio

gold – oro

good (talented) – bravo/a

good – buono/a

good day – buon giorno

good evening – buona sera

good night – buona notte

goodbye – arrivederci

Gothic – gotico/a

grandchild – nipote

grandfather – nonno

grandmother – nonna

gray – grigio/a

great – grande

great-grandparent – bisnonno/bisnonna

Greek – greco/a

green – verde

greet each other – salutarsi

grotto – grotta

grow – crescere

gulf – golfo

H

hair – capelli

hand – mano

happen – succedere, svolgersi

happy – felice

have – avere

have fear (of) – avere paura (di)

have need (of) – avere bisogno (di)

have want (of) – avere voglia (di)

hazelnut – nocciola

he – lui

hear – sentire

heel – tacco

help – aiutare

here (it is) – ecco

her/it [indirect object] – le

hill – collina

him/it [masc. direct object] – lo

himself/herself/itself [reflexive pronoun] – si

historical figure – figura storica

history – storia

hold – tenere

hopefully – magari

horse – cavallo

horseback riding – equitazione

hot – caldo/a

hotel – albergo

house – casa

how – come

how many – quanti/e

how much – quanto/a

however – però

hug each other – abbracciarsi

human being – essere umano

Humanism – Umanesimo

hurricane – uragano

husband – marito

I

I – io

ice – ghiaccio

ice cream – gelato

immediately – subito

in – a, in

in fact – infatti

indicate – indicare

industry – industria

inhabit – abitare

inland – entroterra

inspiration – ispirazione

instead – invece

institute – istituto

international – internazionale

Irish – irlandese

island – isola

Italian – italiano/a

J

Japanese – giapponese

K

kiss each other – baciarsi

knee – ginocchio

know – sapere

knowledge – conoscenza, sapienza

L

lack – mancare

lake – lago

landscape – paesaggio

last – scorso/a

late – tardi

lawyer – avvocato/avvocatessa

learn – imparare

leave – partire

leave each other – lasciarsi

less – meno

lift weights – fare sollevamento pesi

light – luce

light blue – azzurro/a

Ligurian – ligure

lion – leone

lip – labbro

listen to – ascoltare

literature – letteratura

little – piccolo/a, poco

live – abitare, vivere

long – lungo/a

look at – guardare

lose – perdere

love – amare

loved – amato/a

lunch – pranzo

M

made (of) – composto/a (di)

main church – duomo

make – fare

many – molti/e, tanti/e

mask – maschera

maybe – forse

me [direct and indirect object] – mi

mean – antipatico/a

mean to – avere intenzione (di)

medieval – medievale

Mediterranean – mediterraneo/a

meet – incontrare

Mexican – messicano/a

midday – mezzogiorno

midnight – mezzanotte

mineral – minerario/a

moment – momento

money – soldi

monument – monumento

more – più

morning – mattina

mother – madre

mother-in-law – suocera

motorcycle – motocicletta

mountain – montagna

mountain climbing – alpinismo

mountainous – montagnoso/a

movement – movimento

movie theater – cinema

much – molto/a, tanto/a

multicolor – multicolore

mundane – mondano/a

museum – museo

musical – musicale

musician – musicista

myself [reflexive pronoun] – mi

N

national park – parco nazionale

native – natale

near – vicino (a)

neck – collo

need to/owe – dovere

neighborhood – quartiere

neither...nor – né...né

nephew – nipote

nervous – nervoso/a

never – mai

new – nuovo/a

nice – simpatico/a

niece – nipote

night – notte

no one – nessuno

north – nord, settentrione

northern – settentrionale

not even – neanche

noted – noto/a

nothing – niente/nulla

now – adesso, allora

numerous – numeroso/a

O

occur – svolgersi

of – di

of it [particle] – ne

offer – offrire

often – spesso

old – vecchio/a

olive – oliva

olive oil – olio d'oliva

olive tree – olivo

Olympic Games – Giochi Olimpici

on – su

one – un, un', una, uno

one [*si impersonale*] – si

only – unico/a

open – aprire

order – ordinare

originally – d'origine

other – altro/a

otherwise – altrimenti

overall – soprattutto

P

paint – dipingere

painter – pittore/pittrice

painting – quadro

palace – palazzo

panorama – panorama

pants – pantaloni

parents – genitori

part – parte

particular – particolare

pass – passare

passage – passaggio

pastoralism – pastorizia

path – sentiero

patrimony – patrimonio

peninsula – penisola

philosopher – filosofo

photo(graph) – foto(grafia)

picturesque – pittoresco/a

pink – rosa

place – posto, sito

plain (flat land) – pianura

plan – programma

plant – pianta

plate – piatto

play – giocare, spettacolo

playwright – drammaturgo

plaza – piazza

please – piacere

poem – poema

poet – poeta/poetessa

point – punto

popular – popolare

populous – popolato/a

port – porto

portion – porzione

possess – possedere

poverty – povertà

powerful – potente

prefer – preferire

prehistoric – preistorico/a

prepare – preparare

presence – presenza

present – presentare

principal – principale

probably – probabilmente

problem – problema

procession – processione

product – prodotto

prohibited – vietato/a

province – provincia

psychologist – psicologo

purse – borsa

push – spingere

put – mettere

put on (clothing) – mettersi

Q

question – domanda

quiet – piano/a

R

race – corsa

radio – radio

rain – piovere

reach – raggiungere

read – leggere

really – davvero

receive – ricevere

recent – recente

recuperate – ricuperare

reflect – riflettere

reflexive – riflessivo/a

region – regione

relatives – parenti

relax – rilassare

remain – rimanere

remember – ricordare

Renaissance – Rinascimento

Renaissance [adj.] – rinascimentale

repeat – ripetere

research – ricerca

resemble – assomigliare

reserve – prenotare

respond – rispondere

rest – restare

restaurant – ristorante

return – tornare

revisit – risalire (a)

rice – riso

rich – ricco/a

ride – passaggio

right – giusto/a

river – fiume

rock – roccia

rock – sasso

Roman – romano/a

roof – tetto

room – camera

run – correre

Russian – russo/a

S

sad – triste

safe – sicuro/a

sailing – vela

salad – insalata

Sardinian – sardo/a

save – salvare

say – dire

school – scuola

scientist – scienziato

scooter – motorino

screen – schermo

sculpture – scultura

sea – mare

search for – cercare

seat – sede

second – secondo

see – vedere

seem – sembrare

sell – vendere

sensitive – sensibile

sentence – frase

serene – sereno/a

serve – servire

shave oneself – radersi

she – lei

sheep – pecora

sheep's milk cheese – pecorino

shin – stinco

shirt – camicia

short – basso/a

show – mostrare, (television) programma

Sicilian – siciliano/a

sickness – malatia

sign – segno

silent – zitto/a

since – siccome

sing – cantare

singer – cantante/cantatrice

sister – sorella

sister-in-law – cognata

sit – sedere

situated – situato/a

skating – pattinaggio

ski – sciare

skiing – sci

skin – pelle

sky blue – celeste

sleep – dormire

slow – piano/a

small – piccolo/a

smell – sentire

snow – nevicare

soccer – calcio

some [pl.] – alcuni/e

some [sing.] – alcuno/a

someone – qualcuno

something – qualcosa

sometimes – qualche volta

somewhat – quasi

son – figlio

son-in-law – genero

soon – presto

south – meridione, sud

southern – meridionale

space – spazio

Spanish – spagnolo/a

speak – parlare

spend – spendere

spring – primavera

stadium – stadio

stay – restare, stare

steak – bistecca

stepbrother – fratellastro

stepdaughter – figliastra

stepfather – patrigno

stepmother – matrigna

stepsister – sorellastra

stepson – figliastro

stone – pietra

store – negozio

storm – tempesta

story – storia

straight (hair) – liscio/a

strait – stretto

stranger – straniero

street – strada

stressed – stressato/a

stripe – striscia

structure – struttura

student – studente/studentessa

study – studiare

stupendous – stupendo/a

subterranean – sotterraneo/a

suggest – suggerire

suitcase – valigia

summer – estate

summer [adj.] – estivo

sun – sole

sure – sicuro/a

surely – sicuramente

swim – nuotare

swimming – nuoto

swimming pool – piscina

T

table – tavolo

take – prendere

talent – talento

talk – parlare

tall – alto/a

taste – assaggiare

teach – insegnare

telephone – telefono

television – televisione

temperature – temperatura

temple – tempio

terrace – terrazza

terrible – terribile

test – esame

thank you – grazie

that – che, quello/a

the – gli, i, il, l', la, le, lo

theater – teatro

theatrical – teatrale

theme – tema

then – poi

there [particle] – ci

they – loro, [fem. direct object] le

thin – magro/a

thing – cosa

think – pensare

think about – pensarci

this – questo/a

through– per

time – tempo, volta

tired – stanco/a

to – a, in

today – oggi

together – insieme

tomorrow – domani

tonight – stasera

topography – topografia

tornado – tornado

tourism – turismo

tourist – turista

tower – torre

track – pista

train – treno

travel – viaggiare

traverse – percorrere

tree – albero

trip – viaggio

true – verace

turn – tornare

turn off – spegnere

thermal baths – terme

Tuscan – toscano/a

 U

ugly – brutto/a

Umbrian – umbro/a

uncle – zio

underground – sottoterra

understand – capire

unfortunately – purtroppo

unique – unico/a

university – università

usually – di solito

 V

vacation – vacanza

Venetian – veneto/a

vine – vite

vineyard – vigneto

visit (a place) – visitare

visit (a person) – andare a trovare

visited – visitato/a

volcano – vulcano

volleyball – pallavolo

 W

wait for – aspettare

wake up – svegliarsi

walk – camminare, passeggiare, passeggiata

wall – muro

want to – volere

war – guerra

warrior – guerriero

wash – lavare

watch – orologio

water polo – pallanuoto

we – noi, [indirect and direct object, reflexive pronoun] ci

weather – tempo

weekend – fine settimana

well – bene

west – ovest

western – occidentale

what – che, quale

what time is it – che ora è/che ore sono

when – quando

where – dove

which – quale

while – mentre

white – bianco/a

who – chi

why – perché

wide – largo/a

wife – moglie

wild – selvaggio/a

willingly – volontieri

willingness – volontà

win – vincere

wine – vino

winter – inverno

winter [adj.] – invernale

with – con

within – tra/fra

without – senza

wolf – lupo

word – parola

work – lavorare, lavoro

work of art – opera d'arte

worker – lavoratore

worried – preoccupato/a

worse [adj.] – peggiore, [adv.] peggio

worst – peggiore

write – scrivere

writer – scrittore/scrittrice

writing – scrittura

X

xylophone – xilofono

Y

yesterday – ieri

yet – ancora

yogurt – yoghurt

you – tu, [direct and indirect pronoun] ti

you [formal] – Lei

you [formal, pl.] – Loro

you [pl.] – voi, [direct and indirect object] vi

you're welcome – prego

young – giovane

yourself [reflexive pronoun] – ti

yourselves [reflexive pronoun] – vi

Z

zone – zona

zoo – zoo

RESOURCES FOR FURTHER STUDY

In addition to the numerous movies and books listed in the Suggested Films and Novels by Region section, you may wish to supplement your study of Italian with the following resources.

DICTIONARIES

There are several high-quality Italian-English dictionaries that are readily available for purchase: *Harper Collins Italian Dictionary* (both the Sansoni Unabridged and the College editions); the *Oxford-Paravia Italian Dictionary*; the *Cambridge Italian-English Dictionary*; *Webster's New World Italian Dictionary*; *Barron's Italian-English Dictionary*; and the *Langenscheidt Universal Dictionary Italian*. The *Collins Italian Visual Dictionary* and the DK *Italian-English Bilingual Visual Dictionary* are good references for those who appreciate visual learning aids.

In terms of online resources, the most useful dictionary is *Word Reference*: (https://wordreference.com). *Context Reverso* (https://context.reverso.net/translation/) is also excellent for providing examples of words in context.

More intrepid learners may wish to consult single-language dictionaries with definitions in Italian. The *Treccani* dictionary is an Italian dictionary prepared by the Treccani Institute that provides definitions and occurrences of usage in Italian (http://www.treccani.it/vocabolario/). Likewise, *Sapere* (https://www.sapere.it/), prepared by the encyclopedia and dictionary publisher De Agostini, offers many modern examples of usage for entries.

GRAMMAR INSTRUCTION AND MANUALS

In addition to any of the top-ranking Italian-language course textbooks used at the college and high school levels (*Prego*; *Percorsi*; *Avanti!*; *Ciao!*; *Piazza*), strongly recommended are the *English Grammar for Students of Italian*, by Sergio Adorni and Karen Primorac (Olivia & Hill Press, 2001); and *Practice Makes Perfect: The Complete Italian Grammar*, by Marcel Danesi (McGraw Hill). The *Pocket Italian Grammar* by Langenscheidt is a good, quick reference. More specific practice with verbs can be obtained with *Practice Makes Perfect: Italian Verb Tenses* by Paola Nanni-Tate (McGraw Hill).

PRACTICE WITH PHRASES AND VERBS

The *Collins Italian Phrasebook* and *Practice Makes Perfect: Italian Conversation*, by Marcel Danesi (McGraw Hill) , are useful resources. You may also find useful *The Easy Italian Phrasebook: Over 700 Phrases for Everyday Use* (Dover) and *501 Italian Verbs* (Barron's).

ITALIAN JOURNALISM

The main newspapers and weekly magazines produced in Italy are *La Repubblica* (https://www.repubblica.it/); *Corriere della Sera* (https://www.corriere.it/); *La Stampa* (https://www.lastampa.it/); *L'Espresso* (https://espresso.repubblica.it/); and *Il Sole 24 Ore* (https://www.ilsole24ore.com/). Rai Italia is the international television service of Italy's national public broadcaster (http://www.raitalia.it/dl/PortaliRai/Page-ab48738e-506a-4d73-8abb-09248a9db82b.html); however, listening to the intermediate-level Italian podcasts that follow can be a more fruitful experiences for learners of the language.

ITALIAN PODCASTS

Listening to Italian podcasts can greatly improve your comprehension of the language. *The News in Slow Italian* (https://www.newsinslowitalian.com/) is estrongly recommended. Also commendable are *Caterpillar* (https://www.raiplayradio.it/programmi/caterpillar/); *4 Verticale* (https://soundcloud.com/podcast-babbel); and *La Bottega* (https://www.spreaker.com/show/la-bottega-di-babbel-l-italia-in-breve).

HISTORY OF THE ITALIAN LANGUAGE

If the history of the Italian language interests you, you may wish to consult these three titles: *A Linguistic History of Italian*, by Martin Maiden (Routledge, 1995); *The Italian Language*, by Bruno Migliorini and T. Gwynfor Griffith (Faber and Faber, 1984); and *From Latin to Italian: An Historical Outline of the Phonology and Morphology of the Italian Language*, by Charles H. Grandgent (Tiger Xenophon, 2008).

ITALIAN CULTURE

The following books offer different perspectives on Italian culture(s): *La Bella Figura: An Insider's Guide to the Italian Mind*, by Beppe Severgnini (Hodder, 2008); *The Italians*, by John Hooper (Penguin Books, 2016); *The Pursuit of Italy: A History of a Land, Its Regions, and Their Peoples*, by David Gilmour (Farrar, Straus and Giroux, 2012); and *Italian Ways: On and Off the Rails from Milan to Palermo*, by Tim Parks (Norton, 2014).

SUGGESTED FILMS AND NOVELS BY REGION

The films listed below are Italian-language films and have substantial scenes shot on location in the following regions. Titles for these films are provided in English if those titles have been assigned by the distributor. Likewise, the selection of novels is limited to Italian literature in English translation or literature written in English that is set in a specific region. This list is not exhaustive, but a sample of classic and new Italian cinema, as well as classic and contemporary Italian literature, to give you different perspectives of the regions.

Items with an asterisk (*) are listed for multiple regions.

ABRUZZO AND MOLISE

• • • • •
Films

The Road (*La strada*, 1954), by Federico Fellini*

Torture Me but Kill Me with Kisses (*Straziami ma di baci saziami*, 1968), by Dino Risi*

They Call Me Trinity (*Mi chiamavano Trinità*, 1970), by Enzo Barboni

The Desert of the Tartars (*Il deserto dei tartari*, 1976), by Valerio Zurlini

Fontamara (1980), by Carlo Lizzani

Francesco (1989), by Liliana Cavani

Night Sun (*Il sole anche di notte*, 1990), Paolo and Vittorio Taviani*

Parenti serpenti (1992), by Mario Monicelli

La guerra degli Antò (1999), by Riccardo Milani

Bread and Tulips (*Pane e tulipani*, 2000), by Silvio Soldini*

Don't Move (*Non ti muovere*, 2004), by Sergio Castellito*

Neve (2013), by Stefano Incerti

Remember Me? (*Ti ricordi di me?* 2014), by Rolando Ravello

Storie sospese (2015), by Stefano Chiantini

The Tale of Tales (*Il racconto dei racconti*, 2015), by Matteo Garrone*

Omicidio all'italiana (2017), by Maccio Capotonda

The Furlough (*Il permesso - 48 ore fuori*, 2017), by Claudio Amendola

I Am Tempesta (*Io sono Tempesta*, 2018), by Daniele Luchetti

● ● ● ● ● ●
Novels

The Abruzzo Trilogy (series), by Ignazio Silone (Steerforth Italia): *Fontamara, Bread and Wine, The Seed Beneath the Snow*

Bitter Spring: A Life of Ignazio Silone, by Stanislao G. Pugliese (Farrar Straus & Giroux, 2009)

Pescara Tales (1902): Spirit and Flesh—Images of Abruzzo, by Gabriele D'Annunzio (Vladislav Zhukov, 2017)

A Girl Returned, by Donatella Di Pietrantonio (Europa Editions, 2019)

VALLE D'AOSTA & TRENTINO–ALTO ADIGE

● ● ● ● ●
Films

The Great War (*La grande guerra*, 1959), by Mario Monicelli*

The Decameron (1971), by Pier Paolo Pasolini*

All the Fault of Paradise (*Tutta colpa del Paradiso*, 1985), by Francesco Nuti

Le acrobate (1997), by Silvio Soldini*

The Listening (*In ascolto*, 2006), by Giacomo Martelli

Il Divo (2008), by Paolo Sorrentino*

Vincere (2009), by Marco Bellocchio

A Boss in the Living Room (*Un boss in salotto*, 2014), by Luca Miniero

TV Series: *Curon* (2020–)

● ● ● ● ● ●
Novels

The Rocco Schiavone Mysteries (series), by Antonio Manzini (Harper): *Black Run, Out of Season, Adam's Rib, Spring Cleaning*

BASILICATA

Films

The Bandit of Tacca del Lupo (*Il brigante di Tacca del Lupo*, 1952), by Pietro Germi*

Il conte di Matera (1958), by Luigi Capuano

A porte chiuse (1961), by Dino Risi

The Basilisks (*I basilischi*, 1963), by Lina Wertmüller*

The Gospel According to St. Matthew (*Lo Vangelo secondo Matteo*, 1964), by Pier Paolo Pasolini*

Allonsanfàn (1974), by Paolo and Vittorio Taviani*

Christ Stopped at Eboli (*Cristo si è fermato a Eboli*, 1979), by Francesco Rosi

Three Brothers (*Tre fratelli*, 1981), by Francesco Rosi*

Night Sun (*Il sole anche di notte*, 1990), Paolo and Vittorio Taviani*

The Nymph (*La ninfa plebea*, 1996), by Lina Wertmüller

Del perduto amore (1998), by Michele Placido

Terra bruciata (1999), by Fabio Segatori*

I'm Not Scared (*Io non ho paura*, 2003), by Gabriele Salvatores*

Il rabdomante (2007), by Fabrizio Cattani

Afraid of the Dark (Bruises) (*Hai paura del buio*, 2010), by Massimo Coppola

Basilicata Coast to Coast (2010), by Rocco Papaleo

Un giorno della vita (2011), by Giuseppe Papasso

Il pasticciere (2012), by Luigi Sardiello*

The Legendary Giulia and Other Miracles (*Noi e la Giulia*, 2015), by Edoardo Leo

An Almost Perfect Country (*Un paese quasi perfetto*, 2016), by Massimo Gaudioso

Novels

Women of the Shadows, by Ann Cornelisen (Zoland Books, 2001)

Seasons in Basilicata: A Year in a Southern Italian Village, by David Yeadon (Harper, 2005)

Murder in Matera, by Helene Stapinski (Dey Street Books, 2017)

Christ Stopped at Eboli, by Carlo Levi (Farrar, Straus and Giroux, 2006)

The Dawn Is Always New: Selected Poetry of Rocco Scotellaro, by Rocco Scotellaro (Princeton University Press, 2006)

CALABRIA

#####
Films

The Outlaw Girl (*Il brigante Musolino*, 1950), by Mario Camerini

The Bandit of Tacca del Lupo (*Il brigante del Tacca del Lupo*, 1952), by Pietro Germi*

The Gospel According to St. Matthew (*Lo Vangelo secondo Matteo*, 1964), by Pier Paolo Pasolini*

The Brigand (*Il brigante*, 1961), by Renato Castellani

For Love and Gold (*L'armata Brancaleone*, 1966), by Mario Monicelli

A Boy from Calabria (*Un ragazzo di Calabria*, 1984), by Luigi Comencini

The Stolen Children (*Il ladro di bambini*, 1992), by Gianni Amelio*

The Secret Guest (*L'ospite segreto*, 2003), by Paolo Modugno

L'uomo che sognava con le aquile (2006), by Vittorio Sindoni

18 Years Later (*Diciotto anni dopo*, 2010), by Edoardo Leo*

Le quattro volte (2010), by Michelangelo Frammartino

Corpo celeste (2011), by Alice Rohrwacher

Qualunquemente (2011), by Giulio Manfredonia

Black Souls (*Anime nere*, 2014), by Francesco Munzi

Quo vado? (2016), by Gennaro Nunziante*

A Ciambra (2017), by Jonas Carpignano

Il padre d'Italia (2017), by Fabio Mollo*

Amare affondo (2019), by Matteo Russo

Aspromonte: Land of the Forgotten (*Aspromonte - La terra degli ultimi*, 2019), by Mimmo Calopresti

######
Novels

Unto the Sons, by Gay Talese (Random House, 2006)

Stolen Figs: And Other Adventures in Calabria, by Mark Rotella (North Point Press, 2004)

Journey to the South: A Calabrian Homecoming, by Annie Hawes (Gardners Books, 2005)

Black Souls, by Gioacchino Criaco (Soho Crime, 2019)

CAMPANIA

•••••
Films

Paisan (*Paisà*, 1946), by Roberto Rossellini*

Journey to Italy (*Viaggio in Italia*, 1954), by Roberto Rossellini

Yesterday, Today and Tomorrow (*Ieri oggi domani*, 1963), by Vittorio De Sica*

The Decameron (1971), by Pier Paolo Pasolini*

The Scent of a Woman (*Profumo di donna*, 1974), by Dino Risi*

1900 (*Novecento*, 1976), by Bernardo Bertolucci*

The Postman (*Il Postino*, 1984), by Michael Radford

Gomorrah (*Gomorra*, 2008), by Matteo Garrone

Un'estate al mare (2008), by Carlo Vanzina and Enrico Vanzina*

Il Divo (2008), by Paolo Sorrentino*

Benvenuti al Sud (2010), by Luca Miniero

Benvenuti al Nord (2012), by Luca Miniero*

Leopardi (*Il giovane favoloso*, 2014), by Mario Martone*

Naples in Veils (*Napoli velata*, 2017), by Ferzan Ozpetek

TV Series: *My Brilliant Friend* (2018–), by Saverio Costanzo

Ultras (2020), by Francesco Lettieri

•••••
Novels

Gomorrah, by Roberto Saviano (Picador, 2017)

Neapolitan Novels (series), by Elena Ferrante (Europa Editions): *My Brilliant Friend, The Story of a New Name, Those Who Leave and Those Who Stay, The Story of the Lost Child*

Neapolitan Chronicles, by Anna Maria Ortese (Europa Editions, 2018)

Arturo's Island: A Novel, by Elsa Morante (Liveright, 2020)

EMILIA-ROMAGNA

•••••
Films

Obsession (*Ossessione*, 1943), by Luchino Visconti

The Scream (*Il grido*, 1957), by Michelangelo Antonioni*

Red Desert (*Deserto rosso*, 1964), by Michelangelo Antonioni

Fists in the Pocket (*Pugni in tasca*, 1965), by Marco Bellocchio

Oedipus Rex (*Edipo Re*, 1967), by Pier Paolo Pasolini

La califfa (1970), by Alberto Bevilacqua*

The Garden of the Finzi-Continis (*Il giardino dei Finzi Contini*, 1970), by Vittorio De Sica

Amarcord (1973), by Federico Fellini*

What Sign Are You? (*Di che segno sei?*, 1975), by Sergio Corbucci*

And Agnes Chose to Die (*Agnese va a morire*, 1976), by Giuliano Montaldo

The House of the Laughing Windows (*La casa dalle finestre che ridono*, 1976), by Pupi Avati

1900 (*Novecento*, 1976), by Bernardo Bertolucci*

Seeking Asylum (*Chiedo asilo*, 1979), by Marco Ferreri*

The Story of Boys and Girls (*Storia di ragazzi e ragazze*, 1989), by Pupi Avati

Everybody's Fine (*Stanno tutti bene*, 1990), by Giuseppe Tornatore*

Al di là delle nuvole (*Beyond the Clouds*, 1995), by Michelangelo Antonioni and Wim Wenders

La guerra degli Antò (1999), by Riccardo Milani

Un'estate al mare (2008), by Carlo Vanzina and Enrico Vanzina*

Giovanna's Father (*Il papà di Giovanna*, 2008), by Pupi Avati

The Friends at the Margherita Cafè (*Gli amici del bar Margherita*, 2009), by Pupi Avati

The Man Who Will Come (*L'uomo che verrà*, 2009), by Giorgio Diritti

Gli asteroidi (2017), by Germano Maccioni

• • • • • •

Novels

The Garden of the Finzi-Continis, by Giorgio Bassani (Harcourt Brace Jovanovich, 1977)

The Fall of a Sparrow, by Robert Hellenga (Scribner, 1999)

Almost Blue, by Carlo Lucarelli (Vintage Books, 2004)

Back to Bologna, by Michael Dibdin (Vintage Crime/Black Lizard, 2006)

FRIULI-VENEZIA GIULIA

Films

The Great War (*La grande guerra*, 1959), by Mario Monicelli*

Careless (*Senilità*, 1962), by Mauro Bolognini

Va' dove ti porta il cuore (1996), by Cristina Comencini

Vajont - La diga del disonore (2001), by Renzo Martinelli

The Unknown Woman (*La sconosciuta*, 2006), by Giuseppe Tornatore*

The Girl by the Lake (*La ragazza del lago*, 2007), by Andrea Molaioli

Amore, bugie e calcetto (2008), by Luca Lucini

As God Commands (*Come Dio comanda*, 2008), by Gabriele Salvatores

Rumore bianco (2008), by Alberto Fasulo

Different from Whom? (*Diverso da chi?*, 2009), by Umberto Carteni

Missione de pace (2011), by Francesco Lagi

Sleeping Beauty (*Bella addormentata*, 2012), by Marco Bellocchio

The Best Offer (*La migliore offerta*, 2013), by Gabriele Salvatores*

The Invisible Boy (*Il ragazzo invisibile*, 2014), by Gabriele Salvatores

Novels

Zeno's Conscience, by Italo Svevo (Penguin Books, 2002)

Army of the Lost Rivers, by Carlo Sgorlon (Italica Press, 2008)

Trieste and the Meaning of Nowhere, by Jan Morris (Da Capo Press, 2009)

LAZIO

Films

Rome, Open City (*Roma città aperta*, 1945), by Roberto Rossellini

Paisan (*Paisà*, 1946), by Roberto Rossellini*

Shoeshine (*Sciuscià*, 1964), by Vittorio De Sica

Bicycle Thieves (*Ladri di biciclette*, 1948), by Vittorio De Sica

Umberto D. (1952), by Vittorio De Sica

I Vitelloni (1953), by Federico Fellini

The Road (*La strada*, 1954), by Federico Fellini*

Nights of Cabiria (*Le notti di Cabiria*, 1957), by Federico Fellini

The Sweet Life (*La dolce vita*, 1960), by Federico Fellini

Two Women (*La ciociara*, 1960), by Vittorio De Sica

Accattone (1961), by Pier Paolo Pasolini

The Eclipse (*L'eclisse*, 1961), by Michelangelo Antonioni

The Grim Reaper (*La commare secca*, 1962), by Bernardo Bertolucci

Mamma Roma (1962), by Pier Paolo Pasolini

8 1/2 (1963), by Federico Fellini

Torture Me but Kill Me with Kisses (*Straziami ma di baci saziami*, 1968), by Dino Risi*

How, When, and with Whom (*Come, quando e con chi*, 1969), by Antonio Pietrangeli*

Amarcord (1973), by Federico Fellini*

The Scent of a Woman (*Profumo di donna*, 1974), by Dino Risi*

We All Loved Each Other So Much (*C'eravamo tanto amati*, 1974), by Ettore Scola

A Special Day (*Una giornata particolare*, 1977), by Ettore Scola

Everybody's Fine (*Stanno tutti bene*, 1990), by Giuseppe Tornatore*

Dear Diary (*Caro diario*, 1993), by Nanni Moretti*

Ferie d'agosto (1996), by Paolo Virzì

Aprile (1998), by Nanni Moretti*

Facing Windows (*La finestra di fronte*, 2003), by Ferzan Ozpetek

Caterina in the Big City (*Caterina va in città*, 2003), by Paolo Virzì

Don't Move (*Non ti muovere*, 2004), by Sergio Castellito*

Romanzo criminale (2005), by Michele Placido

My Brother Is an Only Child (*Mio fratello è figlio unico*), by Daniele Lucchetti, 2007*

Il Divo (2008), by Paolo Sorrentino*

Un'estate al mare (2008), by Carlo Vanzina and Enrico Vanzina*

18 Years Later (*Diciotto anni dopo*, 2010), by Edoardo Leo*

Rust (*Ruggine*, 2011), by Daniele Gaglianone*

The Great Beauty (*La grande bellezza*, 2013), by Paolo Sorrentino

The Wonders (*Le meraviglie*, 2014), by Alice Rohrwacher*

Quo vado? (2016), by Gennaro Nunziante*

Suburra (2015), by Stefano Sollima

Dogman (2018), by Matteo Garrone

Novels

Rome and a Villa, by Eleanor Clark (Steerforth Press, 1992)

Open City: Seven Writers in Postwar Rome, edited by William Weaver (Steerforth Press, 1997)

The Women of Rome, by Alberto Moravia (Steerforth Press, 1999)

History: A Novel, by Elsa Morante (Steerforth Press, 2000)

Boredom, by Alberto Morava (NYRB Classics, 2001)

Two Women, by Alberto Moravia (Steerforth Press, 2001)

The Late Mattia Pascal, by Luigi Pirandello (NYRB Classics, 2004)*

That Awful Mess on Via Merulana, by Carlo Emilio Gadda (NYRB Classics, 2007)

Suburra, by Carlo Bonini (Europa Editions, 2017)

Raphael, Painter in Rome, by Stephanie Storey (Arcade, 2020)

LIGURIA

......
Films

Attention! Bandits! (*Achtung! Banditi!*, 1951), by Carlo Lizzani

Behind Closed Shutters (*Persiane chiuse*, 1951), by Luigi Comencini

Love on the Riviera (*Racconti d'estate*, 1958), by Gianni Franciolini

General della Rovere (*Il generale della Rovere*, 1959), by Roberto Rossellini

Il peccato degli anni verdi (1960), by Leopoldo Trieste

La congiuntura (1965), by Ettore Scola*

High Crime (*La polizia incrimina la legge assolve*, 1973), by Enzo Castellari

Allonsanfàn (1974), by Paolo and Vittorio Taviani*

The Scent of a Woman (*Profumo di donna*, 1974), by Dino Risi*

Street Law (*Il cittadino si ribella*, 1974), by Enzo Castellari

What Sign Are You? (*Di che segno sei?*, 1975), by Sergio Corbucci*

Merciless Man (*Genova a mano armata*, 1976), by Mario Lanfranchi

A tu per tu (1984), by Sergio Corbucci

Il volpone (1988), by Maurizio Ponzi

Beyond the Clouds (*Al di là delle nuvole*, 1995), by Michelangelo Antonioni and Wim Wenders

Aprile (1998), by Nanni Moretti*

L'amore imperfetto (2002), by Giovanni Maderna

Agata and the Storm (*Agata e la tempesta*, 2004), by Silvio Soldini

Waves (*Onde*, 2005), by Francesco Fei

Days and Clouds (*Giorni e nuvole*, 2007), by Silvio Soldini

Men vs. Women (*Maschi contro femmine*, 2010), by Fausto Brizzi*

L'amore è imperfetto (2012), by Francesca Muci*

Happy as Lazzaro (*Lazzaro felice*, 2018), by Alice Rohrwacher*

• • • • •
Novels

The Path to the Spiders' Nests, by Italo Calvino (Ecco Press, 2000)

Extra Virgin: Amongst the Olive Groves of Liguria, by Annie Hawes (Penguin Books, 2001)

The Late Mattia Pascal, by Luigi Pirandello (NYRB Classics, 2004)*

The Baron in the Trees, by Italo Calvino (Mariner, 2017)

LOMBARDY

• • • • •
Films

Miracle in Milan (*Miracolo a Milano*, 1951), by Vittorio De Sica

Rocco and His Brothers (*Rocco e i suoi fratelli*, 1960), by Luchino Visconti

The Job (*Il posto*, 1961), by Ermanno Olmi

The Night (*La notte*, 1961), by Michelangelo Antonioni

Mafioso (1962), by Alberto Lattuada

Yesterday, Today and Tomorrow (*Ieri oggi domani*, 1963), by Vittorio De Sica*

One Fine Day (*Un certo giorno*, 1968), by Ermanno Olmi

Teorema (1968), by Pier Paolo Pasolini

The Sin (*Bianco, rosso e...*, 1972), by Alberto Lattuada

Allonsanfàn (1974), by Paolo and Vittorio Taviani*

What Sign Are You? (*Di che segno sei?*, 1975), by Sergio Corbucci*

1900 (*Novecento*, 1976), by Bernardo Bertolucci*

The Tree of Wooden Clogs (*L'albero degli zoccoli*, 1978), by Paolo and Vittorio Taviani

Colpire al cuore (1983), by Gianni Amelio

The Icicle Thief (*Ladri di saponette*, 1989), by Maurizio Nichetti

Everybody's Fine (*Stanno tutti bene*, 1990), by Giuseppe Tornatore*

Children of Hannibal (*Figli di Annibale*, 1998), Davide Ferrario*

Cado dalle nubi (2009), by Gennaro Nunziante*

I Am Love (*Io sono l'amore*, 2009), by Luca Guadagnino

Come Undone (*Cosa voglio di più*, 2010), by Silvio Soldini

Happy Family (2010), by Gabriele Salvatores

What a Beautiful Day (*Che bella giornata*, 2011), by Gennaro Nunziante*

Benvenuti al Nord (2012), by Luca Miniero*

The Best Offer (*La migliore offerta*, 2013), by Gabriele Salvatores*

Human Capital (*Il capitale umano*, 2013), by Paolo Virzì

Io, Arlecchino (2014), by Matteo Bini and Giorgio Pasotti

Call Me by Your Name (*Chiamami col tuo nome*, 2017), by Luca Guadagnino

Happy as Lazzaro (*Lazzaro felice*, 2018), by Alice Rohrwacher*

Loro 1 (2018), by Paolo Sorrentino

• • • • • •
Novels

The Betrothed, by Alessandro Manzoni (Penguin Classics, 1984)

The Disappearance of Signora Giulia, by Piero Chiara (Pushkin Vertigo, 2015)

The Bishop's Bedroom, by Piero Chiara (New Vessel Press, 2019)

THE MARCHES

• • • • •
Films

Obsession (*Ossessione*, 1943), by Luchino Visconti

Torture Me but Kill Me with Kisses (*Straziami ma di baci saziami*, 1968), by Dino Risi*

Alfredo, Alfredo (1972), by Pietro Germi

Convoy Busters (*Un poliziotto scomodo*, 1978), by Stelvio Massi

Ciao, cialtroni! (1979), by Danilo Massi

You'll Die at Midnight (*Morirai a mezzanotte*, 1986), by Lamberto Bava

Keys in Hand (*Chiavi in mano*, 1996), by Mariano Laurenti

Dirty Linen (*Panni sporchi*, 1999), by Mario Monicelli

The Son's Room (*La stanza del figlio*, 2001), by Nanni Moretti

David's Birthday (*Il compleanno*, 2009), by Marco Filiberti

Men vs. Women (*Maschi contro femmine*, 2010), by Fausto Brizzi*

Leopardi (*Il giovane favoloso*, 2014), by Mario Martone*

Prendere la parola (2019), by Perla Sardella

• • • • • •
Novels

The Book of the Courtier, by Baldassar Castiglione (Penguin Classics, 1976)

Canti, by Giacomo Leopardi (Penguin Classics, 2010)

Zibaldone, by Giacomo Leopardi (Farrar, Straus and Giroux, 2015)

Moral Fables, by Giacomo Leopardi (Alma Classics, 2017)

The Road to Urbino, by Roma Tearne (Aardvark Bureau, 2020)

PIEDMONT

• • • • • •
Films

Bitter Rice (*Riso amaro*, 1949), by Giuseppe De Santis

Le amiche (1955), by Michelangelo Antonioni

Il peccato degli anni verdi (1960), by Leopoldo Trieste

The Organizer (*I compagni*, 1963), by Mario Monicelli

Made in Italy (1965), by Nanni Loy

The Seduction of Mimì (*Mimì metallurgico ferito nell'onore*, 1972), by Lina Wertmüller

Torino nera (1972), by Carlo Lizzani

The Scent of a Woman (*Profumo di donna*, 1974), by Dino Risi*

The Sunday Woman (*La donna della domenica*, 1975), by Luigi Comencini

Everybody's Fine (*Stanno tutti bene*, 1990), by Giuseppe Tornatore*

Così ridevano (1998), by Gianni Amelio

The Best of Youth (*La meglio gioventù*, 2003), by Marco Tullio Giordana*

The Days of Abandonment (*I giorni dell'abbandono*, 2005), by Roberto Faenza

My Brother Is an Only Child (*Mio fratello è figlio unico*), by Daniele Lucchetti, 2007*

Il Divo (2008), by Paolo Sorrentino*

The Double Hour (*La doppia ora*, 2009), by Giuseppe Capotondi)

Men vs. Women (*Maschi contro femmine*, 2010), by Fausto Brizzi*

The Solitude of Prime Numbers (*La solitudine dei numeri primi*, 2010), by Saverio Costanzo*

Rust (*Ruggine*, 2011), by Daniele Gaglianone*

White as Milk, Red as Blood (*Bianca come il latte, rossa come il sangue*, 2013), by Giacomo Campiotti

Quo vado? (2016), by Gennaro Nunziante*

Il padre d'Italia (2017), by Fabio Mollo*

Happy as Lazzaro (*Lazzaro felice*, 2018), by Alice Rohrwacher*

Golden Men (*Uomini d'oro*, 2019), by Vincenzo Alfieri

• • • • • •
Novels

A Woman, by Sibilla Aleramo (University of California Press, 1983)

The Moon and the Bonfires, by Cesare Pavese (NYRB Classics, 2002)

A Private Affair, by Beppe Fenoglio (Hesperus Press, 2007)

Family Lexicon, by Natalia Ginzburg (NYRB Classics, 2017)

PUGLIA

• • • • •
Films

The White Ship (*La nave bianca*, 1941), by Roberto Rossellini

The Basilisks (*I basilischi*, 1963), by Lina Wertmüller*

Il soldato di ventura (1976), by Pasquale Festa Campanile

Three Brothers (*Tre fratelli*, 1981), by Francesco Rosi*

Pizzicata (1996), by Edoardo Winspeare

Le acrobate (1997), by Silvio Soldini*

Children of Hannibal (*Figli di Annibale*, 1998), by Davide Ferrario*

Prima del tramonto (1999), by Stefano Incerti

Terra bruciata (1999), by Fabio Segatori*

The Knights of the Quest (*I cavalieri che fecero l'impresa*, 2001), by Pupi Avati

I'm Not Scared (*Io non ho paura*, 2003), by Gabriele Salvatores*

My Brother-in-Law (*Mio cognato*, 2003), by Alessandro Piva

Don't Tell (*La bestia nel cuore*, 2005), by Cristina Comencini

Un'estate al mare (2008), by Carlo Vanzina and Enrico Vanzina*

Cado dalle nubi (2009), by Gennaro Nunziante*

L'uomo nero (2009), by Sergio Rubini

Loose Cannons (*Le mine vaganti*, 2010), by Ferzan Ozpetek

What a Beautiful Day (*Che bella giornata*, 2011), by Gennaro Nunziante*

Rust (*Ruggine*, 2011), by Daniele Gaglianone*

L'amore è imperfetto (2012), by Francesca Muci*

Il pasticciere (2012), by Luigi Sardiello*

Fasten Your Seatbelts (*Allacciate le cinture*, 2014), by Ferzan Ozpetek

A Woman as a Friend (*Una donna per amica*, 2014), by Giovanni Veronesi

La scelta (2015), by Michele Placido

The Tale of Tales (*Il racconto dei racconti*, 2015), by Matteo Garrone

Belli di papà (2015), by Guido Chiesa

Quo vado? (2016), by Gennaro Nunziante*

Pinocchio (2019), by Matteo Garrone*

Il grande spirito (2019), by Sergio Rubini

Odio l'estate (2020), by Massimo Venier

Si vive una volta sola (2020), by Carlo Verdone

Novels

Casa rossa, by Francesca Marciano (Vintage, 2003)

Otranto: A Novel, by Maria Corti (Italica Press, 2009)

Guido Guerrieri (series), by Gianrico Carofiglio (Bitter Lemon Press): *A Walk in the Dark, Reasonable Doubts, Involuntary Witness*

The Night Falling, by Katherine Webb (Orion, 2015)

SARDINIA

Films

Altura (1949), by Mario Sequi

Vendetta...sarda (1952), by Mario Mattoli

Bandits of Orgosolo (*Banditi a Orgosolo*, 1961), by Vittorio De Seta

Red Desert (*Deserto rosso*, 1964), by Michelangelo Antonioni

Una questione d'onore (1965), Luigi Zampa

Sardinia Kidnapped (*Sequestro di persona*, 1968), by Gianfranco Mingozzi

How, When, and with Whom (*Come, quando e con chi*, 1969), by Antonio Pietrangeli*

Le coppie (1970), by Mario Monicelli, Alberto Sordi, and Vittorio De Sica

Swept Away (*Travolti da un insolito destino nell'azzurro mare d'agosto*, 1974), by Lina Wertmüller

Dove volano i corvi d'argento (1977), by Piero Livi

Padre padrone (*Father boss*, 1977), Paolo and Vittorio Taviani

Seeking Asylum (*Chiedo asilo*, 1979), by Marco Ferreri*

Piccolo grande amore (1993), by Carlo Vanzina

Le ragioni dell'aragosta (2007), by Sabina Guzzanti

Un'estate al mare (2008), by Carlo Vanzina and Enrico Vanzina*

A Small Southern Enterprise (*Una piccola impresa meridionale*, 2013), by Rocco Papaleo

Quo vado? (2016), by Gennaro Nunziante*

The Man Who Bought the Moon (*L'uomo che comprò la luna*, 2018), by Paolo Zucca

· · · · · ·
Novels

Reeds in the Wind, by Grazia Deledda (Italica Press, 2008)

Cosima, by Grazia Deledda (Italica Press, 2008)

Prison Notebooks, by Antonio Gramsci (Columbia University Press, 2011)

Accabadora, by Michela Murgia (Counterpoint, 2012)

SICILY

· · · · ·
Films

The Earth Trembles (*La terra trema*, 1948), by Luchino Visconti

In the Name of the Law (*In nome della legge*, 1949), by Pietro Germi

L'Avventura (1960), by Michelangelo Antonioni

Il bell'Antonio (1960), by Mauro Bolognini

Divorce, Italian Style (*Divorzio all'italiana*, 1961), by Pietro Germi

Salvatore Giuliano (1962), by Francesco Rosi

I Fidanzati (1963), by Ermanno Olmi

The Leopard (*Il gattopardo*, 1963), by Luchino Visconti

Sedotta e abbandonata (*Seduced and Abandoned*, 1964), by Pietro Germi

We Still Kill the Old Way (*A ciascuno il suo*, 1967), by Elio Petri

Mafia (*Il giorno della civetta*, 1968), by Damiano Damiani

Allonsanfàn (1974), by Paolo and Vittorio Taviani*

Illustrious Corpses (*Cadaveri eccellenti*, 1976), by Francesco Rosi

Kaos (1984), by Paolo and Vittorio Taviani

Nuovo Cinema Paradiso (1988), by Giuseppe Tornatore

Red Wood Pigeon (*Palombella rossa*, 1989), by Nanni Moretti

Johnny Stecchino (1991), by Roberto Benigni

The Stolen Children (*Il ladro di bambini*, 1992), by Gianni Amelio*

Dear Diary (*Caro diario*, 1993), by Nanni Moretti*

The Star Maker (*L'uomo delle stelle*, 1995), by Giuseppe Tornatore

La lupa (1996), by Gabriele Luva

TV Series: *Inspector Montalbano* (1999–)

Malena (2000), by Giuseppe Tornatore

Respiro (2002), by Emanuele Crialese

The Best of Youth (*La meglio gioventù*, 2003), by Marco Tullio Giordana*

A Sicilian Miracle! (*Miracolo a Palermo!*, 2005), by Beppe Cino

Baarìa (2009), by Giuseppe Tornatore

Il 7 e l'8 (2011), by Giambattista Avellino, Salvatore Ficara, and Valentino Picone

Terraferma (2011), by Emanuele Crialese

The Mafia Kills Only in the Summer (*La mafia uccide solo d'estate*, 2013), by Pierfrancesco Diliberto

The Tale of Tales (*Il racconto dei racconti*, 2015), by Matteo Garrone*

Fire at Sea (*Fuocoammare*, 2016), by Gianfranco Rosi

The Goddess of Fortune (*La dea fortuna*, 2019), by Ferzan Ozpetek

Ordinary Happiness (*Momenti di trascurabile felicità*, 2019), by Daniele Luchetti

• • • • • •
Novels

The Leopard, by Giuseppe Tomasi di Lampedusa (Random House, 2007, reprint (1958))

Conversations in Sicily, by Elio Vittorini (New Directions, 2001)

Women of Messina, by Elio Vittorini (New Directions, 1973)

The Inspector Montalbano Mysteries (series), by Andrea Camilleri (Penguin Books)

Six Characters in Search of an Author and Other Plays, by Luigi Pirandello (Penguin, 1996)

House by the Medlar Tree, by Giovanni Verga (Dedalus, 2015)

• • • • •
Films

Paisan (*Paisà*, 1946), by Roberto Rossellini*

The Easy Life (*Il sorpasso*, 1962), by Dino Risi

Family Portrait (*Cronaca familiare*, 1962), by Valerio Zurlini

La congiuntura (1965), by Ettore Scola*

Brother Son, Sister Moon (*Fratello sole, sorella luna*, 1972), by Franco Zeffirelli*

The Night of the Shooting Stars (*La notte di San Lorenzo*, 1982), by Paolo and Vittorio Taviani

Everybody's Fine (*Stanno tutti bene*, 1990), by Giuseppe Tornatore*

Hard-Boiled Egg (*Ovosodo*, 1997), by Paolo Virzì

Life Is Beautiful (*La vita è bella*, 1997), by Roberto Benigni*

The Best of Youth (*La meglio gioventù*, 2003), by Marco Tullio Giordana*

Un'estate al mare (2008), by Carlo Vanzina and Enrico Vanzina*

Pinocchio (2009), by Matteo Garrone*

The First Beautiful Thing (*La prima cosa bella*, 2010), by Paolo Virzì

Men vs. Women (*Maschi contro femmine*, 2010), by Fausto Brizzi*

The Wonders (*Le meraviglie*, 2014), by Alice Rohrwacher*

Tale of Tales (*Il racconto dei racconti*, 2015), by Matteo Garrone

Like Crazy (*La pazza gioia*, 2016), by Paolo Virzì

• • • • • •
Novels

The Light in the Piazza, by Elizabeth Spencer (McGraw Hill, 1960)

The Agony and the Ecstacy: A Biographical Novel of Michelangelo, by Irving Stone (Berkley, 1987)

A Room with a View, by E. M. Forester (Bantam, 1988)

The Divine Comedy: Inferno, Purgatorio, Paradiso, by Dante Alighieri (Everyman's Library, 1995)

Romola, by George Eliot (Penguin Classics, 1996)

Under the Tuscan Sun: At Home in Italy, by Frances Mayes (Broadway, 1997)

Hannibal, by Thomas Harris (Dell, 2000)

The Decameron, by Giovanni Boccaccio (Penguin Classics, 2003)

The Birth of Venus, by Sarah Dunant (Random House, 2004)

The Poetry of Petrarch, translated by David Young (Farrar, Straus and Giroux, 2005)

Galileo's Daughter: A Historical Memoir of Science, Faith, and Love, by Dava Sobel (Bloomsbury, 2011)

Agostino, by Alberto Moravia (NYRB Classics, 2014)

Winter's Child, by R. J. Hervey (Inkdot Press, 2019)

UMBRIA

• • • • •
Films

The Hawks and the Sparrows (*Uccellacci e uccellini*, 1966), by Pier Paolo Pasolini

For Love and Gold (*L'armata Brancaleone*, 1966), by Mario Monicelli

La califfa (1970), by Alberto Bevilacqua*

Brother Son, Sister Moon (*Fratello sole, sorella luna*, 1972), by Franco Zeffirelli*

Io e mia sorella (1987), by Carlo Verdone

Francesco (1989), by Liliana Cavani

Chiedi la luna (1991), by Giuseppe Piccioni

Life Is Beautiful (*La vita è bella*, 1997), by Roberto Benigni*

L'arcano incantatore (1996), by Pupi Avati

TV Series: *Don Matteo* (2000–)

Pinocchio (2002), by Roberto Benigni

The Best of Youth (*La meglio gioventù*, 2003), by Marco Tullio Giordana*

The Unknown Woman (*La sconosciuta*, 2006), by Giuseppe Tornatore*

Lend a Hand (2018), by Raffaella Covino

• • • • • •
Novels

Barbarian in the Garden, by Zbigniew Herbert (Harvest Books, 1986)

After Hannibal, by Barry Unsworth (Gardners Books, 1997)

The Little Flowers of Saint Claire, by Piero Bargellini (Edizioni Porziuncola, 2002)

The Lady in the Palazzo: At Home in Umbria, by Marlena Di Blasi (Algonquin, 2008)

Saint Francis of Assisi, by G. K. Chesterton (Chesterton Books, 2011)

Timoleon Vieta Come Home, by Dan Rhodes (Houghton Mifflin, 2014)

•••••
Films

Paisan (*Paisà*, 1946), by Roberto Rossellini*

Senso (1954), by Luchino Visconti

Count Max (*Il conte Max*, 1957), by Giorgio Bianchi

The Scream (*Il grido*, 1957), by Michelangelo Antonioni*

The Birds, the Bees, and the Italians (*Signore e signori*, 1966), by Pietro Germi

A Place for Lovers (*Amanti*, 1968), by Vittorio De Sica

The Priest's Wife (*La moglie del prete*, 1970), by Dino Risi

Death in Venice (*Morte a Venezia*, 1971), by Luchino Visconti

The Decameron (1971), by Pier Paolo Pasolini*

Io non vedo, tu non parli, lui non sente (1971), by Mario Camerini

Gli ordini sono ordini (1972), by Franco Giraldi

Vacanze di Natale (1983), by Carlo Vanzina

Le acrobate (1997), by Silvio Soldini*

Aprile (1998), by Nanni Moretti*

Little Teachers (*I piccoli maestri*, 1998), by Daniele Lucchetti

Bread and Tulips (*Pane e tulipani*, 2000), by Silvio Soldini*

Holy Tongue (*La lingua del santo*, 2000), by Carlo Mazzacurati

The Best of Youth (*La meglio gioventù*, 2003), by Marco Tullio Giordana*

Greenery Will Bloom Again (*Torneranno i prati*, 2014), by Ermanno Olmi

Youth (2015), by Paolo Sorrentino

••••••
Novels

Death in Venice, by Thomas Mann (Vintage Books, 1989)

Italian Neighbors, by Tim Parks (Grove Press, 2003)

Casanova in Bolzano, by Sandor Marai (Knopf, 2004)

The Floating Book, by Michelle Lovric (Harper, 2005)

Watermark: An Essay on Venice, by Joseph Brodsky (Penguin Classics, 2013)

Blood from a Stone, by Donna Leon (Grove Press, 2014)

The Painter's Apprentice: A Novel of 16th-Century Venice, by Laura Morelli (The Scriptorium, 2017)

Senso: And Other Stories, by Camillo Boito (Dedalus, 2018)

The Master of Verona, by David Blixit (St. Martin's Press, 2007)

IMAGE CREDITS

13: chelovek/Getty Images; **103:** Iurii Buriak/iStock/Getty Images Plus, Ввласенко/Wikimedia Commons/CC BY-SA 3.0; **119:** davidionut/Getty Images; **154:** Franco/flickr/CC BY-SA 2.0.

NOTES

NOTES

NOTES

NOTES

NOTES

NOTES

NOTES